HOUSEPLANT
BASICS

HOUSEPLANT
BASICS

hamlyn

David Squire and Margaret Crowther

First published in Great Britain in 2002 by Hamlyn,
a division of Octopus Publishing Group Limited,
2–4 Heron Quays, London, E14 4JP

Copyright © Octopus Publishing Group Limited 2002

ISBN 0 600 60367 9

A catalogue record for this book is available from the
British Library

Printed in China
10 9 8 7 6 5 4 3 2 1

CONTENTS

INTRODUCTION

A house is not a home without houseplants. Whether the plant is an addition to your home in the form of a pot plant that changes with the seasons or is an old friend in the form of a long-lived plant in a permanent position, it will bring your living space to life.

It may or may not be true that plants respond to being talked to, but they certainly respond to good care. If you are to get the best from your plants, you must be aware of the sort of conditions in which similar plants grow in the wild and try to meet the needs of your plants in terms of compost type, the level of light, the degree of moisture, humidity and temperature in both winter and summer, the amount of fertilizer necessary at different times of year and any other specific requirement they might have. In return, they will reward you with strong growth, a good shape, healthy leaves and beautiful flowers. And whether or not plants respond to people except by flourishing when well cared for, people certainly respond to plants, and feel better for their presence in the home.

Choosing houseplants needs as much care as buying any other item for a home. The plant needs to fit in with its surrounding as well as to create an attractive display in itself. It is essential to buy healthy plants that will last. Buying an inexpensive plant that dies within weeks is a waste of money. Check before buying, and discard plants with roots coming out of drainage holes, those with wilting leaves, any plant with signs of pest and disease and those where the compost and pot are covered with moss or slime. Also avoid plants that are displayed outdoors in hot sunshine or in draughts.

Getting plants home quickly and safely and acclimatizing them to indoor life is also important. Make sure that the garden centre or nursery wraps up the plant to protect it from draughts and to reduce the chance of it being damaged in transit. Do not put a plant in your car boot if the weather is extremely hot or cold: instead, stand it upright in a box inside the car. When you get your plant home, unpack it and stand it in a lightly shaded, draught-free place in gentle warmth for about a week. Water the compost. If a few buds or leaves initially fall off, do not worry unduly because the plant is probably just settling down. During this initial period, check regularly that the plant is not infested with pests and diseases.

Above: A conservatory
provides the opportunity to
create an indoor garden of
ferns and greenery.

1 HEALTHY HOUSEPLANTS

Most houseplants are undemanding, producing attractive foliage or flowers for several years if given the basics of water, food and light. Routine care need not take much time, but your plants will repay your attention.

Left: A sun room provides both ample space and a range of temperature and light conditions that will allow a variety of plants to grow happily.

Right: Pink and red *Kalanchoe blossfeldiana* (flaming Katy) add warmth and colour to a collection of foliage plants, which includes a variegated *Hedera helix* (ivy), *Ficus pumila* (creeping fig) and a young *Ficus benjamina* 'Variegata' (weeping fig).

Providing regular water is, of course, vital. Choose a watering-can with a long spout to make watering easy and buy a mist spray so that you can regularly spray with tepid, lime-free water the many plants that need humidity. Standing plants on clay granules or pebbles in trays or bowls of water is an attractive way in which to provide additional humidity.

Keep plants looking their best by cutting off dead flowers with sharp scissors or secateurs and pinching out growing points to keep them bushy or snip them into shape as necessary. Clean the leaves of foliage plants with a cloth wrung out in tepid water. Watch out for pests and diseases, and treat them promptly (see pages 122–23).

When a houseplant fills its pot with roots it is essential to move it into a larger one. If left where it is, the plant's growth will be stunted and its appearance will deteriorate. Repotting provides the plant with further nutrients

and more space for its roots. It also creates a firmer base for the plant, balancing leaf growth and helping to prevent it falling over. At each repotting, move the plant into a pot that is only slightly larger, especially during its early life. In a pot that is too large, the plant is surrounded by too much compost and its roots can become saturated with water, which eventually causes them to decay and the plant to die. Large plants are generally top-dressed rather than being completely repotted.

The clearest indication that repotting is needed is when the plant's roots are growing out of the pot's base. There are other, less obvious, signs, including a general lack of vigour and deterioration in health, caused by the plant being deprived of nutrients. New leaves are small and old ones become increasingly pale and yellow. Also, pot-bound flowering plants produce fewer flowers. In addition, new leaves will have

pale areas between the veins, and they are also likely to hang limply because they are suffering from a lack of moisture.

A healthy, recently repotted plant soon resumes growth, producing young shoots and fresh, brightly coloured leaves. After repotting, place the plant in light shade until growth restarts. This is indicated by the development of fresh shoots. Until then, keeping the plant out of strong and direct sunlight ensures that the need for water is reduced. Position plants with variegated leaves in good light, so that their colours are enhanced. Strong sunlight, however, should be avoided. Plants with uniform outlines should be rotated about 90 degrees several times a week. If this is not done, leaves turn towards the light. Place the plastic or clay pot in an ornamental outer pot (often called a cache or display pot), selecting a colour that harmonizes with the plant.

Left: Pot chrysanthemums are available throughout the year and remain in flower for about a month.
Right: Large foliage plants such as the variegated *Ficus benjamina* 'Golden King' (weeping fig) gain from being arranged with other leafy plants, such as *Asplenium nidus* (bird's nest fern) and *Kalanchoe blossfeldiana*.

types of houseplant

Houseplants come in all shapes and sizes. They may be slow or fast growing, long or short lived, leafy or flowering. From a designer's point of view they can be roughly divided according to their appearance. There are rosette-forming and bushy plants, from small to large, suitable for table tops and windowsills and for arranging in groups. Plants that climb or trail are candidates for hanging baskets, training on screens and up poles, standing on plinths, shelves and high windowsills, or simply, when young, for training up canes or around hoops as windowsill plants. Finally, there are specimen plants of various kinds, from enormous ferns for containers on stands and high display tables to air-rooting climbers for large mossy poles and weeping figs and other plants with tree-like shapes.

Most houseplants are grown either mainly for their flowers or mainly for their foliage, but within these two groups there is a wealth of choice between: seasonal or almost all-year flowering, perfumed flowers, climbing and trailing plants, plants with bold foliage that reward with a burst of flowers, plants whose leaves are as colourful as flowers, plants for sun rooms and conservatories and plants for cool rooms. Certain plants have special status: palms, ferns and bromeliads, cacti and other succulents all have distinctive features of their own, and then there are plants grown for their colourful berries or fruits, tropical insectivorous plants, and, of course, the wealth of flowering plants grown indoors from bulbs.

Although many plants are widely known by their common names, these can vary from country to country, even from person to person. To be sure that you are identifying a plant correctly it is always safer to use its botanical name. Even botanical names may change from time to time, however, and when this has occurred, both the old and the new names have been included to avoid confusion. This is particularly true of both desert and forest cacti, which have been subject to much reclassification in recent years and some of which may be offered for sale under as many as three specific names.

positioning & displaying plants

Once you have got your plant home and have acclimatized it to your house, you should place it in its permanent position.

CHOOSING A ROOM

Sitting rooms, dining rooms and bedrooms are places of peace and tranquillity, and have more constant temperatures and fewer draughts than other parts of the home. In sitting and dining rooms plants can be displayed in floor-standing groups, in troughs or in fireplaces, on windowsills and on tables. Large floor-standing .

specimens in big pots make superb focal points. Bedrooms are often cooler, and so useful for ferns, azaleas, cyclamen and other plants that need slightly lower temperatures. There are many plants for cooler conditions, from impressive ferns to dainty primroses. Unheated spare bedrooms are often the best place in the house for plants that need a dormant period in winter and for growing plants from seeds and cuttings.

The levels of activity and temperature changes in kitchens

make them inhospitable for many plants. It is best to reserve the kitchen for inexpensive plants and plants that will not get in the way: easy-care green plants, perhaps hung on wall brackets, and undemanding flowering plants on windowsills.

Bathrooms are also primarily functional places, even though they can also be havens of privacy and comfort. They are often advocated as ideal areas for growing plants that love humidity, but not all bathrooms are humid all the time and the

Left: Ferns love humidity and are often displayed in bathrooms. The unusual *Platycerium bifurcatum* (staghorn fern) has quite striking architectural qualities that make it blend well with plain white bathroom fittings and the old-fashioned water taps. *Right:* This *Exacum affine* (Arabian violet), a small and lightly perfumed plant, is ideal for a pretty bedroom.

temperature can fluctuate widely. Again, it may be better to choose tolerant plants.

Halls, landings and passages can be draughty or have low light levels, and people passing to and fro may brush past leaves or even knock over plants that are not carefully positioned. If there is space, large specimens can stand in corners, trailing plants can hang in baskets, and foliage plants or pot plants can stand on a hall table to create a welcoming atmosphere.

Many flowering plants are fragrant, including some not generally known for their scent, such as some cyclamen, daffodils and the houseplant primroses. Conversely, some plants known for their scent have unscented forms. It is always best to be guided by one's nose. Heavily scented plants, such as hyacinths, hoyas, jasmine and stephanotis, must be carefully positioned. While most people like a gentle fragrance in a bedroom, others find these strong perfumes overpowering. Equally, strongly scented plants

are not ideal for a small kitchen or dining room, while plants such as *Cestrum nocturnum* (night jessamine) give out more fragrance at night and are perfect for a sitting room. Scented plants placed in the hall perfume the whole house and add an extra welcome.

DISPLAYING PLANTS

There are numerous ways of displaying plants. The simplest is, of course, to stand a single plant alone in its pot, in a place where it gets the right amount of light – usually on a windowsill. But plants often look better – and grow better – when they are in a group. They can be grouped with their pots on show or arranged with the pots hidden in a container, such as a trough, or they may be planted together in a container to form a sort of indoor garden.

Some plants dictate the way in which they should be displayed. The largest plants need large, floor-standing pots, although they do not necessarily have to be displayed as single

specimens. A group with an architectural plant such as a palm as its main element, grading down through large and medium-sized foliage plants and ferns and softened with trailing ivy, can be a stunning feature in a room with high ceilings, plain-painted walls and simple furniture. This sort of arrangement can be enhanced by a large mirror, which will show the entire arrangement from all sides, or by careful spotlighting to create highlights and shadows.

Climbers and trailers must be allowed the space to grow, and a hanging basket or a plant stand is perfect for trailers. Small climbers can be grown up canes or around hoops, and vigorous climbers can be trained over wires or trellis to form room dividers, to obscure an ugly view or to adorn a conservatory wall.

Moisture-loving, draught-fearing plants can be planted together in a glass terrarium, bottle garden or Wardian case to make a beautiful and interesting centrepiece.

containers & composts

Most plants are sold in plastic pots and in compost that contains sufficient nutrients to sustain them for several months. However, plastic pots are not especially attractive, and you will either wish to disguise them by placing them inside a more decorative cache pot or by repotting them into something more decorative. You will also, if your plant is to last for more than the first year, have to consider repotting it into fresh compost.

CONTAINERS

The sizes of pots, measured across their tops, range from 3.5cm (1¼in) to 38cm (15in) wide. For most houseplants, four sizes are sufficient: 6cm (2½in), 8cm (3in), 13cm (5in) and 18cm (7in), although large, floor-standing plants may need a 25cm (10in) pot. There are complementary saucers available in which pots can be stood.

Clay pots are traditional containers for plants. They create a firm base and harmonize with most leaves and flowers. Their porous nature enables excess moisture to evaporate through the sides and toxic salts can escape in the same way. For some plants, however, especially those that need a peat-based compost, plastic pots are sometimes preferred. Because moisture cannot evaporate through these pots it is important not to overwater the plants.

More or less anything that has sides and a base can be used as a planting pot or an ornamental container for plants in their own pots. Old tea caddies, storage jars and junk-shop finds, teapots and salad bowls, and even wooden boxes can give an original look to a plant display. Plastic containers can be painted in a plain colour and dappled with second and third colours, simple containers can be covered in hessian or printed paper, and baskets can be spray-painted. Blocks of wood can be placed inside a container to raise the height of the plant. Containers made of metal and any material that is not waterproof are best used to hold pots, rather than for direct planting. Place a large plastic box inside, or line with layers of plastic topped with newspaper to absorb excess water draining from the flowerpots.

Left: This beautiful terrarium provides an ideal and unusual container for a pretty display of lush plants. *Right:* All sorts of containers can be used to add character to a plant display. This ornate birdcage shows off a *Kalanchoe blossfeldiana* (flaming Katy) in a novel and attractive way, adding an extra dimension to a simple pot plant.

Planting directly into containers not designed for plants demands some thought and much care because of the lack of drainage. The base of the container must be lined with a good layer of clay pellets, which absorb moisture and give good, natural drainage. Charcoal mixed with the potting medium will help to keep it sweet.

COMPOST

Peat-free composts are becoming increasingly popular as they do not involve the continued destruction of the natural habitat of many plants and animals. The main ingredient in these composts is generally coir, which is obtained from the husk of a coconut and which is a material much used in the past for making ropes and matting.

Gardeners are usually devotees of either peat- or soil-based composts, but it is worth experimenting with a coir-based type. In many ways this will have much the same qualities as peat, such as moisture retention and aeration. Ready-to-use seed and potting composts based on coir are widely available. After use, the compost can be re-used as a mulch around outdoor plants. In future composts formed of materials such as straw, bark and wood fibre may also be available.

Compost provides anchorage for plants and moisture, food and air for roots. Garden soil is unsuitable for houseplants because its quality is variable. It is also badly drained and may contain weed seeds, pests and diseases. Specially prepared composts should be used, therefore, and there are two main types.

Soil-based composts are formed from partially sterilized loam (good topsoil), peat and sharp sand, plus fertilizers. These composts, which are suitable for most houseplants, are heavier than other types and give stability to large plants. In addition, they are unlikely to dry out as fast or so completely as the other types and are richer in minor and trace plant foods than other types of compost.

Most peat-based (and peat-substitute) composts are more uniform in quality than soil-based composts, but they are liable to dry out more rapidly than soil-based types and are difficult to remoisten. They are lighter to carry home by the bag than their soil-based equivalents, but they are poorer in nutrients than soil-based composts (be prepared to feed plants at an earlier stage). They are easily stored even after the bag is opened (just fold over and tie the end), but when these composts are stored in garden centres or nurseries, the peat often becomes compacted. Before using the compost, therefore, shake the bag thoroughly to loosen it.

watering

Without water plants soon die. They also deteriorate when given too much moisture because the compost becomes swamped and airless and roots suffocate and die. The aim of watering is to provide plants with adequate water when they need it. In summer houseplants need more water than in winter, although the compost of winter-flowering houseplants must be kept moist.

APPLYING WATER

The most popular way to water houseplants is by slowly dribbling water from a watering-can directly on the compost. This is known as 'over the rim' watering. At each application of water, fill the complete area between the compost's surface and the pot's rim. An alternative way is to stand pots in a bowl of water until moisture seeps to the compost's surface. Then, remove the pot and allow excess water to drain away. Air plants, such as tillandsias, should be misted (soaking their leaves in water), while bromeliads that form urns

from rosettes of leaves are mainly watered by filling these 'reservoirs' with water.

HOLIDAY CARE

Many houseplants are lovingly looked after throughout the year, only to deteriorate or die when you are away on holiday. Both over- and underwatering could kill them, and it is often better to rely on automatic watering devices than on your neighbours.

Leave large plants in their saucers, but put them on a large polythene sheet in a lightly shaded room. During the week before your holiday, water

several times. If the holiday is for only seven to ten days this will usually preserve them.

Small plants can be placed in large trays with 1cm (½in) of water in the base. This will keep them alive for up to a fortnight, if in light shade. Another way is to place a capillary mat on a draining board and to trail one end in a sink filled with water. Alternatively, trail the end in a bowl of water and stand plants on the matting. This system works best for plants in plastic pots filled with peat-based compost and without crocks in the base.

SAVING A PLANT IN DRY COMPOST

When watering is neglected plants wilt and eventually die. Once a plant is wilting, a point

A simple wick-waterer

A simple method of ensuring that your plants get sufficient water while you are away is to support them over a bowl of water and to insert wicks into the compost through the hole in the bottom of the pot and trail the other end in the water.

WAYS OF JUDGING WHEN WATER IS NEEDED

1 Rubbing a thumb on the surface of compost is a popular way to assess moisture. Only water when the compost is dry and has lost its sponginess.

3 Moisture-indicator strips (watering signals) can be inserted and left in compost. They change colour when the compost is dry.

2 Tapping clay pots with a cotton reel attached to a cane is a well-known method: a dull note indicates moist compost, while a ring tells that water is needed.

4 A moisture meter has a thin, pencil-like probe that is inserted into compost and the moisture level is shown on a dial. It is efficient, but repeated use of the probe will damage roots.

comes when, no matter how much water is given subsequently, it will not recover. However, most plants can be revived if watered soon enough. Stand the pot in a bowl with 3–4cm (1¼–1½in) of water in it. Cut off faded flowers and if the leaves are smooth mist spray them. When moisture rises to the compost's surface, remove the plant and place it in light shade for a few days.

SAVING A PLANT IN WATERLOGGED COMPOST

If compost becomes totally saturated, air is excluded and roots cease to function. The plant wilts, leaves become limp and slime covers the compost. If noticed early enough plants can be saved. Invert the pot and plant and place a hand under the rootball. Tap the pot's rim on a hard surface so that the rootball slips out. Remove any crocks and

wrap several pieces of kitchen towel around the plant to soak up water. Pick off any root mealy bugs. Leave the rootball wrapped until it is lightly dry. If the rootball is packed with roots, leave it fully exposed to the air. When the surface of the compost is dry but not crumbly, repot the plant into a clean pot, using fresh compost. Leave it for a few days, then water. Do not place it in strong sunlight until it is fully recovered.

Left: The yellow pitcher plant *Sarracenia flava* (huntsman's horn) is hardy in temperate climates. This insectivorous plant catches insects but also needs to be given a liquid fertilizer while it is in flower.

feeding & repotting

Houseplants underachieve if they are not fed regularly once they have filled the pot with roots. Regular feeding is essential if they are to remain healthy and to create an attractive display. Both foliage and summer-flowering houseplants are normally fed at intervals of 10–14 days from early spring to late summer.

Winter-flowering houseplants are fed at the same frequency while they remain in flower.

The most popular way to feed houseplants is by diluting and mixing a concentrated liquid fertilizer in clean tepid water. Adhere to the strength that is recommended by the manufacturer. Before applying the fertilizer, make sure that the compost is moist so that it will be quickly and evenly absorbed. Make up just enough fertilizer to feed your plants on each occasion and do not store any surplus. Keep in one container for fertilizer and do not use it for anything else. Store all chemicals safely.

Using feeding sticks and pills is a clean and quick way to feed houseplants. Feeding sticks are gently pushed into compost, about 1cm (½in) from the pot's side. Pills are also inserted into compost. Some devices enable pills to be inserted without having to dirty your hands on compost. Both feeding sticks and pills provide plants with food over a long period, but they encourage roots to become congested around them.

Do not use feeding sticks and pills after midsummer for plants that flower throughout summer. The fertilizer already released will last for the rest of the flowering season and plants will be able to become dormant after this period. Use feeding sticks or pills on winter-flowering plants in autumn and early winter.

REPOTTING PLANTS

When a plant needs repotting, use either a combination of plastic pots and peat-based compost, or clay pots and soil-based compost, depending on the plant's requirements. Soak clay pots for 24 hours before using them so that they do not draw water from the compost.

Although pots are available in sizes from 6–38cm (2¼–15in) wide, only five sizes are usually needed: 6cm (2¼in), 8cm (3in), 13cm (5in), 18cm (7in) and 25cm (10in). When repotting, always use only the next size up. Remember, too, always to leave sufficient space between the surface of the compost and the rim of the pot to allow plants to be watered effectively. This space needs to increase in proportion to the pot size: for 6–13cm (2½–5in) wide pots leave 1cm (½in); for 14–19cm (5½–7½in) pots leave 2cm (3/4in); for 20–23cm (8–9in) pots leave 2.5cm (1in); and for 25–30cm (10–12in) pots leave 3.5cm (1¼in).

Top-dressing

When a houseplant is in a large pot and cannot be repotted the compost needs to be top-dressed every spring. This involves removing the top 25–36mm (1–1¼in) of old compost and replacing it with fresh. Take care that you not damage the plant's roots when removing the compost. Leave a gap between the top of the compost and the pot's rim so that the plant can be easily watered.

1 Water the plant the day before repotting it. Place your fingers over the top of the rootball and invert the pot. Tap the pot's rim on a firm surface. If the rootball resists, run a knife between it and pot to loosen the roots.

2 Inspect the roots and, when repotting a plant in a clay pot, remove the crock from the rootball's base. Tease out the roots: it may be necessary to use a stiff label or stick.

3 Select a clean pot, slightly larger than the present one. If repotting into a plastic pot, no crock is needed. However, for a clay pot it is usual to add one.

4 Place and firm a handful of compost in the pot's base and position the rootball on top. Check that the surface is below the rim, so that the compost can be adequately watered. When the plant is correctly positioned, trickle and gently firm new compost around the old rootball. Do not ram the compost too tightly into the pot.

5 If necessary, add further compost and gently firm it, leaving the recommended space at the top for watering. Finally, gently tap the side of the pot to level the surface. Then, stand the plant where moisture can drain freely and gently trickle water on top of the compost. Completely fill the watering space. Allow surplus water to drain, later placing the pot in an attractive outer container. Do not water again until the compost shows signs of getting dry – the surface assumes a light colouring.

Left: A young plant of *Plumbago capensis* (Cape leadwort) is often trained around a hoop and grown on a windowsill, where its beautiful, phlox-like flowers can be admired throughout summer and into autumn. The plant is vigorous and stems can reach 1.2m (4ft) in length but can be trimmed in spring to keep them shorter.

Right: The exotically perfumed *Stephanotis floribunda* (bridal wreath, floradora) thrives if kept in a fairly cool room in winter and protected at all times from draughts and sudden changes in temperature. Young plants look pretty trained around a hoop.

grooming & care

Unless they are regularly groomed many houseplants become dirty or grow a mass of tangled shoots that dramatically reduce their attractiveness. Dust radically diminishes the ability of leaves to function and create growth. It blocks breathing pores (stomata) and reduces the amount of light reaching growth-activating cells within the leaves.

If large, smooth-surfaced leaves are covered with a thick layer of dirt, use a soft cloth to dust it off lightly before wiping with water. And never place plants in strong sunlight before moisture dries from them: small water droplets act as lenses and intensify the sun's rays, which will burn leaves and cause them to dry and become brown.

Clean, non-chalky soft water is ideal for cleaning leaves; if you live in an area of hard water, use rainwater or tapwater that has been boiled. Although milk, beer and dilute vinegar are also recommended, they do little to shine leaves. Olive-oil is also advocated, but retains dust, which damages leaves. Several proprietary leaf-cleaning substances are available.

LOOKING AFTER LEAVES
Many plants are grown specifically for their attractive leaves. If these become dirty or

TRAINING AND SUPPORTING

Climbing plants need support to prevent stems sprawling, becoming tangled and intruding on their neighbours. Split canes and plastic-mesh frameworks are ideal for climbing foliage plants, but *Jasminum polyanthum* (pink jasmine) has more visual appeal when supported with loops of pliable canes or proprietary supports that hook on pots and form a loop 30–38cm (12–15in) high.

1 When stems are about 30cm (12in) long, insert a pliable cane support into the pot. It should go near to the pot's sides to avoid damaging the roots.

2 Curl the shoots around the support to create a neat shape.

damaged, this diminishes the display. Cleaning leaves is therefore important and the method for doing this depends on their size and texture. Wipe large, smooth-surfaced leaves with a damp cloth. These include *Ficus elastica* (rubber plant) and *Monstera deliciosa* (Swiss cheese plant). Plants with masses of smooth-surfaced leaves can be inverted and dipped in a bowl of clean water. Some plants have hairy leaves and these are best cleaned carefully using a soft brush.

Damaged leaves can be cut out, together with long and misplaced shoots. When vigorous stems spoil the shape of a plant, use sharp scissors to cut them back to just above a leaf-joint. Azaleas often develop long shoots that are best removed. Cut out dead leaves, but avoid leaving small snags that will die back. If dead leaves are at the top of a shoot, these are best removed by using sharp scissors to cut the stem back to its base.

DEADHEADING

Most dead flowers on houseplants are picked off individually and placed on a compost heap. Azaleas produce a profusion of flowers over several weeks; as the first ones fade, hold the shoot and carefully pinch them off. When you are deadheading cyclamen, pull off each faded flower together with its stem. Hold the stem firmly and give it a sharp tug. It will separate from the plant's base. If just the flower is removed, the stem slowly decays and encourages other flowers and stems to decay. It also looks unsightly. Place the flowers and stems on a compost heap; do not leave them at the plant's base.

2 FLOWERING POT PLANTS

Flowering pot plants will generally be less permanent than other indoor plants, either because they are difficult or impossible to keep going once they have flowered or because the plants are not particularly attractive while they are 'resting' in preparation for the next flowering period.

A large number of plants have been developed and introduced commercially in recent years to provide colour for a limited period, and there is now such a wide choice available that it is possible to have something in flower practically all year round. Cyclamens and azaleas, for example, flower in winter or early spring, while scented spring primroses, celosias and calceolarias bloom in summer. Some plants, however, such as chrysanthemums, can be bought in flower all year.

These plants make a colourful, and sometimes fragrant, contribution when they are in flower, but they should be regarded as short-term additions to the indoor scene. They are usually planted in the garden or even thrown away once the flowering period is over. Some

are annuals and so last only one season anyway; others are short-lived perennials, or perennials that have been reared in special conditions or sometimes artificially treated so that they come into flower at an unusual time or retain what is, in fact, an unnatural dwarf habit.

Feeding the plants generously and removing dead and dying flowers should help to extend the flowering period. Most pot plants need good light, but check each plant's own care requirements carefully. Try to protect plants from sudden changes in temperature and from draughts in winter, and remember that many winter-flowering plants need temperatures that are a little lower than those of most living rooms.

A healthy pot plant makes a good centrepiece for a table or

Left: Flowering pot plants are ideal for creating seasonal displays. Once flowering is over, plants can be removed and the next group brought indoors.
Above: Azaleas and pot chrysanthemums mingle with orchids in this cool conservatory. Complementary containers and surfaces at different heights help to enrich the display.

windowsill, and a brightly coloured flowering plant placed in its pot among foliage plants and ferns will bring the arrangement to life. A visit to your garden centre at any time of year will give you a wide choice of pot plants in flower, and many supermarkets now have a good selection.

plant directory

Achimines hybrids (hot-water plant, cupid's bower)

Much grown by Victorians, these plants have masses of slightly fragrant, flaring trumpet-shaped flowers from spring to autumn. Many colourful hybrids, including some with variegated leaves, have been introduced, and the flowers may be purple, mauve, red, white or blue. Plants are easily grown afresh each year from rhizomes.

Achimenes need a position in bright light with shade from full sun. They tolerate normal room temperatures. Water frequently with tepid water and feed once a week.

Astilbe arendsii (plume of feathers)

More often seen in the garden, astilbes make attractive indoor plants for spring and early summer. The flower plumes are usually in shades pink, but red and white cultivars can be found.

In the house astilbes need fairly bright light with shade from full sun and normal room temperatures. Provide high humidity and water well. After flowering, plant in a damp, semi-shaded part of the garden.

Azalea
See **Rhododendron**

Begonia

This is a large genus, containing plants that are grown for their foliage as well as for their flowers. Tuberous begonia hybrids, *B.* x *tuberhybrida*, with their beautiful, mainly double, rose-like flowers, make lovely flowering pot plants for the summer months, and the group also includes Multiflora and Pendula begonias. Multiflora begonias have many small, single or double flowers. Pendula begonias have similar small flowers and rather arching stems, making them good plants for hanging baskets.

Winter-flowering begonias are low-growing evergreen plants, with

masses of single, semi-double or double flowers from late autumn to early spring, such as the justly popular *B.* 'Gloire de Lorraine', with its masses of small pink flowers in winter, and the many Elatior hybrids.

Begonias need bright but indirect light. Keep them in normal summer room temperatures, with spring warmth to bring them into growth, and make sure that the potting compost is evenly moist.

Calceolaria Herbeohybrida Group (slipper flower, pouch flower, pocketbook plant)
These bushy biennials have distinctive puffed flowers, which give the plant its common names. Buy plants in bud and keep them in a bright, sunny but cool place, with a top temperature of 16°C (61°C), for late spring or early summer yellow, orange or red flowers, which last a month or more.

Celosia argentea var. *cristata* Plumosa Group (cockscomb)
This upright perennial, usually grown as an annual, can be a bedding plant, but its colourful of flowers make it popular indoors. Grow in a light, well-ventilated room out of direct sun at normal room temperatures. Feed once a fortnight and discard after flowering.

Chrysanthemum cvs.
Pot chrysanthemums are now available throughout the year, and

they remain in flower for more than a month. When the display ends they are best discarded, although they can be planted out in a sunny border. They need bright light (but not full sun) in a fairly cool room. Keep the compost moist but not waterlogged.

Cyclamen persicum
Also sold as *C. latifolium*, this popular tuberous perennial has beautifully marbled, heart-shaped leaves and pink, red or white flowers from early winter to spring. Grow in bright but filtered light with a temperature of 13–16°C (55–61°F). Place plants out of draughts. They need moderately warm, humid air. Reduce watering after flowering and keep dry during dormancy. Start to water and feed again when new growth appears.

Erica (heather)
Two species make excellent winter-flowering pot plants, *E. gracilis* (Cape heath) and *E.* x *hiemnalis*, but they must be kept in cool rooms and watered with soft water. Both have masses of tubular flowers, which are tiny and pink or rosy-purple on *E. gracilis*, and larger and pink with white tips on *E.* x *hiemnalis*.

These ericas need lime-free, constantly moist compost and good light. They will tolerate temperatures of 4–13°C (40–55°F).

Exacum affine (Persian violet)
This compact, pretty plant has small, fragrant, mauve flowers with bright yellow centres and heart-shaped leaves. It looks good on a coffee table or bedroom windowsill where it will be in good bright light but not strong sun. It will grow in normal room temperatures with fresh air in hot weather. Water generously and keep the humidity high. Pinch out dying flowers and feed every ten days to ensure that you have flowers all summer long.

Hydrangea macrophylla
Pot hydrangeas are available in flower from spring to autumn, and they can be planted out in the garden once they have flowered. The mopheads of flowers are available in white and shades of pale pink and blue. Hydrangeas do best in cool conditions, in temperatures no higher than 20°C (68°F), in good but indirect light. Water well when plants are in flower and feed once a week.

Pericallis x hybrida (cineraria)

Also known as *Cineraria cruentus*, *C. x hybrida*, *Senecio cruentus* and *S. x hybridus*, these colourful perennials are probably best known as cinerarias. From winter to spring they produce daisy-like flowers in bright shades of blue, pink, red and orange. Despite being popular gift plants, they are quite difficult to please. The compost must be kept moist but must also drain freely, and the plants should not be exposed to either draughts or high temperatures. They like indirect light and an even room temperature, which must never be higher than 15°C (60°F).

The plants are usually available in late winter and spring and will flower for up to two months. Feed them once a fortnight and deadhead regularly to encourage new buds to form. Discard plants after flowering is finished.

Primula

The genus includes a number of different species that can be treated as indoor plants. *P. malacoides* (fairy primrose, baby primrose) is a dainty, short-lived plant, which flowers in winter and has a slight but lovely fragrance. It can sometimes be persuaded to flower for a second season if it is kept well. The typical primrose flowers, in a range of pale purples, pinks and white, are carried in whorls on tall, straight stems, growing from rosettes of tooth-edged leaves.

P. obconia (German primrose, poison primrose) has larger flowers, which may be red, pink, blue or white. Contact with the foliage can cause painful allergic rashes in people with sensitive skin, and the leaves are poisonous so handle it only with care.

The flowers of *P. sinensis* (Chinese primrose) have frilly-edged petals and are available in shades of red and orange as well as a muted blue-pink.

Primulas need bright, indirect light and a fairly cool temperature of 10–13°C (50–55°F). Water them generously and maintain a high level of humidity. Feed every two to three weeks.

Top: Sinningia speciosa (gloxinia) has characteristic brightly coloured and bordered petals and large velvety leaves.
Above: A healthy *Pericallis x hybrida* will keep its flowers longer if it is regularly fed and misted. It should not be given too much heat.

Above: A single pot-grown azalea, *Rhododendron* cv., can form a centrepiece for a table or windowsill.
Right: Several tender primula species can be grown indoors for winter flowers. *Primula obconica* (poison primrose) has the largest flowers and these have a lovely fragrance.

Rhododendron

The large genus contains the well-known evergreen garden shrubs but also the group of small to medium-sized plants that are known as azaleas and that produce a mass of flowers in white or shades of yellow, orange, pink and red. Azaleas may be deciduous and evergreen, and there are numerous subdivisions within each group. The evergreen Indica (Indian) hybrids are widely bought for their large, funnel-shaped flowers, which are borne in winter. Azaleas must have ericaceous compost, which should be kept just moist in winter. They need bright but indirect light and high humidity. Keep them in a cool place, with a maximum temperature of 13–16°C (55–61°F), when they are in flower. In summer, after they have flowered, keep them in a shaded, cool place outdoors. Bring them indoors again in the early winter before the first frosts and being to water again as flowerbuds appear.

Sinningia speciosa (gloxinia)

Increasingly exotic-looking hybrids of this plant have been bred in recent years. The rosettes of leaves are soft and velvety, and the large, flaring bell-shaped to tubular flowers, in white or shades of red and violet-blue, often have contrasting throats and may be bordered in white or contrasting colours. Gloxinias need bright, indirect light and a warm temperature, 20–22°C (68–72°F), day and night in summer (when they are in flower). Keep the air humid by standing the pots on a tray of moist pebbles but do not spray the leaves or flowers and water plants from below. Feed once a fortnight in the growing season.

3 FLOWERING HOUSEPLANTS

A well-cared for plant that has 'lived' in a house for several years and that still flowers duly in its season is as much a source of pleasure – and pride – as a well-polished antique. These are the flowering houseplants, as opposed to the flowering pot plants, which come and go and are often dispensed with at the end of the flowering season. Many flowering houseplants can become quite large and will eventually need to be given plenty of room, perhaps in a hall with a high ceiling or standing by a patio door, or even in a conservatory or sun room.

Left: Grouping houseplants of similar sizes or textures enhances their beauty. Here, the delicate flowers of *Saintpaulia ionnantha* (African violets) are echoed by the leaves of *Adiantum raddianum* (maidenhair fern).
Right: The bright yellow flowerheads of *Pachystachys lutea* (lollipop plant) are formed by a cone of overlapping bracts. It flowers from late spring to early autumn and grows well in a room that is cool in summer.
Below right: Euphorbia pulcherrima (poinsettia) has become a classic midwinter plant. The showy bracts make a cheerful seasonal display. Most poinsettias have deep crimson bracts, but white, pink and scarlet cultivars are available.

To stand the test of time, a plant must be well chosen in the first place. There is no point in being seduced by a light-craving hot-house plant if you live in a dark, cool cottage, just as, if your fifth-floor flat gets the full glare of the midday sun, there is little point in buying a plant that needs a position in shade. Choose from the justly popular, well-established favourites that are widely available, or search out something a little different from a specialist grower.

Buy from a reputable supplier. Look out for a healthy-looking specimen that is not pot bound. It should have plenty of new buds and exhibit vigorous, but not soft, growth.

Your plant will need to be repotted, into a pot one size larger, as its roots fill its pot, and this should done at the end of the dormant period. This may have to be done every year, especially while the plant is young and growing quickly. Once the plant has exhausted the minerals in the compost – after approximately six to eight weeks – feed it with proprietary fertilizer during the growing period.

Left: *Anthurium scherzerianum* (flamingo flower) has bold foliage as well as striking red flowers in spring and summer.
Above: *Aphelandra squarrosa* will lose its magnificent leaves very quickly if its roots dry out.
Right: *Bougainvillea* (paper flower) makes a spectacular deciduous indoor climber for a warm, light, sunny position.

plant directory

Acalypha hispida (chenille plant)
An old favourite, this is grown for its softly drooping tassels or catkins, which hang from the stems from midsummer to mid-autumn and give rise to another common name: red-hot cat's tail. These tassels are made up of hundreds of minute flowers, which are usually deep scarlet, although there are forms with cream and greenish tassels. The plant grows to a height of 1–1.2m (3–4ft) with a spread of 30–45cm (12–14in). Stand in bright, indirect light with a normal room temperature in summer but no lower than 15°C (59°F) in winter. Water freely in summer and keep the compost moist in winter. Feed every 10–14 days from spring to autumn.

Aeschynanthus radicans (lipstick vine)
Also sold as *A. lobbianus* and *A. radicans* var. *lobbianus*, this is a trailing perennial, with cascades of little fleshy leaves and tubular red flowers with cream throats. The stems grow to 45–60cm (18–24in) long, and this is an ideal plant for a hanging basket in a sun room or conservatory. It needs bright light, but avoid a position in full sun in summer, and a warm summer temperature. In winter it should be cooler, with a minimum of 13°C (55°F). Water with tepid water, freely in summer, more sparingly in winter, and feed monthly from late spring and throughout the summer. Mist regularly to maintain a humidity.

Allamanda
A. cathartica (golden trumpet) is a vigorous climber with large yellow flowers from summer to autumn and glossy, dark green leaves. Support the stems. *A. schottii* (syn. *A. neriifolia*) is shrubbier, bearing golden-yellow flowers from spring to autumn. Both need good light and indirect sun, with minimum winter temperatures of 18°C (65°F). Water freely in the growing season, feeding every 2–3 weeks. In winter keep the compost just moist.

Anthurium (flamingo flower, tail flower)
A. scherzerianum is a terrestrial or epiphytic perennial with red, palette-shaped spathes, each of which has a

curly, wick-like spire of tiny flowers, from spring to autumn. It is a compact plant, 30cm (12in) high and 30–38cm (12–15in) across, and has attractive, lance-shaped leaves. Similar, but larger – up to 45cm (18in) high and 30cm (12in) across – is *A. andreanum* (painter's palette, oilcloth flower), which has a straight 'tail' and red spathes. There are cultivars with pink, yellow and orange spathes.

Anthuriums need bright but indirect light and normal room temperatures in summer but no lower than 15–18°C (59–64°F) in winter. Water generously in summer but keep the compost just moist in winter. Keep the surrounding air moist and feed every 10–14 days from mid-spring to early autumn.

Aphelandra squarrosa (saffron spike, zebra plant)

This compact shrub is grown for its boldly patterned foliage as well as for the pineapple-like yellow bracts, which form the showy part of its flowerheads. The cultivar 'Louisae' has prominent white ribs on the leaves, and the golden-yellow flower spikes are streaked with red. Plants grow to about 75cm (30in) high and to about 40cm (16in) wide. They need bright, indirect light and normal room temperatures in summer but a winter minimum of 12–15°C (54–59°F). Water generously in summer and moderately in winter. Feed every 10–14 days. Cut off flowerheads when they die and cut the plant back to keep it bushy if necessary.

Begonia

In addition to the many cultivars of tuberous begonias grown for their beautiful flowers, the genus contains several other worthwhile species. *B. scharffii* (syn. *B. haageana*; elephant ear begonia) is a shrub-like begonia with large, curiously shaped leaves, which make the plant interesting all year round. The pale pink summer flowers are a bonus. It will grow to 1.2m (4ft) high with a spread of 60cm (2ft). *B. metallica* (metallic leaf begonia) is best known as a foliage plant, but it, too, has pretty white flowers, borne in clusters in late summer. It grows to about 1m (3ft) high and 60cm (2ft) across.

Both plants need bright but indirect light, with some direct sun in winter. Normal room temperatures are acceptable in summer, but a constant temperature of 13–15°C (55–60°F) is needed in winter. Too much summer heat can be fatal. Keep the atmosphere humid, especially during the summer. Water the plants moderately in summer but only sparingly in winter. Feed every 14 days in summer.

Bougainvillea glabra

A young bougainvillea is a wonderfully showy plant for a sunny windowsill, but it is a scrambler that will need to be trained and given ample space as it grows. The papery, purple 'flowers' are really bracts and grow in clusters through the summer. Bougainvilleas must have ample, bright light all year round. They need to be warm in summer, but with cooler temperatures, 7–12°C (45–54°F), in winter. Water sparingly in summer and keep the compost almost dry in winter. The plants are best grown best in a conservatory when they are more than three years old.

Left: Many calatheas are grown as much for their foliage as for their flowers. *Calathea crocata*, however, makes a pretty focal point.
Right: Columnea hirta has stiff, trailing stems and bears orange-red flowers.
Below right: The quilted leaves of *Episcia cupreata* (carpet plant) have bronze-tinged highlights. The pretty little red, yellow-eyed flowers are almost hidden among the leaves.

not too hot, in summer, with a temperature of 15–19°C (59–66°F), but cooler, 4–10°C (39–50°F), in winter. Keep the compost moist and feed every seven to ten days in summer. Cut back all the stems after flowering and let the plant rest, watering sparingly, in winter.

Cestrum nocturnum (night jessamine)

Similar to jasmine, with an equally strong and beautiful scent. When young this night-flowering plant is ideal for a light living room, but it can grow to 3m (10ft) and then needs a conservatory or large, light space. Train the twining stems up canes and along wires. Position in bright light, but with protection from full summer sun. Plants need a minimum winter temperature of 7°C (45°F). Water generously in summer and moderately in winter.

Columnea (goldfish plant)

There are several popular columneas and all are trailing plants for sun rooms and conservatories. They are useful as they flower throughout winter, from autumn to early spring. *C. microphylla* trails to 1.8m (6ft) and has bright orange-red flowers and hairy leaves. The flowers of *C. x banksii* are similar but have orange markings, the dark green leaves are glossy, and the stems are a more modest 1m (3ft). *C. gloriosa* has stems to 1.2m (4ft) long; it bears scarlet flowers with a yellow patch, and has

Brunfelsia pauciflora (yesterday, today and tomorrow)

This shrubby plant, formerly known as *B. calycina* (syn. *B. eximia*), has pretty flowers that change colour from violet to white as they age. It flowers all summer when growing well and will get to 60cm (2ft) high and 30cm (12in) across. Position plants in bright, indirect light and keep warm in summer, but not above 21°C (70°F); in winter they need a constant temperature of 10–13°C (50–55°F). Water generously and mist the leaves in summer, feeding once a month when plants are in flower. Water sparingly during the dormant period.

Calathea crocata

Most members of the genus are grown as foliage plants (see page 47), but this species produces yellow flowers, resembling small orchids, on erect stems above the leaves. Plants grow to about 30cm (12in) high and 23cm (9in) across. They need bright but indirect light and high humidity. A year-round temperature of 15–21°C (60–70°F) is ideal. Make sure plants are sited out of draughts. Water freely during the growing season and feed every 14 days, but in winter just keep the compost moist.

Campanula isophylla (falling stars, Italian bellflower)

This is a low-growing plant, to 15cm (6in) high, with a spread of 30–45cm (12–18in). The lovely pale blue or white, bell-shaped flowers are borne throughout summer. Its trailing habit makes it ideal for a tall pot or stand or for a hanging basket. Position in good, indirect light. It needs to be warm, but

pale green hairy leaves. *C. gloriosa*
'Purpurea' has purple leaves. *C. hirta*
is one of the smaller species: the
strong, creeping stems bear a mass
of red flowers in spring.

Grow columneas in bright light but
out of direct sun. They need normal
summer temperatures and a winter
temperature of about 16°C (61°F), but
no lower than 13°C (55°F). They need
humid conditions, and the compost
must be kept moist at all times. Feed
weekly once the flower buds appear.

Cuphea ignea (cigar flower)

Formerly known as *C. platycentra*,
this compact shrub produces long,
tubular, bright red flowers, which are
tipped with dark purple and ash
white, from spring until the beginning
of winter or even longer. *C. ignea*
'Alba' has white flowers, and
'Variegata' has yellow-marked leaves.
Cupheas need bright light but with
some shade from full sun in summer.
They will grow in normal summer
temperatures but need a cooler
temperature, 10–13°C (50–55°F),
during the winter rest. Cupheas can
be stood outside in warm summer
weather as long as good humidity can
be maintained. Water generously in
spring and summer and feed every
two weeks. Water sparingly in winter
and do not feed.

Episcia (carpet plant, flame violet)

A close relation of *Saintpaulia* (African
violet), episcias are flowering
houseplants grown also for their
foliage. The variable *E. cupreata* has
flame red flowers and quilted leaves.
E. dianthiflora (syn. *Alsobia
dianthiflora*; lace flower) has plump,
downy leaves and white flowers with
fringed petals, similar to those of
Dianthus (garden pinks). Both species
grow to only about 8cm (3in) high.
They have trailing stems or runners to
30cm (12in) long, from which new
plants can be grown. Position the
plants in good light, avoiding strong
sun. Normal room temperatures are
suitable for summer, but plants need
a winter minimum of 13°C (55°F). Try
to give plants a slight drop in
temperature each evening and make
sure that the air around them is
humid by misting and standing their
pots in a dish of wet pebbles.

Euphorbia (spurge)

This is a large genus, containing plants that can be grown in the open garden as well as several that are normally grown as houseplants. *E. milii* (crown of thorns) is a handsome plant, grown for the colourful, showy bracts – red, yellow or white – that surround the tiny, insignificant flowers, which are borne in spring and early summer and almost non-stop in a really bright light. It has rather sprawling stems with prominent spines and grows to a height of 1m (3ft). This euphorbia is a popular, undemanding plant as long as you can find a sunny spot for it. It needs a bright position, but shaded from midday summer sun. In summer it will grow in normal room temperatures, but it needs a winter minimum of 13°C (55°F). Water sparingly and feed once a month.

    E. pucherrima (poinsettia, Mexican flame leaf) is often available for Christmas decorations, and the bright red bracts are certainly eye-catching and cheerful. It is sometimes treated as an annual and thrown away in spring, because it needs a period of rest, in a cool, shaded position, with two months in darkness for half each day, in summer, which can be difficult to provide in most people's homes. Stop watering after flowering and only begin again when new growth begins.

Gardenia augusta (Cape jasmine)

Also known as *G. florida*, *G. grandiflora* and *G. jasminoides*, these shrubs bear beautiful, fragrant flowers from summer to autumn. Plants grow to 12m (40ft) high in the wild, but when they are grown in pots, heights of 60cm (2ft) are more usual. Grow in good but filtered light. Plants need ericaceous compost. Water freely in summer, using soft water, and feed every month. In winter plants need a minimum temperature of 10°C (50°F).

Hibiscus rosa-sinensis (rose of China)

This is another good plant for a sunny position. Most often seen with deep reddish-pink flowers, it can also have yellow, orange, pale pink or white blooms. The cultivar 'Cooperi' has cream- and pink-variegated leaves. Orange-flowered cultivars include 'Tivoli' and 'Royal Orange'. The large flowers are short-lived, but new buds open regularly through summer. A well-cared for hibiscus can live for many years and grow to 1.5m (5ft) high if not cut back. Grow hibiscus in good light with an even temperature of 18°C (64°F) or above all year round to give non-stop flowering. If you want to give the plant a winter rest, the temperature should be 10–15°C (50–60°F). Water plants fairly generously and feed once a week while they are in flower. In winter water moderately and do not feed if you going to allow the plant a dormant period. Hibiscus, which are native to China, are long-lived plants, but are all too often lost through poor treatment when grown as houseplants. Underwatering causes buds to drop and leaves to fall; underfeeding reduces flowering; low humidity, draughts, sudden temperature changes and over-generous watering are also damaging.

Hoya (wax flower)

H. carnosa (wax plant), which bears clusters of waxy, scented flowers, looks and smells exotic, but it is not too difficult to grow. Its climbing stems will grow up to 4.5m (15ft) and must be trained up canes or trellis or along wires. It looks natural and attractive trained up a moss pole. Position in bright light, with some shade from strong summer sun. It needs a summer minimum temperature of 16°C (61°F), and in winter it needs to be kept at around 10°C (50°F) and not below 7°C (45°F). Give the plant fresh air in summer, but keep the humidity high.

    Another popular hoya is *H. lanceolata* subsp. *bella* (syn. *H. bella*; miniature wax plant), which grows to about 45cm (18in) high and across, and it is perfect for a hanging basket. It needs more warmth in winter, 13°C (55°F), and must be well protected from strong summer sun.

Ixora coccinea (flame of the woods)

This eye-catching plant needs some care. Its big flowerheads are clustered with little red, white, yellow or pink flowers, and it forms an evergreen, bushy plant, which can grow up to 38cm (15in) in a year. It needs bright, filtered light, away from direct sun. Water and mist spray plants regularly, using tepid, boiled water, but after flowering water only sparingly and rest the plant for about two months. Do not repot these plants unless it becomes absolutely necessary, when an ericaceous compost should be used.

Far left: Euphorbia milii (crown of thorns) is grown for the waxy bracts around its tiny yellow flowers. Left: The pinkish-white flowers of Justicia brandegeeana (shrimp plant) project from overlapping bracts. Grown in good sun, the plant is covered with flowers from spring to autumn. Right: Passiflora incarnata (maypops) a strongly growing passionflower, which has beautifully scented flowers in summer, is native to North America.

Jasminum polyanthum (pink jasmine)

The lovely pink jasmine, with its pink buds and clusters of scented white flowers, is fairly easy to grow and flowers indoors in winter. A climber, which can reach 3m (10ft), it is generally restricted and trained over a hoop by wrapping the tendrils around the support. Cut it back after flowering. Grow in bright light. It does best in cooler rooms, heated to 7–10°C (45–50°F) in winter.

Justicia brandegeeana (shrimp plant)

Formerly known as *Beloperone guttata* (syn. *Drejerella guttata*, *J. guttata*), this evergreen shrub is a charming curiosity. The flowerheads consist of shrimp-like bracts, terminating in a white, tubular flower. It makes a small plant, 30–40cm (12–16in) high and across, and is easy to grow, provided you are able to give it a sunny windowsill. Although it needs bright sunlight it will do best with some protection from direct summer sun. In summer grow in normal, warm room temperatures. In winter it needs cooler temperatures, 10–16°C (50–61°F), and will tolerate temperatures as low as 7°C (45°F). Water generously in summer and sparingly in winter. Grow two or three plants together for a good show, and cut them back in spring if they begin to get 'leggy'.

Mandevilla

M. sanderi 'Rosea' (syn. *Dipladenia sanderi* 'Rosea') is a gorgeous and versatile plant. Its large pink flowers appear in profusion throughout the summer if the air is kept warm and humid, and it can be trained as a climber, to 4.5m (15ft) or pruned as a shrub. *M. laxa* (syn. *Dipladenia laxa*, *M. suaveolens*: Chilean jasmine) has white, extremely fragrant flowers. Mandevillas need good light but with protection from strong sun. Try to maintain a constant temperature of about 21°C (70°F) in summer and 15°C (60°F) in winter, with a minimum of 13°C (55°F). Water generously in summer and fairly sparingly in winter. Feed flowering plants once a week.

Manettia luteorubra (Brazilian firecracker)

Formerly known as *M. bicolor* and *M. inflata*, this is a fast-growing, undemanding and attractive plant. It grows well in normal room conditions and flowers almost all year round. Long, red, downy tubular flowers, tipped with yellow, peep out from glossy, deep green leaves. Stems grow rapidly and can reach 3m (10ft). Grow in full sun with a minimum winter temperature of 7°C (45°F). Keep the compost moist at all times, and water more generously in spring and summer. Train the plant up a pyramid of canes, tying in the new shoots as they grow.

Pachystachys lutea (lollipop plant)

A bright and fairly adaptable plant, about 50cm (20in) high, this bears bold, clear, yellow flowerheads made up of overlapping bracts with little, white projecting flowers from spring to autumn. It needs good bright light, but not full sun. Give it normal room temperatures throughout the year, with a winter minimum of 13°C (55°F). Water generously when the plant is in flower but quite sparingly in winter. Keep the surrounding air moist in warm weather. Repot and trim back every spring.

Passiflora caerulea (common passionflower)

Also known as blue passionflower and passion vine, the large and complex summer flowers of this lovely climber can be followed by orange fruits. Although passionflowers can be grown in protected gardens, they are not reliably hardy. Indoors, grow in bright sunlight. They need normal summer temperatures, but should be allowed a winter rest at about 10°C (50°F). Water plants extremely generously while they are flower, but keep the compost just moist in winter. A young plant can be trained around a hoop, but it is vigorous and does justice to a trellis as it grows. Too much feeding can encourage the plant to produce more leaves than flowers.

Left: Pelargonium 'Parasol' is typical of the regal type with its many-petalled flowers splashed in pink and white and streaked with deep red markings.

Pelargonium (geranium)

This old favourite is at home everywhere. There are three main types grown for their flowers: zonal pelargoniums, which often have bold zones of contrasting colour on the leaves; regal pelargoniums, which have bigger, fancier flowers and irregularly edged leaves; and ivy-leaved or trailing pelargoniums, which have lobed, rather fleshy leaves. If you provide plenty of sun and make sure that plants are kept reasonably warm in winter, they will flower cheerfully all year round, but they can be given a cooler winter rest. The bushy types can be quite compact or can reach 60cm (24in) high with a spread of 25–45cm (10–18in). *P. peltatum* (trailing geranium) has shiny, ivy-like leaves. These plants are perfect for hanging baskets or as part of a display on a light, open landing or indoor balcony. They trail for up to 1m (3ft). Pelargoniums, especially zonal and regal types, need full sun. They will survive at normal room temperature all year round, with a winter minimum of 7–10°C (45–50°F). Water fairly generously and feed every two to three weeks when in flower. If plants are resting in lower temperatures keep the compost barely moist. Bushy types become 'leggy' in inadequate light.

Plumbago auriculata (Cape leadwort)

Formerly known as *P. capensis*, this unattractively named plant has the most attractive blue flowers. It can be allowed to trail but is best trained to a support. Like *Passiflora caerulea*, it is fairly tolerant but must have a cool winter rest. Grow in fairly bright light, but not full midday sun, with normal summer temperatures. The winter temperature should be 7–10°C (45–50°F). Water generously when in flower in summer and autumn, sparingly in winter.

Saintpaulia cvs. (African violet)

African violets are one of the most familiar of houseplants, thanks partly to central heating and partly to the ease with which new plants can be propagated from the velvety leaves. These pretty little plants can be kept in flower all year but they can be quite fussy. They usually grow to 8–10cm (3–4in) high and 15–23cm (6–9in) across, but tiny, and exquisite, miniature forms are now becoming popular. African violets look well in groups, and this helps to keep the humidity high, which is essential, as are acid compost and regular feeding. Grow in good, bright light but avoid strong sun. They need steady warmth all year round with a minimum temperature of 15°C (60°F).

Spathiphyllum wallisii (peace lily)

An elegant, rhizomatous plant, this has long, gleaming leaves and tall flowers, consisting of a white, sail-like spathe surrounding a creamy-white flower spike. The flowers are borne from late spring throughout summer. Plants needs warmth, with minimum winter temperatures of 10°C (50°F), and humidity. In summer they should be shaded from strong, direct sun, but in winter need a bright position.

They hate draughts. Feed every ten days throughout the year, but with the fertilizer at half strength in winter.

Stephanotis floribunda (bridal wreath, floradora)

Formerly known as *S. jasminoides*, this lovely and desirable plant has glossy, leathery leaves and headily scented, waxy flowers from early summer to mid-autumn. Stephanotis will climb and spread to 3m (10ft) or so and needs to be trained to a trellis or along wires. Grow in good light with shade from full sun in summer; plants need full light in winter. provide a constant temperatures of about 18–21°C (64–70°F) in summer and a winter minimum of 13°C (55°F). While plants are in flower water generously and provide high humidity, especially when temperatures are high, and feed once every two weeks. Water sparingly in winter.

Streptocarpus cvs. (Cape primrose, Cape cowslip)

Many colourful cultivars have been developed, and there is a wide choice of white-, pink-, mauve-, blue- or purple-flowered plants. The common name seems a misnomer, for the flowers, borne on long, upright stems, resemble single foxgloves or large violets, growing from a loose rosette of rounded leaves. Grow in good, indirect light, with a temperature up to 15°C (60°F) in summer and a steady 10–13°C (50–55°F) in winter. Water freely in summer and stand plants on a tray of wet pebbles to increase humidity. Water more sparingly in winter. Do not mist.

insectivorous plants

Insectivorous plants are of three main types: pitcher plants, sticky-leaved plants and fly traps. They are interesting rather than lovely, but they are not easy to keep in cultivation, requiring both a protected environment and high levels of humidity.

Some types of insectivorous plants, such as the sarracenias, produce enzymes to digest trapped insects. Larger species may also attract larger animals, such as frogs, mice or even small birds.

plant directory

Darlingtonia californica (pitcher plant, cobra lily)
This rosette-forming perennial plant from northern California and Oregon looks just like a cluster of snakes. The nectar attracts insects, which become trapped in the plant's greenish-yellow 'pitcher'. It needs good, indirect light, normal summer temperatures and a cooler winter temperature of 7–10°C (45–50°F). These plant need high humidity and generous watering, especially in summer.

Dionaea muscipula (Venus fly-trap)
This is, perhaps, the best known of the insectivorous plants. It is native to North and South Carolina and can be grown in a conservatory. Plants form rosettes of yellow-green leaves, which are composed of two hinged lobes. Each leaf is edged with spines. When an insect touches a spine, the leaf closes around it. Plants grow to about 45cm (18in) high and to 15cm (6in) across. Grow in good but filtered light and stand the pots in saucers of water to keep the compost moist.

Drosera (sundew, daily dew)
This is a large genus, but only a few species are available. D. binata, an evergreen perennial, has long-stalked, deeply cut leaves, which are covered with red-stalked hairs. They secrete a sticky fluid, which insects mistake for nectar and adhere to. D. capensis (Cape sundew) grows about 30cm (12in) high and to 15cm (6in) across. The spoon-shaped leaves are covered with red or green hairs. Rose-pink flowers are borne from spring to autumn and sometimes winter. Plants should be grown in a mix of equal parts sand and peat or peat substitute. Grow in full light, shaded from hot, direct sun. They need a minimum temperature of 2°C (36°F).

Nepenthes x coccinea (monkey cup, pitcher plant)
This hybrid has broad, arching leaves with 'pitchers', to 15cm (6in) long, hanging from the tips. The pitchers are yellow-green and are mottled with purplish-red. Plants, which can grow to 6m (20ft) but are unlikely to achieve this in cultivation, are good for hanging baskets. Grow in good but filtered light, with protection from direct sun. They need a minimum daytime temperature of 24°C (75°F); the summer night-time temperature should be 21°C (70°F) and the summer night temperature should be 15°C (60°F).

Above: The deep, horn-shaped pitchers of *Sarracenia leucophylla* are veined in purple and decoratively frilled caps. It is very tall – about 75cm (30in) high.

Sarracenia (pitcher plant)
The genus contains several pitcher plants that can be grown in cold or cool greenhouses or even on a sunny windowsill. S. purpurea (huntsman's cup) has purple or green pitchers, veined with purple. S. flava (yellow trumpet, huntsman's horn) has slender, trumpet-like pitchers, which can reach almost 1m (3ft), although they are likely to be shorter in cultivation. S. x catesbaei has green to dark purple pitchers to 75cm (30in).

4 FOLIAGE PLANTS

Plants grown mainly for their leaves often form the backbone of a houseplant collection. Many foliage plants are extremely undemanding and long lived. They can grow to a good size or form the most pleasing shapes, and they can take up a permanent place in the home.

A mature, large foliage plant, such as the ever-popular *Ficus elastica* (rubber plant) or *Ficus benjamina* (weeping fig), can be at its best displayed alone as a specimen plant, standing in a large, handsome container on the floor. Smaller, but equally distinctive, foliage plants provide perfect specimen plants for tables, sideboards and cupboard tops and for broad windowsills and shelves. These include some adaptable plants such as *Araucaria heterophylla* (Norfolk Island Pine). Foliage plants that creep or trail can be shown off in indoor hanging baskets or trailing down from pots placed on high shelves, and almost any green-leaved foliage plant will act as a foil to a flowering plant. Most rooms in the house have a niche for a foliage plant, and they can be excellent in circulation spaces such as halls and landings where ceilings are often high.

Favourites, such as *Monstera deliciosa* (Swiss cheese plant), *Ficus benjamina*, *Schefflera elegantissima* (false aralia), yucca and palm, can grow to well over 1m (3ft) high. Growth may be slow, but eventually you will need a room with a high ceiling. Large entrance halls and landings and half-landings on the stairs can be good places for them as they mature but living rooms are generally ideal in their young days.

Like smaller plants, the large foliage plants can group extremely well when they are young, with their contrasting leaf shapes setting each other off to great advantage. For this sort of arrangement a raised trough works well and gives the plants the height they need at this stage of their lives.

Opposite: Many cultivars of dieffenbachia are grown for their magnificent leaves, spotted and streaked in green, cream and white.
Below: The archetypal plant of the 1970s, *Chlorophytum comosum* (spider plant) is becoming popular once again.

trailing &
cascading plants

Foliage plants that trail or cascade can be shown off to the full in hanging bowls or baskets or trailing down from pots placed on high shelves. The old trick of filtering out a less than perfect view by growing trailing plants in pots on a shelf fixed across the top of the window so that the greenery trails down the glass is well tried and tested. Trailers can grow down from pots placed on small shelves or ornamental wall brackets, and they are perfect for high windows, which allow them to tumble down the wall below the sill. Smaller trailing plants can be grown around other plants in a grouped arrangement, where they can fill in the gaps between the plants and spill over the edges of the container, or they can be planted to cover the base and pot edges of large specimen plants. Plants with arching stems are ideal for display in a pot on a tall pedestal.

All of the following flourish in normal room temperatures unless otherwise indicated.

plant directory

Asparagus

Although they are often called ferns, the plants in the genus are evergreen and deciduous perennials, climbers and shrubs. *A. densiflorus* (asparagus fern) has arching stems with glossy, light green leaves. The cultivar 'Sprengeri' (syn. *A. sprengeri*; emerald feather) had arching stems. It is the larger, more common and more luxuriant of the two popular asparagus ferns, the other being 'Meyersii' (syn. *A. meyeri*; foxtail fern). The hanging stems of emerald feathers are covered with a froth of green needles and quickly grow to 1–1.2m (3–4ft). Grow in semi-shade with a minimum winter temperature of 8°C (48°F). These plants need high humidity, especially when the air is warm. Feed every two to three weeks from spring to autumn.

Callisia elegans (striped inch plant)

Formerly known as *Setcreasea striata*, this is spreading perennial, with oval, dark green leaves with white, longitudinal stripes and purple beneath. White flowers are borne from autumn to winter. These are easy plants, tolerant of a wide range of conditions. Grow in bright or filtered light with a minimum winter temperature of 10°C (50°F). Water regularly during the growing season and feed once a month.

Chlorophytum comosum (spider plant)

This well-known and easy-to-grow plant has arching green leaves and is best known in its striped forms 'Variegatum' and 'Vittatum'. Grow it where its white runners, up to 75cm (30in) long, with their little plantlets, can hang freely. It needs bright, indirect light and a minimum winter temperature of 7°C (45°F). Feed every week from spring to autumn and repot as soon as the roots fill the pot.

Epipremnum aureum (devil's ivy, golden pothos)

Formerly (and still sometimes) known as *Scindapsus aureus*, this is a fast-growing plant with glossy, bright green, heart-shaped leaves that are splashed and spotted with creamy-white. It is a good plant for training up canes, a trellis or a mossy pole in either bright or dim light. Grow it in good but filtered light. It needs a minimum winter temperature of 15°C (60°F). Water plants freely during the spring and summer and feed once a month. In winter keep the compost just moist.

Ficus pumila (creeping fig)

Formerly known as *F. reptans*, this relative of the rubber plant (see page 50) has small, glossy, heart-shaped leaves when young. Its shoots grow to 30cm (12in) per year. The cultivar 'Sonny' has white-edged leaves. Grow in semi-shade with a minimum winter temperature of 10°C (50°F). Water regularly during the growing season and feed once a month. These plants need high humidity.

Opposite: Two young plants of *Fittonia albivensis* Argyroneura Group are a fine contrast with *Spathiphdyllum wallisii* (peace lily).

Above: Like many plants with small, delicate leaves, *Ficus pumilla* 'Variegata' (creeping fig) looks at its best against a plain background.

Fittonia albivensis (net leaf, nerve plant)

These evergreen, mat-forming perennials have small oval leaves, strongly veined in a contrasting colour. The leaves of *F. albivensis* Argyroneura Group (silver net leaf) are pale green with silver-white veining; those of Verschaffeltii Group (painted net leaf) are dark green with red veins. These are good plants for a terrarium. They need soil-less compost in indirect light. Maintain high humidity around the plants and provide a minimum temperature of 15°C (60°F). Do not allow the compost to get too wet, but feed every three to four weeks in the growing season.

Glechoma hederacea 'Variegata' (creeping variegated ground ivy)

This plant used to be known as *Nepeta glechoma* 'Variegata' (syn. *N. hederacea* 'Variegata'). It has white-splashed, scalloped leaves and grows best in cooler rooms. It grows well as a trailer and its stems can reach to 1.8m (6ft) if not kept trimmed. Grow in bright, indirect light with a winter temperature of no higher than 13°C (55°F). Keep the compost moist and feed once a week in summer.

Gynura aurantica (velvet plant)

Sometimes (but wrongly) known and sold as *G. sarmentosa*, this woody perennial is upright at first, but increasingly becomes a trailer as it grows. The purple leaves are hairy, and the yellow-orange flowers appear during winter. It grows fast if it is given plenty of light, and the growing tip should be pinched out regularly in order to keep the plants bushy. Grow in bright, but filtered light, with a minimum winter temperature of 13°C (55°F). Water regularly during the growing season and feed every three to four weeks.

Maranta leuconeura (prayer plant)

These attractive foliage plants have dark green, oval leaves, beautifully marked with shades of green, grey-green and silver. The undersides are reddish-purple. The cultivar 'Erythroneura' (herringbone plant) has wonderful leaves: they are dark green with a lighter central line, red veins and midribs and irregular, lighter green margins. 'Kerchoveana' has light green leaves with bold, dark green-brown splodges. 'Massangeana' has black-green leaves with silver-grey variegation, veins and midribs and purple undersides. Their common name derives from their habit of raising their leaves at night. All grow to about 30cm (12in) high and across. Grow in filtered light or semi-shade away from all draughts. They need high humidity and should be watered regularly in summer, with a liquid feed every three to four weeks. Reduce the water in winter. They need a minimum winter temperature of about 15°C (60°F). They have a trailing habit and can be grown in a hanging basket or trained up a moss pole.

Philodendron scandens (sweetheart plant, heart leaf)

This popular and easy plant has glossy, heart-shaped leaves. It can be trained as a climber if you wish but also spreads and trails beautifully, with shoots growing as much as 0.6–1m (2–3ft) in a year. Grow in good, indirect light, although it will tolerate periods in shade. The temperature should never be higher than 24°C (75°F). Water generously from spring to autumn and feed once a week in summer.

Plectranthus

The genus contains two trailing plants that make attractive houseplants, especially suitable for hanging baskets. *P. forsteri* (syn. *P. coleoides*) has light green leaves with scalloped edges; the cultivar 'Marginata' has leaves that are prettily edged with white. *P. oertendahlii* (candle plant) has bronze-green leaves with creamy-white veins and midribs; the undersides are purplish. Grow plants in good light but sheltered from strong, direct sun, and with a minimum winter temperature of 10°C (50°F). Water plants regularly during

Above left: Maranta leuconeura 'Erythroneura' (herringbone plant), like all the prayer plants, has leaves that point upwards at night.

Above: The trouble-free *Tradescantia pallida* 'Purpurea' (purple heart) can quickly become straggly, but it is easy to grow replacement plants from cuttings.

Above right: Its trailing habit and heart-shaped leaves make *Philodendron scandens* (sweetheart plant) perfect for hanging baskets. Here it is balanced visually by a *Nephrolepis cordifolia* (sword fern), a small-leaved trailing *Hedera helix* (ivy) and the white- and green-leaved *Plectranthus forsteri* 'Marginatus' (candle plant).

the growing season, feeding once a month, but give them less water during winter.

Saxifraga stolonifera (mother of thousands)

This rosette-forming plant, previously known as *S. sarmentosa*, produces a mound of round, hairy leaves and produces wiry, pinkish runners up to 1m (3ft) long threaded with numerous little plantlets that can be potted up. The cultivar 'Tricolor' (syn. *S. stolonifera* 'Magic Carpet') has variegated leaves marked with white and flushed with pink in patches. Grow plants in good, indirect light with a minimum winter temperature of 10°C (50°F). Water from below, fairly generously in summer and more sparingly in winter. Feed every two to three weeks during summer.

Scindapsus pictus 'Argyraeum'

Formerly (and confusingly) known as *Epipremnum pictum* 'Argyraeum', this is a slow-growing climber, with heart-shaped, velvety leaves covered in silvery spots. Grow plants in good but filtered light. They need a minimum winter temperature of 15°C (60°F).

Water freely during spring and summer and feed once a month. In winter keep the compost just moist.

Tradescantia

T. fluminensis (wandering Jew), a trailing perennial, has oval, light green leaves, often purplish beneath. The cultivar 'Variegata' (syn. *T. albiflora* 'Variegata') has leaves that are longitudinally striped with white and green. *T. pallida* (syn. *Setcreasea pallida*; purple heart) is a tolerant plant, with long, narrow, purple leaves with a velvety bloom. The upright stems of young plants soon grow long and can become straggly, but it is easy to grow replacement plants from cuttings. *T. zebrina* (syn. *Zebrina pendula*; wandering Jew) is another trailing plant. It has blue-green leaves, longitudinally striped with purplish-pink and purplish-pink below. Grow in full sun. Plants need a normal summer room temperature, but a minimum winter temperature of 7–10°C (45–50°F). Water moderately in summer, sparingly in winter.

Left: *Syngonium podophyllum* (arrowhead vine) has attractively patterned leaves. Plants can be trained up moss poles or allowed to trail.
Right: Trained up canes, *Cissus antarctica* (kangaroo vine) soon develops into a substantial specimen for a large pot.
Far right: *Cissus rhombifolia* 'Ellen Danica' (mermaid vine) can be trained in a number of ways.

climbing plants

In the wild climbing plants climb up, sprawl over or twine around a host by means of aerial roots, sprawling stems or curling tendrils. In the home, therefore, they need to be given some means of support. Plants with tendrils will soon cling to the support by their tendrils, but other types need to be tied in. Such climbers can equally well be left to their own devices, given no support and not tied in, and grown as trailing plants – it is just a question of training. Most climbers will happily grow up a suitable cane, but plants with aerial roots can be grown up moss poles, and other climbers are often trained into ornamental shapes or up a trellis.

Climbing foliage plants include some of the most tolerant plants, and can be used in many decorative ways. Stately, larger leaved plants, such as *Philodendron domesticum* (elephant's ear), which produces large, fleshy, aerial roots, make a strong statement and are often best in isolation, growing slowly to great height over the years. Scramblers, such as *Cissus rhombifolia* (grape ivy), will travel a long way in a short time and can be trained in many styles.

plant directory

Cissus
C. antarctica (kangaroo vine) has a mass of tooth-edged, glossy green leaves and is tolerant of poor light. As a young plant it is normally grown up a group of canes, but when it is older it can be trained over a trellis. It is vigorous and can be trimmed back at any time of year to keep it within reasonable bounds.

C. discolor (begonia vine) has pointed leaves, which are dark green zoned with silver, grey and pink above and dark red underneath. It can become straggly.

C. rhombifolia (syn. *Rhoicissus rhombifolia*; grape ivy) is a long-lived plant with a mass of glossy, dark green leaves, which are strongly veined and toothed. It bears greenish flowers, which are followed by blue-black berries. It will tolerate some shade but really does best in a fairly bright light. It needs plenty of room and grows well over a trellis or around a doorway.

Grow these plants in bright or filtered light with a minimum winter temperature of 5°C (10°F). Water regularly during the growing season and feed once a month. Water less often in winter.

x Fatshedera lizei (tree ivy)
Although this can be grown in the garden in mild areas, it makes a

handsome houseplant that is easy to look after, eventually growing to about 3m (10ft). The large, glossy, dark green leaves are shaped like ivy leaves. A variegated form, 'Variegata', has leaves edged with cream, but this is less vigorous and less hardy than the species. Plants need a support to grow around. Grow in good light, protecting variegated plants from strong, direct sun. Water regularly during the growing season, feeding monthly, but reduce water in winter.

Hedera (ivy)

H. canariensis (Canary island ivy) is an undemanding plant, usually grown in its variegated form 'Gloire de Marengo'. This has green and white leaves, is easily trained as a climber and is a good choice for draughty halls. It must have reasonably cool conditions, with adequate light. Small-growing cultivars of *H. helix* that are suitable for unheated rooms include 'White Knight' (syn. 'Helvig'), which has small, white-variegated leaves, and 'Melanie', which has leaves that have light purple, slightly crimped margins. Grow in good but indirect light. Water ivies regularly during the growing season, feeding once a month, and keep the compost just moist in winter.

Philodendron domesticum (elephant's ear)

This climber, formerly known as *P. hastatum*, can grow to 6m (20ft) in a greenhouse but is a more modest 1.5m (5ft) in a pot. It needs a big moss pole and a position in semi-shade. Water freely during the growing season and feed every three to four weeks. In winter maintain a minimum temperature of 15°C (60°F) and keep the compost just moist.

Syngonium podophyllum (goosefoot, arrowhead vine)

Formerly known as *Nephthytis triphylla*, goosefoot is a fleshy-leaved climber with aerial roots ideal for training up a moss pole. Many cultivars have variegated leaves, including 'White Butterfly'. 'Emerald Gem' has large, fleshy, spade-shaped leaves. Grow in good light, providing variegated plants with shade from strong sunlight. Maintain high humidity and water freely in the growing season, feeding every three to four weeks, but keep the compost just moist in winter. These plants need a minimum winter temperature of 15°F (60°F).

upright plants

Large architectural plants really come into their own when they stand alone and are displayed as specimen plants in large pots on the floor. The container you use makes all the difference. For large plants it is usually best to have a container that is a quarter to a third the height of the plant and that is in a shape and style that both flatters the plant and complements the furniture and decor of the room. As the plant grows you will need to repot it into a pot one size larger from time to time to prevent it from becoming pot bound. This makes an opportunity to change the cache pot or container to keep it in proportion with the plant.

Plants that are too big to be repotted should be top-dressed – the top 2.5–5cm (1–2in) of the compost is removed annually and replaced with fresh compost, which provides a supply of nutrients and aerates the compost.

Smaller plants with bold forms and patterned leaves, such as the easy *Solenostemon* (coleus) and more demanding *Codiaeum variegatum* var. *pictum* (croton), also look good standing on the floor where you can look down on their leaves, and these plants benefit from being planted in groups of two or three forms together to show off their contrasting leaf coloration. You can also make a floor group of assorted foliage plants of differing heights with a mixture of leaf shapes, colours and forms.

There is often least light at floor level. Fortunately, there are plenty of suitable foliage plants – the many calatheas and marantas, for example – that need shade. Plants that need more light can be raised by, for instance, using a planting trough on legs. Standing plants on the floor is ideal for attic rooms with low windows or for rooms with overhead lighting, where bright light reaches down to floor level. However, having too many pots standing on the floor can be unwelcome when you have to clean around them or move them in order to clean, and having a single container is often the best solution in all but a conservatory room. Alternatively, a low platform on casters, which can be moved for cleaning, will enable you to make a floor-level grouping of plants.

Left: Contrasting types of foliage can be exploited to the full in a mixed bowl. The smooth, shapely leaves of *Aspidistra elatior* 'Variegata' (cast iron plant) are offset by a haze of *Asparagus densiflorus* Sprengeri Group (asparagus fern).
Right: *Begonia rex* hybrids are grown for their foliage rather than their usually insignificant flowers. They tend to look best in plain pots.

plant directory

Aspidistra elatior (cast iron plant)
This well-known indoor plant has long been a favourite for growing in the home. The glossy, dark green leaves are lance-shaped and can grow to 50cm (20in) long. These are tolerant plants, at home in a bright light or semi-shade. Water freely during the growing season, feeding once a month, and reduce the amount of water in winter. They need a minimum winter temperature of about 7°C (45°F).

Begonia
This important genus includes some fine foliage plants. *B. rex* (king begonia, painted-leaf begonia) is a perennial with handsome metallic green leaves that have a broad, silvery band around the margins and pink and purple tones around the darker centre. The undersides of the leaves are brownish-red. Many cultivars, known as Rex-cultorum begonias, have been developed, all with brilliantly coloured foliage. These plants generally grow to about 25in (10in) high and 30cm (12in) across.
    B. masoniana (iron-cross begonia)

is another fine foliage plant, although it does bear clusters of insignificant greenish-white flowers in summer. The leaves, which are to 20cm (8in) long, have a puckered surface. They are green or yellowish-green and are strongly marked with a black-brown central pattern, resembling the German Iron Cross. Plants get to about 45cm (18in) high and across.
    These begonias need good but filtered light and a minimum winter temperature of 10°C (50°F). Never overwater and maintain a humid atmosphere by standing pots in trays filled with clay granules, gravel or the like. Feed every two to three weeks during the growing season and keep the compost just moist in winter. Pot on in spring into good quality potting compost.

Calathea
There are several handsome foliage plants in the genus, the best known and most widely available being *C. makoyana* (syn. *Maranta makoyana*; cathedral windows, peacock plant). The leaves, which grow to 30cm (12in) long, have dark

green central areas surrounded by lighter green with mid-green margins and veining. The undersides are purplish. Plants grow to 45cm (18in) high and about 23cm (9in) across.
    C. sanderiana (syn. *C. majestica* 'Sanderiana', *C. ornata* var. *sanderiana*) has dark green leaves, potentially to 60cm (2ft) long, strongly striped with red-pink, fading to creamy-white. The undersides are purplish. Plants can grow to 3m (10ft) in the wild, although container-grown plants rarely reach that size.
    C. zebrina (zebra plant) has dark green, oval leaves, to 45cm (18in) long, which are edged and veined with mid-green. Plants grow to 1m (3ft) high and 60cm (2ft) across.
    Calatheas are not easy to grow. They tolerate fairly low levels of light but must never stand in a draught. They need an even temperature, with a winter minimum of 16°C (61°F), and a constantly humid atmosphere. Mist and water freely during the growing season and feed once a month. In winter the compost should be kept just moist.

Left: Dracaena fragrans Deremensis Group make superb foliage plants. They will eventually grow to 1.2m (4ft) or more.
Right: The vividly coloured leaves of *Codiaeum variegatum* var. *pictum* (croton) make it a striking focal point in any home.
Below right: Fatsia japonica (Japanese aralia) will thrive almost anywhere except in direct sun. With its finger-like lobes, this plant is an attractive feature in halls and landings and also in rooms that are not overheated in winter.

Codiaeum variegatum var. pictum (croton)

A large number of colourful cultivars has been developed from this foliage plant. The narrowly oval, glossy, rather leathery leaves, to 30cm (12in) long, are usually mid-green splashed with yellow, ageing to shades of red. The young, mid-green leaves of 'Flamingo' have cream-coloured veins, turning yellow and ageing to red or purple. The striking leaves of 'Evening Embers' are blue-black, with red veining and red and green marks. Plants can grow to about 1m (3ft) high and to 60cm (2ft) or more across.

All crotons must be kept out of draughts. They need a minimum winter temperature of 10°C (50°F) and a position in good light but out of any strong, direct sunlight. Water freely during the growing season, misting frequently and feeding every two to three weeks. In winter keep the compost just moist, using tepid water. Crotons are particularly susceptible to scale insect and red spider mite.

Cordyline (cabbage palm)

Many cordylines come from Australia and New Zealand, and although some of the larger forms can occasionally be grown outside in mild areas, they are best regarded as foliage houseplants. All cordylines have an erect central stem from which sword-shaped or lance-shaped leaves are borne. *C. fruticosa* (syn. *C. terminalis*; good luck tree, ti tree) has dark green leaves, which can grow to 60cm (2ft) long. These plants can achieve heights of 5m (15ft), although this is unlikely in a container. There are many colourful cultivars, including 'Baby Ti', which has leaves that are boldly edged in red; this is a good choice for indoors because it grows to only 60cm (2ft) high and across. 'Tricolor' has leaves that are boldly splashed with green, reddish-pink and cream.

C. stricta is lower growing and has more arching leaves. The species has dark green leaves, but those of the cultivar 'Rubra' are flushed with red and those of 'Discolor' are bronze-purple.

Cordylines need a bright position, although variegated forms do best in filtered light. Water regularly in the growing season, feeding once a month, and reduce the amount of water in winter. They need a minimum winter temperature of about 10°C (50°F).

Dieffenbachia seguine (dumb cane)

The species is also sometimes available as *D. amoena* and *D. maculata*. All dieffenbachias exude a sap that can irritate the skin; do not touch your mouth or eyes if you have been handling one of these plants. There are several cultivars, all with handsome, oval leaves, which are variably patterned in white, cream and shades of green. The cultivar 'Amoena' has creamy-white bands and marbling; 'Exotica' has dark green leaves with bold white and greenish-white marks; 'Maculata' has bright green leaves with creamy-white veins and splodges. All these plants grow to about 60cm (2ft) high and across.

Dieffenbachias need a bright position but sheltered from strong, direct sun and high humidity. Water and mist freely in summer, feeding every three to four weeks, and reduce the water in winter. Plants need a minimum winter temperature of 15°C (60°F).

Dracaena

Plants in the genus are similar to cordylines; indeed, much renaming has occurred between the two genera, and plants offered for sale as belonging to one genus may well belong to the other. Dracaenas are architectural plants, which look splendid grown on their own where their overall shape can be admired. *D. fragrans* is an erect plant, growing to 15m (50ft) tall in the wild and with leaves to 1.2m (4ft) long. There are several cultivars more suitable for growing indoors. Plants in Deremensis Group have leaves that are variegated in various ways: 'Lemon Lime', for instance, has lime green leaves with yellow edges and central lines; 'Warneckei' has dark grey-green leaves with white stripes.

D. marginata (Madagascar dragon tree) has red-edged, dark green leaves; it will grow to 5m (15ft) tall. The cultivar 'Tricolor' has narrow leaves that are edged with red and creamy-white.

D. sanderiana (ribbon plant) is a slender plant, growing ultimately to 1.5m (5ft) tall. The narrow leaves are glossy green with silver-white stripes. An added attraction is that the leaves are slightly wavy.

Dracaenas need to be grown in good light, although plants will all-green leaves will tolerate some shade. They need a minimum winter temperature of about 13°C (55°F). Water freely throughout the growing season, feeding every three to four weeks. Reduce the amount of water in winter.

Fatsia japonica (Japanese aralia)

Also known as *Aralia japonica*, this is a large, handsome plant, which can be grown in gardens in mild areas, where it will grow to 4m (12ft) high and across; plants rarely achieve those dimensions in containers. The large, dark green, glossy leaves are deeply divided into 7–11 lobes and can be to 40cm (16in) long. In autumn little creamy-white flowers appear, and these are followed by round black fruit. There is an attractive variegated form, 'Variegata', which has leaves with broad cream margins; it is less hardy than the species. Grown as houseplants, fatsias need good light, although variegated plants should be protected from strong summer sun. Water regularly during the growing season, feeding every three to four weeks, but reduce the water in winter.

Ficus (fig)

The genus contains two handsome but quite different looking, upright foliage plants, in addition to the smaller *F. pumila* (see page 41). *F. benjamina* (weeping fig) is a small tree with fluttering, dark green leaves on weeping branches. Although weeping figs grow to 30m (100ft) in the wild, container-grown plants are usually about 1.8m (6ft) tall. There are a number of cultivars: 'Exotica' has leaves with extended, twisted tips; the leaves of 'Starlight' have gold-coloured variegations; 'Variegata' has white-edged leaves.

While the leaves of *F. benjamina* are 5–13cm (2–5in) long, those of *F. elastica* (rubber plant, India rubber tree) can be 45cm (18in) long. They are dark, glossy green, often flushed with red and prominently ribbed, and they have a leathery texture. In the wild *F. elastica* can achieve heights of up to 60m (200ft), but as a houseplant a height of 3m (10ft) is more usual. Cultivars are available from time to time: the leaves of 'Decora' have cream ribs and are reddish beneath; the grey-green leaves of 'Doescheri' are variegated with creamy-white and yellow; 'Robusta' has large leaves opening from red or orange shoots.

Grow in good light but shaded from strong, direct sun. These plants need a minimum winter temperature of 15°C (55°F). Water regularly during the growing season, taking care that the compost does not become waterlogged, and give a high-nitrogen feed once a month. Keep the compost just moist in winter.

Monstera deliciosa (Swiss cheese plant)

This well-known houseplant has large, glossy, dark green leaves. When they are young, the leaves are heart-shaped, but as they age they develop large oblong holes between the veins. In its native Central America it is a huge plant, but in a container a plant will grow to about 3m (10ft) tall. Plants grow well when they are supported

Below left: Schefflera arboricola grows quickly to a height of 1.5–1.8m (5–6ft). to form a bushy plant. Its leaves consist of leaflets radiating on parasol 'spokes' from the tips of leaf-stalks.
Below: Ficus elastica (rubber plant) are good, bold specimens to stand in pots on the floor.
Right: Monstera deliciosa (Swiss cheese plant) has large, leathery leaves, which develop holes like Swiss cheese as they grow.
Far right: Yucca elephantipes makes a permanent houseplant feature. Bold plants such as this need sturdy pots, both visually and to take their weight. This yucca produces leaves to 1m (3ft) long.

on a moss pole, and mature plants develop aerial roots, which can be trained into the moss or down into the compost. They are tolerant of a range of conditions but do best in a bright position, shaded from strong, direct sunlight, and with high humidity. Water well throughout the growing period, feeding every three to four weeks, but reduce the amount of water in winter.

Schefflera

S. actinophylla (syn. *Brassaia actinophylla*; octopus tree, Australian ivy palm) has large, bright green leaves divided into leaflets that are borne in rosettes at the end of the leaf stalks, so that they resemble a parasol. The young plants that are available as houseplants can reach 3m (10ft), although in the wild they will get to 12m (40ft) or more.

S. arboricola (syn. *Heptapleurum arboricola* grows to 1m (3ft). It has glossy green leaves, divided into 7–16 arching leaflets, which surround the

leaf stalk. The form 'Variegata' has yellow-variegated leaves.

S. elegantissima (syn. *Aralia elegantissima*, *Dizygotheca elegantissima*; false aralia) is an attractive but difficult plant. The dark green-brown, glossy leaves are finely divided and are flushed with bronze beneath; the midribs are white. In the right position plants will grow to 3m (10ft) tall.

Scheffleras should be grown in good light but sheltered from direct sun. The need a minimum winter temperature of about 13°C (55°F). Water regularly throughout the growing season, feeding every three to four weeks, but keep just moist in winter. These plants do not like being moved around, so once you have found a spot that suits your plant, try to keep it there.

Solenostemon scutellarioides (coleus, flame nettle)

Formerly sold as *Coleus blumei* var. *verschaffeltii*, these bushy plants have

brightly coloured foliage, often vividly patterned, in shades of green, yellow, orange, red and brown. Pinch out the growing tips to keep plants bushy. They will grow to about 60cm (2ft) high and across. They need a fairly light position, but away from direct sun, and a minimum winter temperature of 4°C (39°F). Water freely in the growing season and feed every two weeks. Keep compost just moist in winter and pot on in spring.

Yucca

The genus contains plants that can be grown outside in mild areas, but *Y. elephantipes* (syn. *Y. gigantea*, *Y. guatemalensis*; boundary plant, spineless yucca) is a popular indoor plant, growing to 1.8m (6ft) high. It needs good light and fairly cool winter conditions, with a winter minimum of 10°C (50°F). Water freely during the growing season, feeding once a month, and keep the compost just moist in winter. If well cared for it will eventually produce white flowers.

Left: Capsicum annuum (ornamental pepper) are cheerful plants for autumn and winter with their brightly coloured fruits. They do best in direct light where several of the plants arranged together will make a colourful show.

Right: Nertera depressa (bead plant) is usually grown as a pot plant for its bright autumn and winter berries. It needs bright light, cool air and plenty of summer moisture. If given a dry, late winter rest, and a spring and summer outdoors, it will produce its shiny 'beads' year after year.

Far right: Fortunella japonica (kumquat) is highly decorative if rather temperamental. Given plenty of light, warmth and moisture, it will produce attractive fruit.

berried & fruiting plants

Some of the most decorative houseplants are grown for their fruits or berries. Fruiting plants can give double value, some having beautiful, fragrant flowers, as well but in general, plants with attractive berries, such as

Nertera depressa (bead plant), have negligible flowers.

Most fruiting plants require extra care, especially those with edible fruit, such as miniature orange, lemon and kumquat. They need a conservatory or at

least an airy, sunny room, and do not produce fruit without the right amount of warmth, light and humidity. However, some of the best ornamental fruiting plants, such as *Capsicum annuum*, are easily grown as annuals.

plant directory

Capsicum annuum (ornamental peppers)
These plants are grown as annuals. They come in many colours, from red and yellow to white, purple and black, all starting off green. Sow the seed in spring, cover the seed tray and keep at a temperature of 21°C (70°F). Germination takes about two weeks. Pot up as the plants grow and pinch out at the tips to make them bushy and fruitful. Give plenty of humidity, water well and feed once a fortnight as peppers appear.

Citrus limon (lemon)
Many members of the genus can be grown as houseplants, and it is possible to obtain fruit from many, but this species is one of the most widely available. It grows into a large, spiny shrub with light green leaves and, in summer, fragrant white flowers. The yellow fruit follow the flowers. The cultivar 'Meyeri' (syn. *C. meyeri*; Meyer's lemon) is similar but bears small, ornamental lemon fruits. Grow in good light but shade from direct summer sun. Mist and water freely, feeding every two to three weeks in the growing season. Reduce the water in winter and maintain a temperature above 5°C (41°F). Plants benefit from standing outside during the summer.

x Citrofortunella microcarpa (calamondin, Panama orange)
Formerly known as *C. mitis*, this large shrub grows slowly to a height of 1m (3ft). If it is well watered in summer, given plenty of light all year and a cool, 13°C (55°F), winter rest, it should produce white, scented, waxy flowers and small, edible fruit. Even if it fails to flower it is an attractive, bushy, evergreen shrub.

Ficus deltoidea (mistletoe fig)
The small, slow-growing shrub has grey-gold, sometimes red-flushed, berries borne singly on little stems sprouting from the leaf-joints. The dark green leaves are small and oval. Plants usually grow to 45–75cm (18–30in) across and 45cm (18in) across, although it can grow much bigger if kept in a tub. The plant will stand a winter low temperature of 10°C (50°F).

Fortunella japonica (kumquat)
This large, spiny shrub has glossy green leaves and fragrant flowers in spring and summer. These are followed by the small golden-yellow fruits. Grow in good light with a winter minimum temperature of 7°C (45°F).

Nertera depressa (bead plant)
This is a stem-rooting, spreading perennial, to 2.5cm (1in) high, with bright green leaves. In summer it produces yellow-green flowers, and these are followed by a mass of small orange or red berries. Grow in filtered light and water freely during the growing season, feeding once a month. Water less often in winter.

Solanum capsicastrum (winter cherry)
This plant has nothing to do with cherries and the shining, berries, which turn from green through yellow to orange or red in winter, are poisonous. Do not overwater and keep in a cool room at 10–15°C (50–60°F) but in bright light. *S. pseudocapsicum* (Christmas cherry) is similar but has larger berries.

5 PALMS, FERNS & BROMELIADS

Palms, ferns and bromeliads are not, of course, related plants, but they all have, in their own ways, highly distinctive foliage and something exotic about them. All three groups of plants make fine and worthwhile houseplants.

Most of the palms grown as houseplants are tropical or subtropical plants that require warmth and humidity and bright but filtered light, although there are some, such as *Chamaedorea elegans* (parlour palm) and the much larger *Howea forsteriana* (kentia palm), that will tolerate ordinary, fluctuating living-room conditions. A palm takes dedication and time to produce, and it is a long-term investment, to be chosen with care and looked after equally carefully.

Ferns have been popular since Victorian times, when they were collected and housed in glass cases or in glass ferneries built on outdoor balconies. They can look exotically redolent of the jungle or be light and fragile. Ferns from temperate regions are often less than ideal as houseplants, because they require cooler conditions than centrally heated homes can

offer, but numerous tropical and subtropical ferns flourish in the temperatures we prefer for ourselves as long as they are given plenty of humidity and are not subjected to sudden temperature changes.

In the wild many bromeliads grow on other plants or on rocks, taking their nourishment from the air and from organic debris, although a few root in shallow soil. Many species will adapt to being grown in pots indoors as exotic plants, and although they are grown as foliage plants some occasionally produce spectacular flowers. Others can be grown on stones and driftwood or up moss poles, and some are suitable for hanging baskets.

While palms and ferns and some types of bromeliad are coming back into fashion after a period of neglect, some bromeliads have only recently been introduced to cultivation as

Opposite: A large conservatory is a stunning setting for a few large specimen plants.
Above: *Phoenix canariensis* (Canary Island date palm) makes a striking architectural plant.

houseplants. Many of these plants have to be sought out, as only the most popular are widely available. Some palms, especially young ones, can be bought from nurseries and garden centres and even the plant sections of large supermarkets and chain stores, but others will have to be obtained from specialist houseplant growers. Commoner ferns and bromeliads can also be found in many garden centres and other shops, but the more unusual specimens of these plants have to be obtained from specialist growers.

palms

Palms are widely associated with ideas of elegance and splendour and of exotic lands. They make us think of oases in the hot, dry desert and palm-fringed beaches of white sand or even of the palm courts and palm court orchestras of fashionable watering places of days gone by.

In Victorian and Edwardian times the most demanding and largest palms were grown in glass houses, where they could be given the warmth and lush humidity they needed. Surprisingly, perhaps, the resilient fronds of the most tolerant species swayed over the

comings and goings in hotel foyers and restaurants in all sorts of public rooms. The entrance halls and drawing rooms of late nineteenth- and early twentieth-century homes were also often graced with parlour palms.

As simpler styles replaced the opulence and clutter and dim

light of Victorian and Edwardian interiors, palms went out of fashion, but now they have found their way back into our homes in interiors of a different style. With its well-defined fronds and stark but graceful shape, a palm is an outstanding plant, which makes a striking feature and one that is especially well suited to a large, bright, plainly furnished and decorated interior.

Traditionally, palms were displayed on ceramic palm stands, with the palm planted in an ornamental jardinière balanced on top of a matching pedestal. Displaying them in this way, using original or reproduction palm stands (both of which are expensive), is perfect for a room in a period house decorated in the appropriate style. But it could also successfully supply an unusual feature in an otherwise simple, modern interior. Any pedestal or pedestal table is a good way of giving prominence to the smaller palms, but a large palm generally looks best standing on the floor in a pot or cache pot of good quality, and it will, in any case, be too heavy to be raised on any kind of stand. Containers can be patterned porcelain, glazed earthenware, brass or copper, basketware or even plain, well-made plastic planters, depending on the setting.

Palms grow in two rather extreme situations: in arid deserts and in lush, green jungles. Either of these can be expressed in the way the plants are displayed. Palms in a bare room, with polished or varnished wooden floors, echo the idea of plants growing in a barren, desert landscape, but palms

growing with other foliage plants, perhaps in a room with a green carpet or a green-patterned wallpaper, bring out the tropical jungle theme. This can also be achieved in miniature with a group of foliage plants, such as foliage begonias, selaginellas and small ferns, grown in a glass case with a small, young palm, such as *Chamaedorea elegans* or *Lytocaryum weddellianum* (Weddell palm).

Perhaps more than any other plant, palms lend themselves to creating shadows and reflections. A palm standing in an alcove that is lined with a mirror creates a stunning effect, and one each side of a fireplace reflected in this way is doubly stunning. The shadows cast by a palm's fronds can pattern a plain wall in a most dramatic way. Spotlights create a good strong light for bold shadows but generate heat so should not be positioned too close to the plant. Lighting the plant from below creates shadows on the ceiling as well as the walls, and a plain blind (as opposed to a curtain) provides a good, smooth surface for shadows.

Above left: Palms are are long-lived. *Howea forsteriana* (kentia palm), creates a dramatic feature (left), and *Chamaedorea elegans* (parlour palm), has a feathery outline (right). *Above*: *Phoenix canariensis* (Canary Island date palm) will make an eye-catching focal point. Its graceful foliage looks best against a plain background.

Left: Although *Howea forsteriana* (kentia palm) will eventually become a large plant, it retains the lightness and grace shown by this small young specimen. A window position is ideal for winter, but some shade from summer sun is needed.

Right: Dypsis lutescens (areca palm) may be sold as butterfly palm, yellow palm, golden feather palm, yellow butterfly palm, cane palm and golden cane palm. It enjoys temperatures of 13–16°C (55–61°F) in winter and up to 27°C (80°F) in summer.

CARE AND CULTIVATION

In the wild many – although not all – palms grow to great heights, but in the main they are slow-growing plants and can remain at living-room size for many years. These are not plants for impatient indoor gardeners. New fronds unfurl in a leisurely way at the rate of only two or three a year. In many of the palms grown as houseplants several fronds are produced from ground, or compost, level, whereas the large palms, which generally require extremely high temperatures – *Phoenix* (date palms), for example – have a single stem (the trunk) with a flourish of fronds at the top. A frond is really a compound leaf and each apparent leaf is really a leaflet, forming part of the whole frond. In each frond, all the growth develops from a single growth point, known as the terminal bud, and if this is

damaged the whole frond is affected. If you cut a stem it will not re-grow. Palms are among the few plants that grow best in relatively small containers.

The most popular palms are adaptable specimens. They like a winter rest in cooler conditions, although not normally in temperatures below about 10°C (50°F), but they tolerate central heating. They prefer good but not strong light, especially when young (in the wild they would be growing in the shade of other, taller plants), but can survive in quite dim corners. They dislike draughts and sudden changes of temperature, although some prefer a regular slight drop in temperature at night.

Palms grow best if their roots are allowed to fill the pot, and they should not be repotted unnecessarily. They need a soil-based potting compost, with plenty of drainage material at the

bottom of the pot. In summer, or in warm rooms, they need plenty of watering, but in lower temperatures the compost should be allowed to dry out a little between waterings. The plants should never be allowed to become waterlogged and must not stand with their pots in any excess water that has drained out. They should be regularly fed in summer. Palms appreciate humid conditions, and they should be misted frequently in warm rooms. They can also be stood on a tray of wet pebbles to keep the atmosphere humid. The fronds should be cleaned from time to time by being wiped with a cloth that has been wrung out in tepid water.

Palms are sensitive to chemicals and will be damaged if exposed to aerosol sprays. If you need to treat them with insecticides make sure that these are suitable for palms.

Left: Chamaedorea elegans (the parlour palm) has a more feathery outline than many of the kentia palms. *Above: Cycas revoluta* (Japanese sago palm) is not a true palm, although it is often sold as one in garden centres. Its strong, fan-like fronds sprout from a conical base, which is part of its attraction. *Right: Rhapsis excelsa* (miniature fan palm) has erect stems and spreading, fan-shaped leaves.

plant directory

Caryota (fishtail palm)
These palms come from India, Sri Lanka, Southeast Asia and Australia, and the unusual leaves are more like those of a fern than a palm. In the wild they can grow to 12m (40ft) tall, but container-grown specimens generally grow to a maximum of 3m (10ft). *C. mitis* (Burmese fish-tail palm, clustered fish-tail palm) has mid-green leaves, with lopsided leaflets. *C. urens* (jaggery palm, sago palm, toddy palm, wine palm) has dark green, arching leaves, which are irregularly toothed.

Chamaedorea
These Central and South American palms have bamboo-like stems and pinnate leaves. *C. elegans* (syn. *Neanthe bella*; parlour palm, dwarf mount palm) has mid-green leaves, to 1.2m (4ft) long, formed of 21–40 narrow leaflets. Plants will grow to 3m (10ft). The cultivar 'Bella' is more compact, growing slowly to 1m (3ft). *C. metallica* (miniature fish-tail palm) grows to 1m (3ft) tall and about 50cm (20in) across. The blue-green leaves are shaped like a fish's tail. *C. seifrizii* (reed palm) is a small, clump-forming plant, growing to about 1.8m (6ft) high, with mid-green leaves, to 60cm (2ft) long, composed of 24–28 leaflets.

Chamaerops humilis (dwarf fan palm)

This palm, which is native to the western Mediterranean, is suitable for a cool conservatory or even an unheated porch. It will grow to no more than about 1.5m (5ft) tall. The fan-shaped leaves, with 12–15 leaflets, are blue-green or grey-green.

Cycas (fern palm, sago palm)

These plants – cycads rather than true palms – are from Madagascar, Southeast Asia and Australia, and they produce whorls or rosettes of stiff leaves and stout, woody trunks. They make fine architectural plants but need space to look their best. C. circinalis (false sago, fern palm, sago palm) is slow growing, eventually getting to 1.8m (6ft) in a container. The glossy, dark green leaves are composed of up to 100 leaflets. C revoluta (Japanese sago palm) will grow to about 1.5m (5ft) in a container. It develops a stout trunk, with the leaves, to 75cm (30in) long, crowded in a rosette at the top.

Dypsis lutescens (areca palm)

Formerly known as Chrysalidocarpus lutescens (syn. Areca lutescens), this small palm is also known as the yellow palm, butterfly palm and the golden feather palm. It is native to Madagascar, where it grows to 6m (20ft) tall, but in a container it will grow to 3m (10ft) or so. The arching leaves can grow to as much as 1.8m (6ft) long, even on container-grown plants. They are formed of numerous linear leaflets, which are usually yellow-green.

Howea (sentry palm)

The two species in the genus originated on Lord Howe Island. The popular H. belmoreana (syn. Kentia belmoreana; curly palm) will grow to about 3m (10ft). The leaves, to 1m (3ft) long, arch strongly. The widely available H. forsteriana (syn. Kentia forsteriana; kentia palm, thatch leaf palm) will also grow to about 3m (10ft) tall in a container. The leaves have long-stalked leaflets, which point downwards at the end.

Lytocaryum weddellianum (Weddell palm)

Formerly known as Microcoelum weddellianum (syn. Syagrus weddelliana), this palm from Brazil has an erect stem and leaves, to 1.2m (4ft) long, with red-black scales.

Phoenix

These palms come from tropical and subtropical Asia and Africa. P. canariensis (Canary Island date palm) has flat, finely divided, feather-like leaves arising from a dense crown. The date palm, P. dactylifera, is quicker-growing than P. canariensis and has grey-green leaves with small leaflets; it is easily raised from date stones. P. roebelenii (miniature date palm, pygmy date palm) has glossy, dark green, arching leaves.

Rhapsis (lady palm)

Rhapsis excelsa (syn. R. flabelliformis, miniature fan palm) will grow to about 1.5m (5ft) in a container. It has dark green, lustrous, deeply lobed leaves, with three to ten leaflets. R. humilis is a smaller, slimmer palm, with leaves that are composed of between 9 and 20 leaflets.

Trachycarpus fortunei (windmill palm, Chusan palm)

This single-stemmed palm has large, fan-shaped, dark green leaves, which are deeply divided into many pleated segments and the leaf stalks are covered in fine teeth. This palm will survive outdoors in a very sheltered garden, but it must be protected from cold, drying winds to survive the winter. Indoors it will tolerate both bright sun and semi-shade.

Washingtonia

There are two palms in the genus, which are native to southwestern United States and northern Mexico. W. filifera (syn. W. filamentosa; desert fan palm, petticoat palm) grows to 15m (50ft) or more in the wild but to 1.8m (6ft) in a container, where it rarely forms a trunk. It is quite short-lived. The leaves have white filaments on the margins and the stem has coarse teeth. W. robusta (syn. W. gracilis, Pritchardia robusta; Mexican washingtonia) has bright green leaves and grows to about 1.8m (6ft) or so in a container. It has a more upright habit than W. filifera and is more slender.

Left: Ferns and baskets go well together. The arching, wiry stems of *Adiantum capillus-veneris* (maidenhair fern) bend over the basket's edge and reach towards the handle. A begonia adds colour and highlights the fern's light foliage.
Above: Ferns flourish when grown in a group, and smaller ferns can be planted together. Different species and cultivars of *Pteris* offer a range of foliage shapes and shades of green.
Right: The sedately arching fronds of a mature *Nephrolepis exaltata* 'Whitmonii' are seen at their best on a plant stand.

ferns

Ferns are not difficult to grow, but draughts, dry air and extremes of temperature will do them no good at all. A fern that is pampered and protected from these ills will reward its owner with a wealth of luxuriant green fronds all year round.

There are many species of tropical and subtropical ferns, but there are also many ferns that are native to areas with temperate climates. These are well-suited to cooler parts of the house but will not survive in rooms that are too well heated. Tropical ferns are at home in warmer air and are better suited to centrally heated homes.

All ferns thrive on moisture and must be given humid conditions. In living rooms this usually means standing them on trays of damp pebbles or clay granules or putting each fern's pot in a larger pot and packing the gap with peat that is kept moist. Ferns should also be misted regularly with tepid, soft water unless the humidity of the whole room is kept high through the use of a humidifier.

Providing the right compost is also important, because most ferns are forest or woodland plants and have tender, delicate roots adapted to the light forest soil, which is rich in leaf mould and decayed vegetable matter.

Left: The height of *Asplenium scolopendrium* (hart's-tongue fern) makes an excellent background for low-growing or trailing plants. The Cristatum Group ferns have particularly attractive fronds, which are branched and crested.

CARE AND CULTIVATION

The first requirement for ferns is a light, moisture-retaining compost, but it must be freely draining so that the roots are never waterlogged. A compost based on peat, or fibrous peat substitute, containing plenty of fine sand and small, sharp stones, is best. The compost should never be allowed to dry out, and this may mean giving plants a little water every day in a warm, dry atmosphere.

Although ferns grow in moist, shady places, this does not mean that they need no light. Their normal situation in the wild is dappled light, and light levels that are too low cause poor growth and yellowing fronds. Give ferns a position near to a window that gets morning or late afternoon sun or somewhere that receives good light within the room. Do, however, keep them away from strong sunlight, particularly during the summer, as it will soon make them lose their intense colouring and turn them a pallid or greyish-green, and it can also scorch their fronds, making them brown and dry around the edges.

Ferns can be kept in dim light as long as they are given regular holidays in bright light. They can also be given artificial light, but this should be from a special bulb or a fluorescent strip, because ordinary light bulbs generate too much heat.

Temperature is just as important as light and growing medium, but this depends on the individual fern's place of origin and adaptability. As a rule, most ferns dislike cold; ferns from temperate regions thrive at 10–15°C (50–60°F) – slightly cooler than most heated rooms – and those from tropical and subtropical areas need an average of 15–21°C (60–70°F). Most ferns like a winter rest at slightly lower temperatures, but few will survive at temperatures lower than 7°C (45°F), and for many ferns 10°C (50°F) is the absolute minimum.

In summer feed ferns every two to four weeks with weak liquid fertilizer. Do not mix to full strength because this can damage the delicate root systems. A few drops of fertilizer can be added occasionally to the water used for misting. Ferns should not be fed in winter if they are given a resting period. Mist as often as you like to keep the air around ferns moist, but never in low temperatures, at night or when the plant is standing in bright sunlight.

Repot ferns in spring, but only when their roots are filling the pot. Otherwise, simply gently scrape out and replace the top layer of the compost. When you are potting up ferns or planting them in containers make sure that you leave their crowns exposed and always take great care not to damage the vulnerable fronds. When making arrangements for glass containers such as Wardian cases, arrange the plants first on a piece of card the same size and shape as the container so that you will not need to move them in and out of the container. Cut off any damaged fronds to encourage new ones to grow in their place.

You can divide large ferns when repotting them, and some produce tiny plantlets that can be detached and potted up. You can also grow new ferns from the powdery spores that are produced in little capsules visible as rows of rusty-brown patches, usually on the undersides of the fronds. These grow into a green film of minuscule prothalli from which true ferns develop. The process can take several months, however. Collect spores in a bag tied around a frond and grow them on moist, peaty compost in a seed tray or on a brick in a container of water. Pour boiling water over the compost to sterilize it and powder on the spores, using the tip of a knife. Alternatively, lay a frond spore-side down on the surface. Place the container in a polythene bag and keep it warm and semi-shaded until small plants develop from the green film that appears on the surface. Pot these up and give them more light and constant warmth.

Left: *Adiantum raddianum* (Delta maidenhair fern) has a mass of delicate branching fronds with light green foliage and some people find it easier to grow than other adiantums. The cultivar 'Fragrantissima' has dense and large foliage.
Right: A young *Blechnum gibbum* (hard fern) can be kept moist by having its pot plunged into a peat-filled cache pot. This palm-like fern grows into a large specimen and develops a trunk as it ages.

are decoratively crimped and frilled. This and their bright, clear green coloration make a good contrast to smoother and darker foliage.

Blechnum (hard fern)

These terrestrial ferns are found in sheltered sites in temperate and tropical areas. They need acid soil. *B. chilense* (syn. *B. cordatum*, *B. magellanicum*) has dark green, pinnate fronds, to 1m (3ft) long. It can grow to 1.8m (6ft) high. *B. gibbum* (syn. *Lomaria gibba*) has bright green fronds, to 1m (3ft) long, forming a wide-spreading rosette.

Cyrtomium falcatum (holly fern)

This unusual plant has glossy, leathery pinnae, shaped like holly leaves. It will grow to 50–60cm (20–24in) high and across and does well in low temperatures and dim light. Provide extra humidity to compensate if temperatures rise to around 21°C (70°) or more.

Davallia

D. canariensis (hare's foot fern, deer's foot fern) has feathery foliage. The sturdy, hairy rhizomes, which grow over the surface of the compost, form part of its attraction. *D. fejeensis* (rabbit's foot fern) has mid-green, finely divided fronds. Grow in medium light with a minimum winter temperature of 10–15°C (50–60°F).

plant directory

Adiantum (maidenhair fern)

The evergreen *A. capillus-veneris* (true maidenhair fern) has light green, triangular fronds made up of fan-shaped pinnae. Plants grow to 30cm (12in) high and 40cm (16in) across. *A. raddianum* (syn. *A. cuneatum*; delta maidenhair fern) has black stalks and triangular fronds with rounded pinnae. This is a variable species, which has given rise to many popular cultivars, including the larger 'Fragrantissimum' and 'Lawsoniana', which has sharply triangular fronds.

Asplenium (spleenwort)

A. bulbiferum (mother fern, hen and chicken fern) produces new ferns rather like laying eggs: they grow from small brown bulbils on the fronds and drop off to grow in the soil below. Mature fronds are to 1m (3ft) long and 23cm (9in) wide. The plant likes medium light and average summer temperatures, with a winter minimum of 10°C (50°F). *A. nidus* (bird's nest fern) is an epiphytic plant with bright green fronds to 1m (3ft) long. They are semi-erect and form a broad, spreading funnel. *A. scolopendrium* (syn. *Phyllitis scolopendrium*, *Scolopendrium vulgare*; hart's tongue fern) has irregularly shaped, shuttlecock-like crowns. The fronds are bright green and to 40cm (16in) long. Cultivars in the Crispum Group

Right: With its broad, glossy leaves, about 8cm (3in) wide and 45cm (18in) long, *Asplenium nidus* (bird's nest fern) makes an excellent plant for a pot standing alone on a table. *Below right: Cyrtomium falcatum* 'Rochfordianum' (holly fern) is a dependable fern, which is less susceptible to draughts and dry air than most. Standing the fern's pot in a saucer of wet pebbles provides adequate moisture.

Nephrolepis (sword fern)

The genus contains one of the finest indoor ferns, *N. exaltata* 'Bostoniensis' (Boston fern), which has broad, lance-shaped fronds that arch gracefully. Several other attractive cultivars have been developed, including 'Mini Ruffle', which grows to only 5cm (2in) tall and 8cm (3in) across, and 'Golden Boston' (syn. 'Aurea'), which is similar to 'Bostoniensis' but has golden-yellow fronds. 'Whitmannii' (lace fern) has fronds to 45cm (18in) long with small pinnae. *N. cordifolia* (sword fern, ladder fern) has almost erect fronds to 60cm (2ft) long. The pinnae are sharply toothed. These ferns need bright, indirect light and average summer temperatures, with winter temperatures of 13–16°C (55–61°F).

Pellaea rotundifolia (button fern)

This fern from New Zealand has deep green fronds to 30cm (12in) long on wiry stems with button-shaped pinnae. It grows to 25–30cm (10–12in) high and 40cm (16in) across. It needs fairly bright, indirect light, normal summer temperatures and winter temperatures of 10–13°C (50–55°F).

Platycerium (staghorn fern)

The genus contains some large ferns. *P. alcicorne* (South American staghorn) has kidney shaped, mid-green leaves. It can grow to 80cm (32in) high and across. *P. bifurcatum* (which is sometimes sold as *P. alcicorne*; common staghorn fern) is variable but has glossy green fronds that are deeply lobed. It will grow to almost 1m (3ft) tall and about 80cm (32in) across. *P. superbum* (syn. *P. grande* has grey-green, deeply lobed fronds. This is a huge, epiphytic fern, growing to 1.8m (6ft) tall and 1.5m (5ft) across.

Polystichum (holly fern, shield fern)

The genus contains species that are perfectly hardy and can be grown in gardens, but in a cool room they can be treated as houseplants. *P. setiferum* (soft shield fern) is a well-known garden fern with dark green fronds forming attractive shuttlecocks. Cultivars in the Actutilobum Group develop tiny plantlets along the upper surface of the fronds. *P. tsussimense* (Tsusina holly fern, Korean rock fern),

Left: A larger fern in a pot, such as *Polystichum tsussimense* (Tsusina holly fern), can leave a bare space below it when standing alone on a table. A trailing ivy and a bright blue pot will fill the space.

Above: The popular *Platycerium bifurcatum* (staghorn fern) is an epiphyte and grows well without a pot.

Right: The variegated *Pteris cretica* var. *albolineata* stands in a white pot with nothing to detract from its slender, rippling fronds.

which is native to China and Japan, has dark green, broad, arching fronds, to 30cm (12in) long, which form a broad shuttlecock. It grows to about 40cm (16in) high and across.

Pteris (brake)

The genus is found in tropical and subtropical forests all over the world. *P. argyraea* (silver brake) is particularly attractive, having a silver-white stripe down the centre of each of the pinnae. The fronds can grow to 60cm (2ft) long, and plants grow to 1m (3ft) high and across. The best known species in the genus is *P. cretica* (brake fern, ribbon fern), which has narrow, ribbon-like pinnae. The pale green fronds grow to about 60cm (2ft) long, and plants can grow to 75cm (30in) high and 60cm (2ft) across. *P. cretica* var. *albolineata* has a broad white line along the centre of each pinna. Several cultivars have been developed from the species, including 'Alexandrae', which has undulating fronds with crested tips, and the compact 'Wimsettii', which has irregularly lobed pinnae. *P. tremula* (shaking brake, tender brake), which is native to Australia and New Zealand, will eventually grow to 1.5m (5ft) tall and 1m (3ft) across. It has a feathery appearance. All varieties need indirect light with some shade in summer and fairly low temperatures, 10–18°C (50–64°F), in the summer, which should not drop below around 7°C (45°F) in winter.

bromeliads

The typical houseplant bromeliad is a pineapple-like plant with a rosette of firm, fleshy leaves and, occasionally, an exotic, brightly coloured central flower. Some, similar in form, have an 'urn' or 'vase' at their centre, while a third group, the tillandsias or air plants, have less form and wander rootlessly.

The roots of a bromeliad are used simply for anchoring it to a support, such as the branch of a tree, rather than for getting nourishment from the soil, and the plants flourish when grown in a pot that would be much too small for other plants of the same size. The bolder strap-leaved bromeliads, such as *Ananas* spp. (pineapple), *Aechmea* spp. and *Vriesea* spp., make striking plants grown in pots and also adapt well to hanging baskets.

There are also tillandsias that grow well as specimens in pots and baskets, and the larger grey-leaved tillandsias are good plants for a hanging basket as they have arching foliage, are light and need no watering. Tillandsias are, however, often grown without pots because they can take their nourishment entirely from the surrounding air. Many tillandsias make interesting centrepieces attached to pieces of bark or driftwood or set in large shells and getting food from the air as they do in their native forests. *Cryptanthus* spp. (earth star, starfish plant) and *Fascicularia* spp. are ground-growing air plants, and these can be grown on stones, shells or bark. Cryptanthus are particularly well suited to being grown in open-topped bottles and other glass containers.

Above: The leaves of *Neoregelia carolinae* f. *tricolor* are attractively striped in cream, and the whole plant flushes deep pink as it flowers and keeps this colouring for several months.
Right: A group of tillandsias, some planted in pebble-covered compost, others attached to bark, looks well in plain pots. Air plants also have an affinity with sea shells. Simple surroundings and hard surfaces suit these plants best.

CARE AND CULTIVATION

Most of the pineapple-type and vase or urn bromeliads grow in the humid environment of the rain forests of Central and South America, dwelling in dappled light on the branches of trees. Xerophytic bromeliads, such as fascicularia, and cryptanthus (earth stars), are generally ground dwellers that have adapted to the moist air of coastal areas or the inhospitable slopes of high mountain ranges.

Except for tillandsias, most of which do not take to being grown in pots at all, bromeliads for the home should be grown in

Far left: Ananas comosus (common pineapple) will eventually bear colourful flowers, but they are principally grown for their striking, spine-edged leaves. A. comosus 'Variegatus' has the advantages of a compact form and attractive cream-colour variegation.
Left: The larger, grey-leaved tillandsias are good plants for a hanging basket where the arching foliage can be seen to good effect.

pots that are small for their size, in well-drained fibrous or peaty, preferably lime-free, compost, which has some added charcoal.

Bromeliads must have their specific needs for moisture met. All benefit from frequent misting with tepid, lime-free water, and this is essential for the tillandsias growing without pots. Many bromeliads grown in pots have a rosette of leaves and a central reservoir, and these central vases or urns should be filled with fresh, soft, tepid water, which is emptied and replaced from time to time, but the compost itself should be watered only moderately.

All bromeliads are tropical or subtropical plants that make for dramatic displays. In general they need high humidity and temperatures of 13–15°C (55–60°F), and up to 20°C (70°F) when actively growing in summer. They need warm air,

and a test of this is that the water in the centre of vase and urn types should evaporate away – if it does not, it will become stagnant. In the wild they get their nourishment from organic debris in the air and, in the case of vase and urn types, the detritus that falls into their centres. In the home they should be watered with a balanced fertilizer, diluted to half-strength, every six to eight weeks. This can also occasionally be added to the water with which they are sprayed and to the water in their central reservoirs. Like most flowering plants, bromeliads need to be watered more when flower buds appear and during active growth. To maintain a good level of humidity you can stand the plants on trays of wet pebbles, which can look attractive, or use a mister.

The main attraction of bromeliads is their leaves and

forms, but many also bear beautiful flower spikes, generally consisting of colourful bracts and small, insignificant flowers. Be prepared to wait, because flower spikes normally appear only on mature plants. After flowering the plant may die, but not before it has produced offsets, which can be potted up to make new plants.

plant directory

Abromeitiella brevifolia

Formerly known as *A. chlorantha*, which is still sometimes offered as a separate species, these South American bromeliads eventually form large mats, to about 15cm (6in) high, of spiky-leaved rosettes, and they should be grown in large pans rather than in a 'normal' flowerpot. They have tapering, almost triangular leaves ending in a pointed tuft. In summer greenish flowers are borne on mature plants.

Aechmea

The bromeliads in this genus have strap-shaped leaves that arise from the centre, whey they form a pronounced reservoir. The offsets that grow around the parent plant should be detached when they are about 15cm (6in) high and grown on in small pots. *A. chantinii* (Amazonian zebra plant) has beautifully marked leaves, banded in grey, and edged with spines. The flowerheads are orange-yellow.

The best known species is, perhaps, *A. fasciata* (urn plant, silver vase), which has strong, broad, curving leaves of a dull, bluish-green, marked all over with powdery silver-white. Mature plants have leaves to 50cm (20in) long and 5cm (2in) or more wide and bear a flower spike of pink bracts and tiny, blue flowers. The flowers can last for several months but the plant begins to die after flowering. As long as the air is kept moist the plant will enjoy

Left: The bold architectural form and pale blue bloom of the leaves of *Aechmea fasciata* (vase plant) make it a striking plant.
Right: Ananas comosus (common pineapple) was introduced and cultivated for its fruit, but is now grown as an ornamental plant.
Below right: Cryptanthus spp. (earth stars) have wavy-edged leaves, which may have contrasting bands of colour.

temperatures of up to 26°C (79°F) in summer. It should be kept cooler in winter but not below 15°C (60°F).

The common name of *A. fulgens* (coral berry) is derived from the red berries that follow the blue flowers. It has dark green, spine-edged leaves. It can grow to 50cm (20in) high and 40cm (16in) across. *A. fulgens* var. *discolor* has leaves with purple undersides.

Ananas (pineapple)

Pineapples will eventually bear colourful flowers and even, in a warm greenhouse, fruit, but they are principally grown for their striking spine-edged leaves. *A. bracteatus* (red pineapple, wild pineapple) has spiny leaves and, in summer, red and yellow flower spikes. The form 'Tricolor' (syn. *A. bracteatus* 'Striatus') has lovely yellow-striped leaves. *A. comosus*, the pineapple grown commercially, can be grown by cutting off the top of a fruit, leaving it for a couple of days to form a callus and planting in well-drained compost. It will eventually grow to about 1m (3ft) high and 50cm (20in) across. *A. comosus* var. *variegatus* (ivory pineapple) is a compact form with attractive cream-edged leaves. *A. nanus* is similar to *A. comosus* but smaller, growing to about 45cm (18in) high and 60cm (2ft) across.

Billbergia

Billbergias are especially easy bromeliads to grow. They produce spectacular flowerheads on long, arching stems from the centres of the rosettes, and although each rosette dies after it has flowered, the plant has several at once, in different stages of development. One of the most popular billbergias is *B. nutans* (friendship plant, queen's tears), which has grey-green, sometimes red-tinged, leaves, forming a funnel-shaped rosette. In summer yellow, pink and green flowers, surrounded by red bracts, are borne on arching stems. *B.* x *windii* has mid-green leaves, which are arching and slightly twisted, forming a tubular rosette. Green-yellow flowers with pinkish-red bracts are borne on arching stems in late summer.

Cryptanthus (earth star, starfish plant)

Many bromeliads are large, 'stand alone' plants. The earth stars or cryptanthus are small in comparison. There are many species, but all are grown for their striped or banded foliage, arranged in the typical rosette and often with wavy or saw-toothed edges. They produce numerous offsets, and the best way to detach these to form new plants is first to remove the parent plant from its pot and then to pull off the offsets before replanting the parent. Earth stars need normal summer temperatures and a steady 15°C (60°F) in winter. They thrive in glass containers.

C. bivittatus is the most popular species. Its leaves have wavy, serrated edges and are 10–15cm (4–6in) long, striped green and pinkish-yellow. *C. bromelioides* also produces spreading rosettes of strap-

shaped, arching leaves, which are finely toothed and wavy edged. *C. bromelioides* var. *tricolor* is larger and has leaves olive green leaves longitudinally striped with white and pink. *C. fosterianus* (pheasant leaf) has ginger-brown leaves brindled in grey, resembling the tail feathers of a pheasant. *C. zonatus* (zebra earth star) has finely toothed, green-brown leaves that are beautifully banded with grey-buff.

Dyckia

This South American genus contains rosette-forming plants. *D. fosteriana* has attractive silver-grey, toothed leaves, which curve back to form a spreading rosette about 20cm (8in) high and 12cm (5in) across. *D. remotiflora* has dark green leaves, which are edged with hooked spines. Orange flowers appear in late spring. It grows to 30cm (12in) high and 50cm (20in) across.

Hechtia

These bromeliads are native to the southern United States and Central America. *H. argentea* (syn. *Dyckia argentea*) is a rosette-forming plant with long, tapering leaves, to 60cm (2ft) long, which are silvery-grey and edged with spines. It is a striking plant, growing to 1m (3ft) across and high. *H. epigyna* has bright green leaves, to 45cm (18in) long, which are edged with white teeth and which form rosettes to 60cm (2ft) high and across.

Neoregelia

The most popular neoregelia is *N. carolinae* (syn. *Aregelia carolinae*, *Nidularium carolinae*). It has mid-green, copper-tinged leaves, which form an open rosette. When plants begin to flower, the centre of the rosette turns red. The leaves of *N. carolinae* f. *tricolor* (blushing bromeliad) are glossy and striped longitudinally in cream and pink. The whole plant blushes red from the centre before it flowers and retains this colouring for several months. The low flowerhead appears at the centre of the rosette.

    N. spectabilis (fingernail plant) has red-tipped, green leaves which become purple-brown at the centre. The flue flowers emerge from purple-banded, green bracts.

Nidularium

N. fulgens (syn. *Guzmania picta*), sometimes known as blushing bromeliad, has toothed, bright green leaves that form a spreading rosette to 60cm (2ft) across. The white, purple-blue and red flowers are surrounded by bright red bracts. At the centre of *N. innocentii* (bird's nest bromeliad) is a rosette of short leaves, which turn red before the flowers appear. They are surrounded by longer, broader, green leaves.

Tillandsia

The species that grow well in pots have long, grassy, rather untidy-looking leaves and spectacular flat, fish- or quill-shaped flowers, made up of overlapping bracts. Many of these are delightful, fairly small plants between 23cm (8in) and 45cm (18in) high. *T. cyanea*, for example, with its vivid-pink flowerhead, is 23cm (9in)

Fascicularia

These rosette-forming plants are mostly from Chile. *F. bicolor* (syn. *F. andina*) has stiff, spiny toothed leaves to 45cm (18in) long; at flowering time the inner leaves turn bright red. *F. pitcairniifolia* has blue-green, rather glaucous leaves, which can get to 1m (3ft) long. At flowering, the inner circle of leaves turn vivid red around the blue-purple flowerheads.

Guzmania

The most widely grown species is *G. lingulata* (scarlet star). It has fairly narrow green leaves, to 50cm (20in) long, and eventually produces a flowerhead consisting of flaring red bracts. This is another relatively easy bromeliad, which tolerates a range of normal room temperatures as long as it has plenty of humidity. It should not be fed but its funnel should always have fresh, soft water. It will grow to about 45cm (18in) high and across. *G. sanguinea* produces almost flat rosettes of dark green leaves, to 40cm 916in) long, which become flushed with yellow, red and orange when the plants produces flowers. The flowers themselves are yellow, green or white and are surrounded by vivid red bracts. Plants grow to 20cm (8in) high and about 35cm (14in) across.

high. All tillandsias prefer high summer temperatures of up to 27°C (80°F) and 10–15°C (50–59°F) in winter although they are tough plants and can survive at temperatures as low as

Above left: Vriesea hieroglyphica (king of bromeliads) forms a rosette of yellow-green leaves irregularly patterned with darker green and purplish on the underside.
Above: Neoregelia carolinae 'Flandria' has particularly broad leaves, generously edged and narrowly striped in cream.
Right: Tillandsia flabellata is one of the green-leaved tillandsias that are normally grown in a pot. Its leaves are long and tapering and can take on reddish tints.

5°C (41°F) as long as the compost is kept only just slightly moist.

Among the tillandsias that can be included in pot-free displays are *T. circinnatoides* (pot-bellied tillandsia), which has spiralling leaf blades, 20–45cm (8–18in) high; *T. ionantha* (blushing bride), 8–10cm (3–4in) high, which has rosettes of silver-grey leaves, flushing red before flowering; *T. geminiflora*, which has bracts of rosy-pink with tiny, violet flowers and grows to 15–20cm (6–8in) high; and *T. ixioides*, which has a narrow, yellow flowerhead and grows to 13cm (5in) high.

Vriesea
These plants, which are closely related to tillandsias, have deeply cupped rosettes of strap-shaped leaves, and many are grown for the attractive leaves alone. *V. fenestralis* has yellowish-green leaves that are speckled with dark green on the upperside and reddish-purple on the underside. Plants can grow to 1m (3ft) high and 50cm (20in) across. *V. hieroglyphica* (king of bromeliads) has purple-marked, yellowish-green leaves that can be up to 60cm (2ft) long and 10cm (4in) wide. The

individual rosettes are to 1m (3ft) high and across. *V. splendens* (flaming sword) produces a succession of long-lasting flowerheads of bright red, overlapping bracts on stems 60cm (2ft) high from a rosette of dark green, banded leaves about 40cm (16in) long. The rosette, which forms a central 'cup', dies slowly when the flowering has finished. It needs a temperature of up to 27°C (80°F), with high humidity.

6 CACTI & SUCCULENTS

People become addicted to growing cacti, and they are certainly collectable plants and ideal for a sunny windowsill. We associate cacti with the desert, and many do, indeed, grow in the desert regions of Central and South America, but other cacti come from as far north as Canada, and many are native to rainforests. Like bromeliads, many cacti are epiphytes, and the forest-dwelling species grow over forest trees.

Desert-dwelling cacti can survive for long periods without rainfall, getting their moisture from dew or mist and storing nutrients and moisture in their tissues. This is a defining characteristic of succulent plants and it is this capacity that defines cacti as succulents. Botanically, what makes a cactus a cactus is that it has growths, known as areoles. These are cushioned growing points, which are technically compressed lateral branches. Spines, 'wool', flowers and offsets all grow from the areoles. Many succulents resemble cacti in almost every way – even to growing spines – but not in this distinguishing feature. In all but one genus of cactus, *Pereskia*, the plants do not have leaves, but spines or scales.

Because it has leaves, a cactus stores nutrients and water in its body, which consists, botanically, of a stem. The 'bodies' of cacti are generally globular or cylindrical in shape, although opuntias have round, segmented stems, which are flattened, and epiphyllums have stems that look more like strap-shaped leaves, which are again segmented. Many cacti have prominent spines, barbs or bristles, and some have woolly hair. In fact, every cactus has spines even though these may be small and seemingly insignificant. It is not always known or appreciated that all cacti are actually flowering plants, which will flower regularly if well looked after.

The word succulent means juicy, and succulent plants have leaves or stems that are swollen with juices, the stored water and nutrients that enable the plants to survive in harsh conditions all over the world. They normally have a glossy or leathery appearance, and the texture

Left: An imaginatively arranged group of cacti makes an absorbing display. Here barrel, columnar and 'lollipop' shapes mingle with two opuntias, which may be recognized by their flattened pads.
Above: Displaying related plants in similar pots gives the group added coherence.

helps to protect them from excessive moisture loss. There is a huge range of succulent plants that can be grown in the home and some of them are among the easiest plants to care for, making them ideal for beginners, for children and for people who have to be away from home a lot. But, as with all plants, you have to understand their nature to grow them successfully.

Left: Many cacti are rounded and attractively ribbed and spined. *Parodia claviceps* has golden spines and quickly forms clusters of spheres topped with patches of white areoles.

Right above: *Epiphyllum* 'Reward' is one of the forest cacti that produce beautiful flowers. These rainforest plants hybridize readily and many cultivars have been produced.

Right below: A mixed group of small cacti is perfect for a broad, sunny space. Patience is required for the first three or four years, and then many of the cacti will burst into bloom.

CARE AND CULTIVATION

From the breathtakingly beautiful, such as *Nopalxochia ackermanii* and the large-flowered epiphyllums (orchid cactus), to the frankly weird and wonderful, such as *Astrophytum asterias* (sea urchin cactus) or the hairy *Cephalocereus senilis* (old man cactus), cacti and succulents make a fine display, and it is a shame that they are not more widely cultivated. This probably stems from their undemanding natures: they will survive almost any treatment except overindulgence. This has resulted in cacti and succulents that are neglected and left to gather dust on people's windowsills at one extreme

and plants that are rotting from overwatering at the other. They need bright light, fresh air and a cool, dry winter rest.

Forest cacti tend to have a trailing habit and large flowers, making them perfect for individual display in hanging baskets, but the interesting shapes and textures of the desert types, and of many succulent plants, can be highlighted by a grouped display where they can be compared and contrasted. A group of small cacti or succulents planted in a single bowl is particularly effective, although larger specimens, such as aloes and agaves, look best in a pot of their own, as can the more curious

plants, such as *Heliocereus speciosus* (sun cactus).

Any large, shallow dish can be used as a container for a cactus garden. Select desert cacti and small succulents for this, so that the plants share similar growing and care requirements. Because these plants all need maximum light, you need to select a container that is the right shape and size to fit in the lightest place that you can offer. Arrange the plants fairly closely to avoid the 'spotted dick' or 'dot' effect – this is an effect caused by groups of plants that have been arranged with little form or structure – and choose a variety of shapes and sizes. A layer of fine grit spread over the compost provides an attractive and suitably dry surface for the cacti, and clean pebbles arranged between the plants completes the effect.

Cacti can look charming in a row, potted in matching pots.

Cacti such as mutant cultivars of *Gymnocalycium mihanovichii*, which come with differently coloured heads but are otherwise alike, look best displayed in this simple but attractive way.

Most cacti and succulents need the maximum light possible and are therefore suitable for the sunniest of windowsills. This light-loving characteristic can be exploited to the full by fixing shelves across a sunny window and standing rows of neatly potted cacti on them. You could also arrange the pots in a low-sided basket or a wicker tray. Make sure that the plants are turned frequently so that all parts get equal exposure to the full light. A mixed group of small cacti is perfect for a broad, sunny windowsill.

There is an almost bewildering range of cacti to grow at home, and every garden centre has a fairly wide selection. Some cacti – the forest-growing *Hatiora rosea* (Easter cactus) and *Schlumbergera* x *buckleyi* (Christmas cactus), for example – are sold as seasonal gift plants in department stores, too. It is best to buy cacti that are in flower, because they can take several years to reach maturity and flowering age. Check them carefully, making sure they are sound with no trace of rot or areas that are dry or shrivelled. They should be just the right size for their pot: not too small but not showing signs of roots being cramped. Make sure that they are not exposed to sudden draughts of cold air on their way home. Once you get a taste for cacti you will find that you need to go to a specialist nursery for the more unusual specimens.

Above: Echinopsis chamaecereus (peanut cactus) has short stems. The bright red flowers are produced in abundance in spring and summer.
Left: Astrophytum capricorne (goat's horn cactus) gets more columnar as it ages and has dark, curled spines (left). *A. myriostigma* (bishop's cap) is covered in silvery-white scales (right).
Opposite: Cereus. uruguayanus typifies desert cacti with its spines and well-defined shape.

desert cacti

Desert cacti must have well-drained compost. Special cactus compost, or any potting compost to which added sharp sand or gravel has been added, can be used. The cacti should be well watered with tepid water in spring and summer, but the compost should be allowed to become almost completely dry between waterings. In winter they should be kept almost completely dry, especially if they are in cool conditions. Cacti should be fed about every three weeks during periods of active growth, with well-diluted tomato plant fertilizer.

Most desert cacti do best if kept in winter temperatures of 10–13°C (50–55°F) but can withstand temperatures as low as 5°C (41°F). Repot only when the roots absolutely fill the pot.

plant directory

Astrophytum

These slow-growing cacti come from the southern United States and Mexico. *A. asterias* (syn. *Echinocactus asterias*; sand dollar cactus, sea urchin cactus) is hemispherical, growing to 10cm (4in) high and across, with six to ten almost flat ribs. Yellow flowers with red throats are borne in summer. *A. myriostigma* (syn. *Echinocactus myriostigma*; bishop's cap cactus) has ribbed sides, gathered up in the shape of a bishop's mitre. It is smooth and greyish-green, speckled with white, and the four to eight ribs are marked with white, felty blobs (areoles); it eventually grows to about 23cm (9in) high and to 30cm (12in) across. When four or five years old it produces a succession of scented, lemon-yellow flowers in summer. Astrophytums grow best in a light, sunny position and should be fed once every two weeks in summer with tomato fertilizer.

Cephalocereus

The three cacti now included in the genus are from Mexico. They all columnar and have numerous spines. The best known species is *C. senilis* (old man cactus), which will grow to 12m (40ft) tall in the desert but is extremely slow growing. Young plants have 12–15 ribs, and the yellow spines are produced from closely set areoles, which produce 20–30 soft, white hairs. These hairs, which give the cactus its appearance, can be 13cm (5in) long. In summer nocturnal pink flowers are borne. Eventually, at home, the beards need to be washed with detergent; this should be done outside on a warm, dry day.

Cereus

The genus contains tree-like cacti from South America and the Caribbean. *C. uruguayanus* (syn. *C. peruvianus*; Peruvian cereus) can grow to 90cm (3ft) fairly quickly in a warm, sunny room. Its columns are blue-green, ribbed and spined. Under the name *C. uruguayanus* 'Monstrosus' (or 'Monstruosus') a number of mutations with gargoyle-like side branches are sold.

Cleistocactus

These cacti from mountainous areas of South America have tall, slender stems, with the narrow ribs ornamented by neat spines and woolly areoles. One or two forms are branched or trailing. *C. strausii* (silver torch), which has silvery-white spines that are covered with fine bristles and grows to about 1m (3ft) high and across.

Echinocactus

These slow-growing cacti originate in the southern United States and Mexico. *E. grusonii* (golden barrel cactus, mother-in-law's cushion) is a popular non-flowering cactus. It has sharp golden-yellow spines and a deeply ribbed stem, ultimately 60cm (2ft) high and 80cm (32in) across, which is topped with a depression and a crown of yellow hairs.

Left: Many ferocacti are grown for their fierce curling spines, but *Ferocactus echidne* has short erect spines on its barrel-shaped stem and is crowned with flowers.

Right: Mammillarias are often densely covered with downy or spiky spines, and are generally globular. They remain small and produce neat coronets of brightly coloured flowers, as in *M. hahniana* (old lady cactus).

Far right: Intriguing forms of *Gymnocalycium mihanovichii* are produced by grafting brightly coloured heads (which lack chlorophyll) on to the green stems of *Hylocereus*. This is 'Red Cap'.

and often barbed spines. *F. latispinus* is bright green, with 15–23 ribs and pinkish-yellow coloured spines. It is slow growing, eventually getting to 40cm (16in) high and across, and in summer has red, white, purple or yellow flowers.

Gymnocalycium

There are more than 50 species in the genus, and they are found throughout South America. *G. bruchii* (syn. *G. lafadense*) forms clumps of dark green stems with 12 ribs and each to about 4cm (1½in) high. In summer pink flowers are borne. *G. mihanovichii* is a globular cactus with a grey-green stem and eight prominent ribs. It has given rise to a number of mutant forms that lack chlorophyll and that are grafted on to robust plants of *Hylocereus*. These plants grow to about 13cm (5in) tall.

Heliocereus

The cacti in this genus are native to Central America. They vary widely in habit and appearance, some being more or less erect, while others are trailing. *H. cinnabarinus* is a trailing

Echinopsis

The common name of the much re-named *Echinopsis chamaecereus* (syn. *Cereus silvestrii*, *Chamaecereus silvestrii*, *Lobivia silvestrii*; peanut cactus, gherkin cactus) is derived from its rather marrow-shaped stems, each to about 10cm (4in) tall, which look like bristle-covered gherkins or peanut pods. It is fast growing and produces red or deep orange flowers in late spring. Several hybrids are available but these are less fast growing. It should be brought out of its winter rest in early spring.

Espostoa

The genus includes ten species of columnar cacti, which are slow growing, eventually tree-like. *E. lanata* (snowball cactus) is columnar, with 20–30 ribs, and in the wild it grows to 1.5m (5ft) or more. White or yellowish hairs emerge from the areoles, giving the plant its common name. *E. melanostele* has a grey-green stem, covered with brown areoles. Plants will grow to 1.8m (6ft) in the wild. In summer white, yellow or brown flowers are produced.

Ferocactus

Native to southern parts of the United States and to Mexico and Guatemala, these cacti are usually solitary. They are mostly spherical in shape and can very slowly reach 60cm (2ft) or more in height. They have ferocious, stiff,

cactus, with dark green stems with white, yellow or brown spines. In summer it bears bright red flowers. *H. speciousus* (syn. *Cereus speciosus*) is semi-erect, with branched, green stems that have three to five ribs. The small spines are white or brown and the carmine flowers are borne during the summer.

Mammillaria
The genus includes the most popular and widely available of all cactus species, of which there are more than a hundred. They form cushions, mounds – some cylindrical – and 'cauliflower' heads, all covered in numerous tiny spines. In spring they bear either a few large flowers or more smaller ones, which are followed by fruits. But beware: many mammillarias also have vicious hooks. *M. longimamma* (syn. *Dolichothele longimamma*) is a small, long-lived cactus with several narrow, fleshy projections, each of which has a lightly spined tip. In summer this plant produces shiny, bright yellow, upright, bell-shaped flowers that have many petals.

Opuntia (prickly pear)
Most opuntias are the multiple-lollipop type, with flattened stems that grow in rounded segments. Among those species popular as houseplants are

O. brasiliensis, which makes a large plant that grows to 6m (20ft) or more high; *O. microdasys* (bunny ears) has round, golden-tufted pads; and *O. microdasys* var. *rufida* (syn. *O. rufida*; red bunny ears), which has brownish-red tufts and grows to about 60cm (2ft) high and across. *O. subulata* (awl cactus) is unusual in that it has cylindrical, many-branched stems that are covered in projecting awl-shaped, green leaves and yellowish-spined areoles. Although this plant grows to 3m (10ft) in the wild it is seldom taller than 75cm (30cm) in the home.

Oreocereus
Formerly known as *Borzicactus*, this genus contains cacti that come from mountainous areas in South America. *O. aurantiacus* (syn. *Borzicactus aurantiacus*, *Matucana aurantiaca*), which grows to about 15cm (6in) high and across, has a slightly flattened globe shape, and bright orange-yellow flowers sprout from the top of the stem in summer. Bright light, and fairly generous watering and fortnightly feeding in summer encourage flowering.

Parodia
The genus contains cacti that were previously classified as *Eriocactus*, *Notocactus* and *Wigginsia*. They are

mostly small, taking ten years to reach up to 18cm (7in), and are generally spherical and spiny, some becoming cylindrical as they age. The flowers, which can sometimes be disproportionately large, are produced on the top of the 'ball'. *P. leninghausii* (syn. *Eriocactus leninghausii*; golden ball cactus) grows to 60cm (2ft) but only about 20cm (8in) across, and is liked for its golden spines. *P. ottonis* (syn. *Notocactus ottonis* is a typical small ball cactus, which has a mass of yellow flowers in spring. Ball cacti are easily grown from seed.

Rebutia
This genus now also includes plants that used to be known as *Sulcorebutia* and *Weingartia*. These small cacti are perhaps the easiest to grow. They are often known as crown cacti, a common name that describes the way flowers often form a ring around the base of the plant. They have funnelled, many-petalled flowers and form mounds 10–15cm (4–6in) high. *R. aureiflora* is studded in late spring with yellow flowers; *R. minuscula* (syn. *R. violaciflora*) comes in forms with red or violet flowers; *R. senilis* has flowers in red, yellow or lilac in late spring and early summer. Rebutias may die quite soon after flowering, but they produce offsets from which replacement plants can be grown.

Left: Aporocactus flagelliformis (rat-tail cactus) makes an ideal plant for a medium hanging pot.
Above: Nopalxochia ackermanii flowers very prolifically, especially if not repotted for several years.
Above right: Hatiora gaertneri is the red-flowered 'Easter cactus'.

forest cacti

Forest cacti are very different from desert cacti. They usually have spectacularly beautiful hanging flowers growing from the tips of segmented stems, which look like chains of fleshy leaves. They grow in a trailing manner because of their habit of growing over trees. Because of this habit they are used to dappled shade, although, being tropical and subtropical plants, they need quite bright light; they should be kept in good light but protected from strong sun. Like all rainforest plants they need light, lime-free, well-drained compost and high humidity, and they should be frequently misted with tepid, soft water. These cacti should be rested in a cool place at a temperature of 10–13°C (50–55°F) after flowering and watered sparingly until flower buds appear; then water them moderately and feed weekly with a fairly weak solution of balanced fertilizer and move them to a position that has higher temperatures.

plant directory

Aporocactus

These epiphytic cacti from Mexico are trailing plants, grown for the slender stems and colourful flowers. *A. flagelliformsi* (syn. *Cereus flagelliformis*) has grey-green stems with 10–14 ribs and red-brown spines. Each stem can grow to 1.8m (6ft) long. Bright pink flowers are borne in spring.

Epiphyllum (orchid cactus)

Epiphyllums are forest cacti: rainforest plants that, in summer, produce some of the most beautiful of all flowers. They cross-breed readily, and many hybrids have now been bred to be grown as houseplants, including 'Reward', which has yellow flowers, and 'Cambodia', which has purplish-red flowers with ruffled petals. Epiphyllum flowers are usually about 10–15cm (4–6in) wide. Some epiphyllums have been reclassified in *Nopalxochia*.

Hatiora

Formerly known as *Rhipsalidopsis*, the genus contains the well-known Easter cactus, *H. rosea* (syn. *Rhipsalidopsis rosea*), a shrubby plant with flat, green segments and, in the early spring, vivid pink flowers. *H. gaertneri* (syn. *Rhipsalidopsis gaertneri*, *Schlumbergera gaertneri*), which is also sometimes called the Easter cactus, is a spreading plant with leaf-like stems. Bright red, funnel-shaped flowers are produced during the spring.

Nopalxochia

Many of the plants now classified in this genus were formerly known as epiphyllums, including *N. ackermannii* (syn. *Epiphyllum ackermannii*), which is an erect plant with flat, fleshy stems. In late spring to early summer it bears orange-red flowers. There are now many named cultivars (still sometimes named as epiphyllums),

including 'Celestine', which has pale pink-red flowers, 'Jennifer Ann', which has yellow flowers, and 'Moonlight Sonata', which has purplish-pink flowers.

Schlumbergera (Christmas cactus)

The genus is closely allied to *Hatiora* and is sometimes also known as *Zygocactus*. However, most of the plants offered for sale are cultivars that are grown for their reliable and colourful flowers. They have the typical, segmented, flattened stems and make spreading plants, suitable for a hanging basket, although they are enormously dull when not in flower. There are many named forms to choose from, including 'Gold Charm', which has yellow flowers, 'Joanne', which has red and purple flowers, and 'Weinachtesfreude', which has pale and dark red and purple flowers.

succulents

Apart from the cacti, there are 50 or more families of plants that can be classified as succulents. The cacti are in origin confined almost exclusively to the Americas, but the rest of the succulents come also from Africa and parts of Europe. Like the desert cacti they are dry land plants (many of them grow side by side with cacti), and nearly all have the same needs for plentiful sun and a free-draining compost. The need to be watered freely in summer but only when the compost has become nearly dry, and during winter water should be reduced and they should be kept at temperatures around 10°C (50°F).

In summer most succulents need some well-diluted fertilizer every three to four weeks and fresh air rather than humidity. Some succulents store water and nutrients in their swollen, fleshy leaves (the leaf succulents), others, the stem succulents, have tough, fleshy stems; a third kind, the root succulents, have swollen roots of various kinds in which their reserves of water are stored.

Left: Aloe aristata has orange-pink flowers on tall stems, which spring from dense rosettes of sharply pointed, white-edged leaves. The rosette is only 10–15cm (4–6in) high, with the flower stems 30cm (12in) high.
Right: Agave americana 'Marginata' has the characteristic broad, wavy leaves, which in this variety are edged and narrowly striped with creamy-yellow.

plant directory

Adenia
These plants come from Africa, Madagascar and Burma, and the tiny flowers are followed by yellow, green or red fruits. *A. digitata* (syn. *A. buchananii, Modecca digitata*) grows from a caudex (swollen root), which can get to 30cm (12in) across. The dark green leaves are borne in a cluster on top of the caudex. Yellow flowers are followed by red fruits. *A. spinosa* has a huge caudex, 1.8m (6ft) across and spiny branches. White flowers are followed by yellow fruit.

Adenium obesum (desert rose, impala lily)
This variable, caudex-forming plant comes from Africa and the Arabian peninsula. It is also known as *A. arabicum, A. micranthum, A. speciosum* and *Nerium obesum*. The bottle-shaped caudex, up to 1m (3ft) long, is topped by brown stems and grey-green leaves. Red, pink or white flowers are borne in summer. Plants can reach 1.5m (5ft) in height.

Agave
These rosette-forming plants from the Americas include many popular houseplants, although some species are potentially large and are best grown in a cool greenhouse. *A. utahensis* has grey-green leaves with spines along the wavy margins. It grows to 30cm (12in) high but spreads

indefinitely. *A. victoriae-reginae* (syn. *A. consideranti*) is perhaps the favourite as a houseplant. The many dark green, spine-tipped leaves are neatly edged with white, and plants eventually grow to 50cm (20in) high and across.

Aloe
Aloes have rosettes of stiff, leathery, tooth-edged leaves, broad at the base and tapering to a point. The leaves are often blotched, striped, banded or striated. The flowers are bell-shaped – generally orange – and grow in cones on tall, erect stems. There are small aloes, such as *A. humilis* (hedgehog aloe), with bluish, white-toothed leaves and growing to 10cm (4in) high, and *A. aristata* (*A. ellenbergeri*; brush aloe, lace aloe), which has white-spotted leaves and reaches some 10–15cm (4–6in) high. Medium-sized species include the 30cm (12in) high *A. variegata* (syn. *A. ausana, A. punctata*; partridge-breasted aloe) with its white-patterned leaves. One of the giant species is *A. arborescens* (tree aloe), which can easily grow to 1m (3ft) in a container.

Cotyledon
These African succulents have fleshy leaves borne in opposite pairs. *C. orbiculata* grows to 60cm (2ft). It has white-grey leaves covered with waxy white bloom and edged with

red. *C. orbiculata* var. *oblonga* (syn. *C. undulata*; silver crown) has red-edged leaves, like fleshy cabbage leaves, with undulating margins.

Crassula
There are many crassulas, generally with small, rounded or sometimes triangular leaves and succulent, sometimes twisting stems. One of the best known species is *C. ovata* (syn. *C. arborescens, C. argentea*; jade plant, money tree) It looks like a tiny, exotic tree with a sturdy, fleshy stem and equally fleshy deep green, waxy leaves. It can grow to 1.8m (6ft) tall but is usually less in a container. The cactus-like *C. muscosa* (syn. *C. lycopodioides*; rat tail plant, lizard tail) shows how different plants of the same genus can be. It has upright branching stems in light green, completely covered in little triangular, fleshy leaves from top to bottom.

Echeveria
This is another rosette-forming group of plants from southern United States and Central America. *E. derenbergii* (painted lady) has rosettes of piled-up fleshy leaves with blue bloom and orange flowers on towering stems. It grows to 10cm (4in) high to about 30cm (12in) across. *E. elegans* has pale blue-green leaves forming small rosettes, to 5cm (2in) high and forming clumps to 30cm (12in) across.

Euphorbia

This large genus contains plants that are suitable for the garden as well as for growing as houseplants. *E. obesa* (living baseball) is a cactus-like pincushion with grey and yellow gingham marking and crimped ridging. It grows to 15cm (6in) high and 13cm (5in) across.

Gasteria

These clump-forming succulents from southern Africa have fleshy leaves arranged in tiers. *G. carinata* var. *verrucosa* (syn. *G. verrucosa*; ox tongue) has grey-green, tapering leaves, which have thick margins and are covered in white tubercles (warts). Each rosette of leaves grows to 15cm (6in) high and to 30cm (12in) across. *G. obliqua* (syn. *G. pulchra*) has almost triangular, grey-green leaves with white margins. Plants are to 30cm (12in) high and 45cm (18in) across.

Haworthia

Haworthias have strong, rather plump, broad tapering leaves, which grow from small stems in packed rosettes and are often said to be 'warty'. *H. pumila* (syn. *H. margaritifera*; pearl plant) has such dense rosettes that they are almost spherical and the leaves are encrusted with decorative pearly 'warts'. *H. retusa* is a rosette-forming succulent, with fleshy leaves to 5cm (2in) long.

Kalanchoe

The genus is best known for the hybrids of *K. blossfeldiana* (flaming Katy), which have red, orange, yellow and pink flowers. Among the other species are *K. daigremontiana* (syn. *Bryophyllum daigremontianum*; Mexican hat plant), which has green leaves spotted with red. Adventitious plantlets form around the edges of the leaves and can be potted up. *K. fedtschenkoi* is an upright succulent with blue-green leaves with boldly scalloped edges.

Kleinia

The plants are related to the familiar garden genus *Senecio* but look quite different. *K. stapeliiformis* (syn.

Far left: The broad yellow margins of *Sanseveria trifasciata* 'Laurentii' (mother-in-law's tongue) help the plant to make a bold statement against a plain background.
Left: The many euphorbias have no one distinctive form. The remarkable *Euphorbia obesa* (living baseball, gingham golfball) is dome shaped, but other euphorbias have branching, tree-like stems.
Left below: The bright green leaves of *Sedum morganianum* (donkey's tail) are easily detached, so care must be taken when handling these plants.
Right: Kalanchoe blossfeldiana (flaming Katy) can be bought in flower at any time. Red, orange, pink, yellow and white cultivars are available.

Senecio stapeliiformis) is an erect plant with fleshy, glaucous green stems with dark green longitudinal lines. Red-orange flowerheads are produced in summer.

Lithops (living stones)
These dwarf succulents from southern Africa consist of two opposing 'bodies' topped with large, daisy-like flowers. *L. marmorata* has pale grey bodies and scented white flowers. *L. turbiniformis* (syn. *L. hookeri*) has brown-grey bodies and red and yellow flowers.

Pachyphytum
These rosette-forming perennials from Mexico have fleshy, swollen leaves. *P. longifolium* has glaucous blue leaves, which are elongated at the tips. Racemes of flowers are borne in spring. *P. oviferum* (sugar almond plant) has pale green-grey leaves tinged with blue. The rosettes grow up to 13cm (5in) tall and as much as 30cm (12in) across.

Sansevieria
The genus includes the well-known *S. trifasciata* (mother-in-law's tongue) from western Africa, which has sword-shaped, upright leaves, to 1.02m (4ft) tall. The leaves are banded and marbled. 'Golden Hahnii' and 'Silver Hahnii' are dwarf forms; 'Laurentii' has leaves with broad yellow margins.

Sedum
As well the many sedums that will grow in the garden, there are several species that can be grown as houseplants. Some have fleshy and some have cylindrical 'jelly bean' leaves. Many of them have branching, prostrate stems. *S. morganianum* (donkey's tail, burro's tail) comes from Mexico and has stems that can trail as much as 1m (3ft). It makes an ideal plant for a hanging basket, sometimes bearing clusters of pink flowers at the ends throughout the summer. These stems are crowded with bright green leaves. In the similar *S. sieboldii* 'Mediovariegatum', which comes from Japan, the leaves are a pink-patterned, cool blue-grey.

7 BULBS

Many of the best loved indoor flowering plants are grown from bulbs, corms (technically stems) or tubers (underground storage organs). Most of all we associate bulbs with spring, and some of the long-time favourites are spring-flowering, with early indoor hyacinths, crocuses, daffodils and other forms of narcissi and tulips reminding us that winter is coming to an end. Specially prepared bulbs make spring narcissi and hyacinths available for Christmas in the northern hemisphere, a long time before they will be flowering in parks and gardens. But bulbs, corms and tubers can produce lovely flowers at all times of year.

It is usually best to consign all hardy bulbs that have been grown indoors to the garden after they have flowered because they cannot be relied upon to give a good repeat performance, but there is really no reason for not keeping most tender indoor bulbs, such as amaryllis, begonia tubers and cyclamen corms, for indoor flowering the following year. If they are correctly treated they should perform indoors year after year.

A pot of bulbs in flower is a visual delight in its own right, but a large part of the pleasure is lost if you do not grow them yourself. This is really simple, and bringing your own bulbs into flower provides an extra thrill, as well as saving money and giving you a much wider choice of plants.

You can just wander into your local garden centre at the last minute to see what they have in stock; or you may find yourself buying bulbs on impulse without even knowing what you plan to do with them. But sending for the catalogues of the major bulb producers and selecting and ordering bulbs in good time can become a pleasant ritual. If you order from a reputable supplier you can be guaranteed good bulbs in perfect condition. If you buy from retailers, go early in the season (late summer for the majority of spring bulbs) to get the best choice and the freshest bulbs.

Select bulbs or corms that are firm and of good size for the type of plant, and that feel heavy for their size. Make sure that they show no sign of mould, damp or damage. Remember to check that bulbs for early indoor flowering have been specially prepared for 'forcing'.

Bulb fibre (which is made up of peat or coir fibre, mixed with crushed oyster shells and charcoal) is light, convenient and cheaper than potting compost. If you do not intend to keep your bulbs after their first flowering it is an adequate growing medium, but it contains no nutrients and is intended for short-term use only. Soil-based potting compost contains a balanced mix of nutrients and is more akin in structure to the bulbs' natural growing medium, enabling bulbs to develop and replenish themselves after flowering, and is more suitable for bulbs that are to be grown on in future years.

When you buy bulbs, get the bulb fibre or compost for planting them in, the pots and anything else you will need, such as charcoal to add to the compost if you are using pots without drainage. Plant the bulbs without delay so that they do not have a chance to deteriorate through being stored, and to get them off to an early start.

Always give careful consideration to the pot or container for indoor displays because this can make or mar the effect you are hoping to create. Hyacinths, daffodils and the other narcissi, tulips and crocuses are normally grown in bowls that have no drainage, and although simple and practical plastic bowls are sold for this purpose, an attractive china, glazed earthenware or terracotta pot is much more suitable. The container should be wide and shallow, and preferably non-porous, because if it is of porous material (as are most terracotta pots), its damp base will damage table tops and other surfaces. The remedy is to place a saucer or plate under it, which can spoil the effect, or to stand porous containers on a tiled windowsill or kitchen top.

Larger bulbs, such as the various lilies that are grown as individual specimens, are usually best grown in standard flowerpots that are stood in saucers; there is a good choice of ornamental versions of these. Ordinary clay pots can also be used, but plastic pots are always best hidden by a decorative container that suits both the flower and the room.

daffodils

Probably the favourite among the bulbs grown for indoor flowers are daffodils (and other popular narcissi), and there is such a wide range that it would be possible to have different types in flower from early winter until well into the spring.

Daffodils belong to the *Narcissus* genus, and the word daffodil, although used loosely to describe all narcissi, is used more specifically for those flowers that have prominent trumpets and a single bloom on each stem. We usually think of them as being yellow, but there are white and cream cultivars. The other members of the genus have cups and trumpets of varying sizes, some have several flowers on each stem, some are highly scented, and some have double flowers.

If you want an early performance from all bulbs, not just narcissi, you must make sure that you use bulbs that have been prepared for forcing, because they will have been artificially subjected to a cold 'winter' period and can be made ready to begin growing indoors

Left: Hardy daffodils make a good show indoors. Tall cultivars, such as 'King Alfred' and 'Dutch Master', or shorter stemmed varieties, such as 'Tête-à-Tête' and 'February Gold', grow well as houseplants.
Right: Bright yellow daffodils are symbolic of spring, and an indoor display is at its best when the bulbs are planted close together.

INDOOR PLANTING

much earlier than normal. They can be brought into flower especially early or introduced gradually to warmth so that they are only just ahead of their natural seasons. Ordinary, unprepared bulbs can be used if you do not want an unnaturally early show.

Small and miniature narcissi, such as 'February Gold' and 'Tête-à-Tête', are among the best for growing early indoors. Bulbs planted in late summer can be brought into good light in winter for Christmas flowering (in the northern hemisphere). For scented flowers grow *N. papyraceus* (syn. *N.* 'Paper White'; paper white narcissus), which has as many as ten intensely fragrant, gleaming white flowers on each stem. These narcissi can also be forced in glass containers of water and pebbles, with a little charcoal added to keep the water sweet.

1 Plant daffodils in late summer using one cultivar per bowl. Half-fill a clean bowl with damp, sterilized compost or bulb fibre.

2 Check the height of the compost, using a bulb to measure. When planted the tops of the bulbs should be just about level with the rim of the bowl. Space the bulbs in the bowl so that they are close together but are not quite touching. A full bowl will give the best display with a host of flowers.

3 Starting from the middle, add more compost or fibre, pushing it gently between the bulbs. Fill the bowl to within 1cm (½in) of the rim. If the bowl has drainage holes, water it well and allow to drain. Otherwise water lightly.

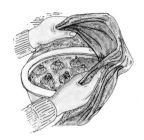

4 Wrap the bowl in polythene and keep in a cool spot. Check regularly to see that the compost is still damp: water if not. Bring the bowl indoors and gradually increase warmth when the shoots are 5cm (2in) high.

crocuses & tulips

After narcissi, crocuses and tulips are the most popular spring bulbs. As with naricssi, many cultivars have been developed, and there are now flowers in every imaginable shade and many new shades.

When you are choosing tulip species to force for winter flowering indoors, bear in mind that you should pick early types that will cope with a certain degree of warmth as these are more likely to get good results.

The best place to keep tulips and crocuses once they have begun to flower is in a relatively cool room, away from radiators or fires, as they will soon cease flowering, wilt and die off if kept in a warm, dry atmosphere.

Forcing tulips

Plant tulips in late summer or early autumn for indoor flowering. Early tulips, both single and double forms, are the best types for growing indoors. To help their roots to form quickly you can peel off the outer brown skin. Keep the pots in the coldest part of the garden, covered with a thick layer of soil topped with black polythene, or in the coolest, darkest place you can provide. Check every ten days or so to make sure the compost is still damp. Bring the pots into a warm room in early winter but keep them in dim light. When there is about 10cm (4in) growth, give the tulips full light and a temperature of about 20°C (68°F). They should then flower around Christmas (in the northern hemisphere). Introduce them only gradually to warmth and light for later flowering.

Crocus pots

Spring-flowering crocuses are among the earliest flowers to appear in the garden, and corms bought for forcing will bring a splash of colour indoors even earlier. Crocuses planted in autumn open their goblet-like flowers in late winter or early spring. Most spring-flowering crocuses are hybrids of C. chrysanthus, and they are available in a wide range of colours, from the silvery pale blue of 'Blue Pearl' to the dramatic yellow and purple-striped 'Gipsy Girl'.

It is possible to obtain special containers with holes in the sides, and these are perfect for crocuses. Soak the pot for 24 hours, then put a layer of clay pellets or other drainage material in the bottom of the pot. Put in some damp compost or bulb fibre and position the corms into the holes from the inside, so that their 'noses' are just sticking out on the outside. Firm in, adding more compost as necessary to fill the pot. Add more corms at the top. Cover to keep out the light, taking care not to damage the 'noses'.

Opposite left: Crocus corms are usually sold by cultivar name and are available in many shades of cream and yellow, blue and purple, as well as white.

Opposite right: Indispensable for brightening up garden borders in early and mid-spring, tulips will also add colour and cheer to any room in the house.

Above left: The bright red tulip 'Red Riding Hood' has attractive maroon or purple-brown markings on the leaves.

Above: The vibrant hues and strong forms of tulips make them popular indoor bulbs.

hyacinths

Cultivars developed from *Hyancinthus orientalis* are the most popular indoor hyacinths, with fragrant flowers in white and shades of pink, blue, yellow and red. New cultivars are appearing all the time, some with double flowers, but 'Carnegie' (pure white flowers), 'City of Haarlem' (cream-coloured flowers), 'Hollyhock' (bright red, double flowers), 'Ostara' (blue flowers) and 'Sheila' (pale pink flowers) have stood the test of time.

Plant the bulbs from late summer to early autumn, keeping bulbs of the same cultivar in one pot. For a good show, the bowl should be just large enough to allow a little space between the bulbs. After flowering, hyacinths can be planted in the garden, and they will flower in subsequent years. Over time, however, the flower spikes will become less dense.

PLANTING HYACINTH BULBS

 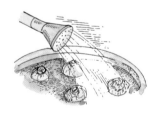 

1 Make sure the pot is clean, to prevent the risk of mould and infection, and half-fill it with damp potting compost or bulb fibre. Position the bulbs on the surface of the compost. If you are using an odd number of bulbs, start with one central bulb and arrange the rest around it.

2 Seat the bulbs in the compost, with a gap of 1cm (½in) between them. Add more compost – to within 1cm (½in) of the rim – and leave the bulb tops showing. Firm the compost gently. Water pots with drainage thoroughly and allow to drain; water pots without drainage sparingly.

3 Store, wrapped in black polythene, in a cool place such as a shed, cellar or cupboard in an unheated room. Check occasionally that the compost is still moist and water if necessary. Bring the pot into a cool room when when the shoots reach 5–8cm (2–3in) high.

Left: The heavily scented flowerheads of *Hyacinthus orientalis* (Dutch hyacinths) are one of the pleasures of late winter and spring.
Right: A bulb glass makes a lovely container for a single hyacinth. The bulb sits neatly within the rim, and its white, fleshy roots fill the rest of the glass, so that the whole plant is visible.
Below: Even one hyacinth can brighten up a whole room.

Using a Bulb Glass

Hyacinths are the best plants for a bulb glass. They should be started off in late summer or early autumn, using bulbs that have been prepared for forcing. Fill the glass up to the neck with water and sit the bulb in the container with its base just in the water. Keep the glass in a cool, dark place until the leaves begin to show, when the roots should be 8–10cm (3–4in) long, then bring it into the warmth and light in gentle stages. Keep the water level topped up so that the bulb base is just in the water, especially until the hyacinth's roots have developed.

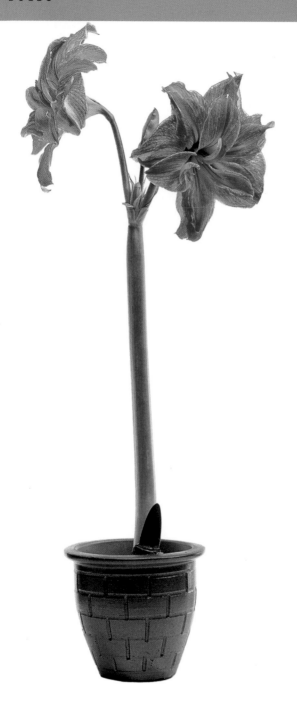

range in colour from beautiful deep red to the palest of pinks, and double flowers, flowers with frilled petals and even striped flowers are increasingly available. Hippeastrums will produce between two and six flowers on each stem.

Use a soil-based compost for the large bulbs, which should be planted so that the neck and shoulders are above the compost. Water sparingly but never let the compost dry out completely until a shoot emerges from the bulb. Increase the amount of water given and feed the plants once a week with a balanced liquid fertilizer diluted to half strength. Position the plants in good light but not direct sun. After flowering has finished gradually reduce the amount of water while the leaves die back. The bulbs should be kept completely dry during their dormant period and then brought back into growth in late autumn for early spring flowering.

Hippeastrums do not respond well to having their roots disturbed at all, and they grow perfectly well in pots that would appear to be too small for the large bulbs. After three to four years, however, bulbs should be potted up. This should be done in autumn before they are brought into growth again to avoid stressing the plant.

New cultivars are appearing every year, but reliable favourites include 'Apple Blossom', which has white flowers shading to a delicate pink at the edges, 'Picotee', which white flowers finely edged in red, 'Red Lion', which has scarlet flowers, and the double-flowered 'Lady Jane', which has pink and white striped flowers.

hippeastrums

These exotic looking flowers – usually (though incorrectly) known as amaryllis – are increasingly popular houseplants, bearing their huge, showy flowers on erect stems above the strap-shaped leaves in winter and early spring. The funnel-shaped flowers, which can reach as much as 15cm (6in) across,

Opposite: With care and summer dormancy, hippeastrums can be brought into flower for several seasons.
Left: In order to force a *Clivia miniata* (Kaffir lily) to flower this well, it must be given a resting period and very little water until the flower stalk is at least 15cm (6in) long.

tender bulbs

While hardy bulbs – narcissi, tulips, hyacinths, crocuses and the like – can be grown outside in temperate climates and can be persuaded to flower indoors in late winter and early spring, there are many tender bulbs that can be grown as houseplants and that will flower at various times of the year. Unlike the hardy bulbs, these plants do not need to be forced.

Pot them in soil-based compost in pots with good drainage and keep them in the light at normal temperatures. Water fairly sparingly until shoots appear and then increasingly generously. All but the evergreen tender bulbs need an annual rest. After they have flowered continue watering until the leaves and flower stems have died down, then cut them off at the base. Store the bulbs – either in their pots or in a box of peat – in a cool, frost-free, dark place without watering. Bring into a warm room and begin to water again in the planting season.

Left: Commonly known as Kaffir lilies, clivias will flower year after year if given a cool winter rest. The pot should not be moved once the plant is in bud or while it is flowering and the plant should not be repotted.

Right: Bulbous irises can all be grown indoors, and the reticulatas make particularly lovely, softly scented, spring-flowering houseplants. The many named cultivars in this group are mainly in shades of blue.

Far right: Lilies make excellent pot plants. They can be persuaded to flower at any time of year, depending on when they are planted, as long as they are kept cold before planting.

plant directory

Babiana stricta (baboon root)
This cormous species is native to
South Africa and requires a minimum
winter temperature of 5°C (41°F). It
has upright stems and leaves, with
small, scented flowers growing up the
stems in spring. The funnel- to
tubular-shaped flowers may be
purple, mauve, blue or, occasionally,
yellow, and plants grow to 15–30cm
(6–12in) high. Flowering and planting
times can be varied, but corms that
are planted in the spring will flower in
the following autumn. Among the
available cultivars are 'Purple Star'
and 'Tubergen's Blue'.

Clivia miniata (Kaffir lily)
This is an evergreen perennial from
South Africa, which needs a farily
warm minimum winter temperature of
10°C (50°F). It is not technically a bulb
but develops a swollen, bulb-like
base. Plants grow up to 45cm (18in)
tall and from late spring to summer
produce flaring, tubular flowers in
orange, light red or cream on a
sturdy stem that is surrounded by
strap-shaped, glossy, green leaves.
Plant them in spring. Clivias do not
like their roots to be disturbed and do
best when their root growth is slightly
restricted, making them excellent
container plants.

Freesia cvs.
Familiar from florists' bouquets, these
cormous plants can be grown in
containers for flowers in early spring.
Use prepared corms of florists'
freesias (some freesias can be grown
in the garden and are not suitable for
forcing). There are many named
cultivars, bearing flowers in a range of
delicate colours, but all exquisite
scented. The flowers are borne on
wiry, branching stems to 45cm (18in)
tall from late winter to late spring.
Plant the corms in late summer to
early winter for spring flowers. After
flowering, reduce watering gradually
and store the dry corms until autumn,
when they can be replanted.

Iris
More often seen as early-flowering
garden plants, *I. reticulata* and its
cultivars can be grown in containers
of well-drained compost. The typical
iris flowers are fragrant and to 6cm
(2½in) across. They should be planted
outside after flowering.

Lachenalia aloides (Cape cowslip)
Formerly known as *L. tricolor*, these
bulbous perennials have sturdy
stems, to 30cm (1ft) tall, hung with
rows of narrow, yellow bells with
green and red markings. The arching,

strap-shaped leaves have contrast
markings. These plants are native to
South Africa and will not survive in the
garden in cooler areas. Flowers
appear from winter to early spring
from bulbs planted in late summer.

Lilium
There are many lovely lily cultivars
that can be grown in containers, and
they are a beautiful addition to a
conservatory or cool greenhouse.
Colours range from pure white to
gleaming reds and yellows, and many
lilies are sweetly scented. After
flowering and during the dormant
period, lilies can be propagated by
removing scales, offset or bulblets.

Nerine
The genus contains the familiar and
hardy *N. bowdenii*, but *N. flexuosa*,
also from South Africa, is tender. In
late autumn the bulbs produce whorls
of flowers with backward curving,
pink petals on stems to 45cm (18in)
tall; 'Alba' has white flowers. The
flowers are followed by attractive
grass-like leaves. Plant bulbs in late
summer. *N. sarniensis* (Guernsey lily)
is similar to *N. flexuosa*, but the
flowers have narrower petals in
white, orange or red and are borne
on stems to 45cm (18in) tall.

8 PROPAGATION

Growing your own plants, whether from seed or by one of the vegetative methods, such as cuttings or layering, is an immensely satisfying pastime.

Left: Growing your own plants from seed, from bulbs or by dividing plants is not only satisfying, but is an excellent means of obtaining large displays of plants at relatively little expense.
Right: Although *Streptocarpus* (Cape primrose) can be grown from seed, they are unlikely to come true to type, so vegetative propagation is the best way of ensuring that new plants are like the parent plant.

Of the many plants that can be raised from seed it could be best to begin with flowering annuals. Most seeds are available only in fairly large quantities, but you cannot have too many summer-flowering *Impatiens* (busy Lizzie) and *Schizanthus* (butterfly plant), *Thunbergia* (black-eyed Susan) and *Calceolaria* (slipper flower) – and, if you find you have, there will be no problem in finding homes for the spares. Few houseplant annuals are generally available as bought plants, and it is certainly much cheaper to raise your own.

Short-lived pot plants, such as *Primula sinensis* (Chinese primrose) and *P. malacoides* (fairy primrose), give extra pleasure at reduced cost when you have raised them from seed. Move on to the rarer plants, such as some of the succulents and cacti, and once you have started to raise these you will be hooked.

Plants can be grown from cuttings, by dividing the roots or by growing on small plantlets and offsets produced by the parent plant. These are known as

vegetative means of propagation. When you grow plants from seed you cannot always be sure exactly what the results will be, because, except with F1 hybrids, nature is free to choose some of the details, such as exact flower colour or markings. Vegetative propagation methods allow you to reproduce the parent plant exactly, so that you get a miniature replica of it. Taking leaf cuttings, for example, is a form of vegetative propagation. It involves detaching leaves from a parent plant and encouraging roots to form on them. Some leaf cuttings are taken from whole leaves, while others are cut into squares, triangles or cross-sections. Early to midsummer is the best time to encourage roots to form on leaves, thereby ensuring that young plants are well established by autumn.

Succulent plants are popular and, once established, are ideal for brightening sunny windowsills throughout the year. They tolerate extremes of temperature better than any other type of plant. Many of these plants can

be raised from seeds and are sold in mixtures or individual species, but a much quicker way to produce replicas of a plant is to grow new ones from cuttings.

Division is an easy way to increase some congested houseplants, and if they are not split into exceptionally small pieces there is an opportunity to produce several attractive plants instantly. Always use young, healthy pieces from around the outside of a clump; discard old parts from its centre. Houseplants that can be increased in this way include *Saintpaulia* (African violet), *Spathiphyllum wallisii* (peace lily), *Maranta* (prayer plant), many ferns and some succulents. Cane cuttings are thick pieces of bare stem from plants with cane-like stems, such as yuccas and cordylines, cut into small lengths and either inserted vertically into or pressed on the surface of well-drained compost. They offer a good way to increase plants that are bare of leaves and so unattractive that otherwise they might have to be thrown away.

sowing seed

To grow plants from seed you must provide somewhere where seed trays can be kept in warmth at a fairly constant temperature, in good light, undisturbed and away from draughts, and when you pot up seedlings the pots will take up quite a lot of room. Otherwise, little equipment is needed and you certainly do not need a greenhouse – a sunny spare room or even a kitchen windowsill is ideal.

Use small trays (seed pans) for small quantities of seed and standard seed trays for larger quantities. Trays should be washed and scrubbed clean. Keep each container for seeds of one species only as the plants grow at different rates, and use plastic labels and waterproof ink to label the trays.

Check the compost every day, without disturbing the tray. Water it from below when necessary to keep it constantly moist but not wet. Keep the trays in a draught-free place and at an even temperature. If there is no specific recommendation on the packet, maintain them at 16–21°C (61–70°F).

Keep seeds that germinate best in the dark in a cupboard or place a folded newspaper over the glass or propagator lid until the seedlings appear. As soon as this happens give the seedlings good light (but not strong sunlight) and remove the glass cover or polythene bag or open the ventilators of the propagator to allow fresh air in. Remove the cover altogether as seedlings grow. When the seedlings are large enough to handle, they should be pricked out.

GROWING PLANTS FROM SEED

1 Place a layer of peat or peat substitute in the tray. Clay trays and pans should be soaked for 24 hours and lined with small, clean crocks. Top with seed compost, which is light and sterile and contains well-balanced nutrients at the correct strength. Firm in the compost, carefully packing it into the corners and all around the edges.

2 Add more compost to fill the tray completely. Smooth and level the surface by passing a straight piece of wood over it. Firm down the compost with the flat of your hand, a jam jar or a convenient piece of wood cut to the right size. When firmed the compost should come to about 2cm (¾in) below the edge of the tray.

3 Fold a piece of paper in half and pour the seeds into the V. Tap the edge of the paper gently to spread the seeds finely and evenly over the compost. Avoid sprinkling the seeds too close to the edges because the compost dries out quickly there. Label the tray with the name of the plant and the date.

5 Water the compost by standing the tray in a dish filled so that the water comes half way up the sides of the tray. Leave the tray in the container until water appears on the surface of the compost to make sure that the compost is evenly wet. Remove the tray and allow all excess water to drain away. If your seed tray is part of a propagator place the lid over the tray. Leave the cover on the tray until seedlings appear.

7 As soon as the seedlings are big enough to be handled, transfer them to another tray. Prepare a tray of compost and firm it as before. Have ready a wad of wet newspaper on which to stand the seedlings so that the roots do not dry out. Use a plant label or a fork to 'dig' up small clumps of seedlings. Separate them, taking care not to handle the roots, which are easily damaged, but hold them gently by their leaves.

4 Most seeds germinate better when covered with a thin layer of compost (check the seed packet for details). Sprinkle a fine layer of compost over the surface by passing it through a sieve. The layer should be three or four times the diameter of the seeds. Only the finest sprinkling is needed for small seeds.

6 If you do not use a propagator you can slide the seed tray into a polythene bag, and tie loosely with a tag. Alternatively, cover the top with a sheet of glass, making sure that it does not actually touch the compost. Cover seeds that germinate in the dark with newspaper. Remove the glass or polythene every day and wipe off the condensation before replacing it.

8 Use a pencil or small dibber make holes in the new compost, spaced 4–5cm (1½–2in) apart. Drop the seedlings into the holes one by one, handling them gently, and firm them in with their seed 'leaves' just above the compost surface. Water from below and allow to drain as before. Keep the tray in bright light (but not strong sun). True leaves will develop as the seedlings grow. Pot plants into individual pots when their leaves show signs of beginning to touch.

taking cuttings

Propagating plants from cuttings can be a good way to grow replacements for short-lived plants and much-loved plants which are outgrowing their space. It can also, of course, be an ideal way to increase the numbers of plants of which you would like more. By way of equipment you need nothing more than clean flowerpots, a sharp knife, cuttings compost, which is well aerated and well draining but also moisture retentive, a polythene bag and a few short sticks to support it.

Mists, hormone rooting powder and propagating units are optional extras, and you must provide a light place with an even temperature of 13–18°C (55–64°F), or more for tropical plants. Several cuttings can be grown in one pot.

TIP CUTTINGS

Select a healthy specimen with plenty of well-developed stems, taken from the outside of the plant. Soft new growth does not readily root. Water the plant well the day before taking cuttings. Keep the cuttings in good light (but not direct sun) and steady warmth until new growth indicates that roots have formed. Then remove polythene and pot the plants on in potting compost. Pinch them out at the growing points as they grow to encourage bushy growth.

1 Use a sharp knife, scalpel or craft knife to cut a 8–13cm (3–5in) length of stem, with a growing tip at the end. Make the cut just above a leaf joint (node) and cut it at an angle sloping away from the joint.

2 Trim the stem, cutting it off just below the bottom of the leaf joint (the point from which new roots develop). Cleanly slice off the lower leaf or pairs of leaves. If preparing several cuttings keep in water until all are ready.

Rooting cuttings in water

African violet leaf petiole cuttings can be rooted in water. Cover the top of a bottle with kitchen paper, held in place with a rubber band. Pierce a hole it and insert the cutting. Keep it warm, light and draught-free, ensuring the end remains in water, until roots develop. Tear away the paper, remove the cutting and pot it up in a small pot.

3 Make a hole in a pot of compost. Dip the cutting in rooting powder. Insert it in the compost, making sure the leaves are not touching it.

4 Water the compost from above. To conserve moisture make a 'tent' around the cutting with a polythene bag (with holes for air) supported on split canes.

TAKING STEM CUTTINGS

Plants such as *Hedera* spp. (ivy), and others which have long, trailing, woody stems with leaves growing at intervals along their whole length can be propagated from stem cuttings taken from a length of stem, without the need for growing tips on the individual cuttings.

One long piece of stem is divided into several cuttings that can be planted up into pots of cuttings compost, watered in and covered in a polythene 'tent' until new growth appears, indicating that the young cuttings have taken root and can safely be potted on.

1 Cut off a good length of young, supple stem, using a sharp knife. Cutting just above the leaf joints, divide the stems into small pieces, each with a leaf.

3 Water the pot, then cover with a 'tent' of polythene as for tip cuttings, making sure that the leaves do not touch the polythene.

2 Insert the cuttings into a pot of cuttings compost, several to a pot, using a pencil or dibber to make the holes. Avoid placing the cuttings too close to the edges of the pot where compost quickly becomes dry.

4 When small new leaves appear the cuttings have rooted and should be transferred to separate small pots of potting compost.

LEAF PETIOLE CUTTINGS

A leaf petiole cutting uses a leaf and its stalk (the petiole). Soft-stemmed plants root particularly well in this way, and the method is often used for *Saintpaulia* (African violet).

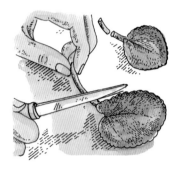

1 Choose a plant with plenty of leaves, and make sure that the leaves you select have firm, fleshy petioles. Cut off leaf stalks at the base, using a sharp knife. Trim down the stems so that they are 3–4cm (1¼–1½in) long.

2 Dip the petiole tips in hormone rooting powder and insert the cuttings in a pot of cuttings compost, using a dibber or pencil to make the holes. Firm in the cuttings and stand the pot in water, to make sure the leaves do not get wet. Put the pot in a polythene 'tent' and keep it warm until new growth appears.

leaf cuttings

Before severing a leaf, water the parent plant thoroughly several times, preferably during the previous day so that the leaf is full of water and will not deteriorate before roots have formed. Check that the leaf is healthy, pest- and disease-free and a good copy of the parent plant. Each leaf used as a cutting should be relatively young and without surfaces that have become hard and old. These do not root rapidly.

After the cuttings have been inserted in compost, position them out of strong and direct sunlight; small leaf-squares and triangles soon shrivel when in strong sunlight. It is better to place them on a cool, well-shaded windowsill than on a sunny one. Keep the compost moist during rooting. As soon as roots and shoots develop, remove the plastic covering and lower the temperature.

WHOLE-LEAF CUTTINGS

Plants such as the *Begonia rex, B. masoniana* (iron-cross begonia) and cultivars of *Streptocarpus* (Cape primrose) can be increased from whole-leaf cuttings, a means of propagating a number of plantlets from one leaf.

1 Sever the stalk of a healthy leaf close to its base, taking care not to leave a short snag on the plant that later would die back. Place the severed leaf upside down on a wooden board and cut off the stalk, close to the leaf.

2 Use a sharp knife to make cuts, 20–25mm (¾–1in) apart, across the main and secondary veins, taking care not to cut completely through the leaf.

3 Place the leaf vein-side down on equal parts moist peat and sharp sand. Use small stones or pieces of U-shaped wire, inserted astride the veins, to hold the leaf in contact with the compost.

4 Lightly water the compost, allow excess moisture to evaporate, then cover with a transparent lid. Put in gentle warmth and light shade. When the young plants are large enough, transfer them to pots.

LEAF SECTIONS

In addition to positioning whole leaf cuttings on the surface of compost, cultivars of *Streptocarpus* (Cape primrose) can be increased by severing leaves into sections. Sever a healthy leaf and place it on a flat board. Use a sharp knife to cut it laterally into pieces about 5cm (2in) wide. Use the blade of a knife to make 2cm (¾in) deep slits in the compost, into which cuttings can be inserted and firmed.

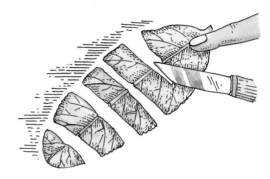

LEAF TRIANGLES

These are easier to insert in compost than leaf squares, and they tend to be slightly larger, which gives them a greater reserve of food while they are developing their roots. Water a mother plant and the following day remove a healthy leaf. Sever it close to the plant's base and then again next to the leaf. Place the leaf on a flat board and use a sharp knife to cut triangles, each with its point towards the position where the stalk joined it. Fill and firm a seed tray with equal parts moist peat and sharp sand. Use a knife to make slits into which cuttings can be inserted to half their depth with the point facing down. Firm the compost around them and place in light shade and gentle warmth.

LEAF SQUARES

Many more cuttings of this type can be taken from an individual leaf than the triangular type (see below). After severing a leaf from a healthy plant, cut off the stalk and place the leaf on a board. Cut it into strips about 3cm (1¼in) wide, each with a main or secondary vein running down the middle. Then cut each of the strips into squares. Each square is inserted separately and by about one-third of its depth into equal parts of moist peat and sharp sand. It is vital that cuttings are inserted with the side that was nearest to the leafstalk facing downwards or they will not root.

Make a slit in the compost with a knife and insert a cutting. Firm the compost around it, lightly water the surface and place it in gentle warmth and light shade. Cover with a plastic, translucent lid. When the cuttings have developed plantlets, transfer them into small, individual pots. Water the compost gently and place the plantlets in light shade until they are properly established.

Horizontal leaf squares

Small leaf squares can be pressed flat on the surface of compost formed of equal parts moist peat and sharp sand. These leaf cuttings are about 3cm (1¼in) square and they need to be carefully secured horizontally on the compost's surface. Because they are small, hooked pieces of wire are easier to use than pebbles.

cane cuttings

This type of cutting involves cutting bare stems into pieces 8–13cm (3–5in) long and either inserting them vertically into pots of sandy compost or pressing them horizontally on the surface. Plants like yucca and dieffenbachia can be are increased in this way. Specially prepared cuttings of yucca are sometimes available; these can be inserted vertically into cuttings compost and kept at a gentle, even temperature until roots form and shoots appear.

Old plants of dieffenbachia often have several long, bare stems that have small tufts of leaves at their top. Instead of discarding these plants, cut their stems into pieces about 8cm (3in) long. When you handle dieffenbachia either wear gloves or make sure that you do not touch your mouth and eyes if your hands have come into contact with the sap.

TAKING CANE CUTTINGS

1 Use a sharp knife to cut a thick, healthy stem from the congested base of a dieffenbachia. Cut low down to ensure that an unsightly stub does not remain, and take care not to damage the plant.

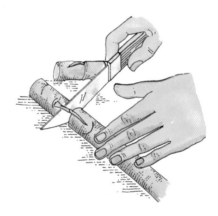

2 Cut the stem into several pieces, each about 8cm (3in) long. Make sure that each length has at least one strong, healthy bud to create good upward growth and develop into healthy new shoots.

3 Fill a wide pot with equal parts moist peat and sharp sand and firm it to 1cm (½in) below the rim. Press each cutting to half its thickness into the compost and secure with pieces of bent wire.

4 Water the compost, allow to drain and place a plastic dome over the pot. Alternatively, insert small pieces of split cane around the pot's edge and draw a plastic bag over. Secure it with an elastic band.

division

One of the easiest ways of increasing some overcrowded houseplants is by division.

Saintpaulia (African violet), for example, are easily increased by removing congested plants from their pots and teasing them apart. Tap the edge of a congested pot on a hard corner to remove the rootball. Gently pull the plants apart and repot the young pieces into small, individual pots. Water the compost gently from below.

Plants that have variegated leaves, such as *Sansevieria trifasciata* 'Laurentii', have to be propagated by division if the variegation is to be maintained as they will not breed true.

DIVIDING SANSEVIERIAS

1 A plant such as sansevieria will eventually fills its pot with fibrous roots, with many stems and leaves arising directly from the roots. When the rootball completely fills the pot, the quality of the plant's leaves deteriorates. At this point, it becomes necessary to divide the plant. Water the compost the day before dividing it to make sure that the roots, stems and leaves are full of moisture. Dehydrated plants are less likely to survive division than those that have been well watered.

2 Invert the plant and knock the pot's rim on a corner of a hard surface. As you ease out the plant, support the rootball, so that it gently slides from the pot but does not break up or fall on the floor. Using your fingers, gently tease and pull apart the rootball, dividing it into several substantially sized pieces. It may be necessary to cut through some roots, but you should never just slice through the rootball. Discard old pieces from the plant's centre and use only young, outer parts.

3 Select a clean pot, slightly smaller than before but large enough to accommodate the roots. Place compost in its base and position a divided piece in the centre. Hold the plant so that the soil-mark which indicates its earlier depth in a pot is about 1cm (½in) below the pot's rim. Then, gently trickle compost around the roots, spreading it evenly and in layers. Fill and firm compost to within 1cm (½in) of the rim, then lightly but thoroughly water it. Allow excess moisture to drain.

runners & plantlets

Many houseplants produce plantlets or offsets from which new plants can be grown. Some send out runners or stolons (creeping stems), which travel along the ground, developing tiny new plants that root in the soil. Others develop roots along their arching stems, wherever these touch the ground. These can be pegged down into the ground along their length to encourage rooting. In houseplants stolons and their little plantlets can be an attractive feature of the plant and are usually left to hang. Other plants produce their plantlets around, and attached to, the parent, and these miniature plants, usually known as offsets,

can be detached and grown on. Some plantlets begin to produce their own roots while hanging on the plant, while others develop them when they come in contact with a suitable growing medium.

TRAILING OFFSETS

Chlorophytum comosum (spider plant) and *Saxifraga stolonifera* (mother of thousands) are among the easiest plants to grow from offsets. Both produce small versions of themselves at the end of long, arching stems. Stand the plant on a tray and surround it with small pots of cutting or potting compost. Water them all. Arch the stolons over so that the plantlets are resting on the

surface of the compost, one per pot. Use a hairpin or a piece of bent wire to anchor each stolon in place. Keep the compost moist, and sever the stolons when new growth appears.

DETACHABLE OFFSETS

Some plants have offsets that grow on the plant itself, either on the leaf surface or (more usually) around the rosettes of leaves that form the plant. These offsets can be severed from the parent plant and grown on. Typical are *Kalanchoe delagoensis* (syn. *K. tubiflora*; chandelier plant), with offsets that grow at the leaf tips, and *K. daigremontiana* (syn. *Bryophyllum daigremontianum*; Mexican hat plant, devil's backbone), in which they grow around the leaf edges.

OTHER OFFSETS

Many succulents and bromeliads have offsets that grow on, or around the base of, the plant. Sometimes these are easily identifiable as new plants, as in many of the cacti, while in other cases they are attached to the parent, as in many bromeliads. The best time to remove the offsets is during repotting. Cut them off with a sharp clean knife; for those growing up around the base, try to make sure that you get a bit of root. Allow cactus offsets to dry for a few days before planting them in cactus compost, but pot up other plants in potting compost straight away. Half-fill the pot first and hold the plant with the roots in the pot as you trickle in more compost. Firm in and water from below.

ROOTING DETACHABLE OFFSETS

1 Water the parent plant the day before taking offsets. Fill an 8cm (3in) pot with potting compost and water it. Remove only a few plantlets from each leaf with your fingers or tweezers (to avoid altering the appearance of the plant), handling them carefully.

2 Arrange the plantlets on the surface of the compost, so that each has its own growing space. Keep the compost moist by watering from below. When the plants grow, roots will have formed and they should be potted in individual pots.

layering

Propagating from runners and arching stems is called layering, and *Hedera* spp. (ivy) and other climbers can be reproduced in this way. The method produces a replica of the parent plant, so a healthy parent is essential. Water the plant well the day before.

Place a pot filled with cuttings compost next to the parent plant. Fold over a stem (without cutting it off) near a node, about 15cm (6in) from the tip, to form a V in the stem and anchor the V of the stem into the compost with bent wire. Firm compost over the V

and water the compost from above. Keep the compost moist as new roots develop. When fresh growth appears at the tip of the stem, this indicates that roots have formed; sever the new plant from its parent with a sharp knife or scissors.

AIR LAYERING

This is an ideal way to give a tall, leggy plant that has lost its lower leaves a new lease of life, and it is often used on *Ficus elastica* (rubber plant), and sometimes on dieffenbachias, dracaenas and

monsteras. Air layering involves encouraging roots to develop just below the lowest leaf; when these are established the stem is severed and the plant is re-potted. This is not a rapid method of propagation.

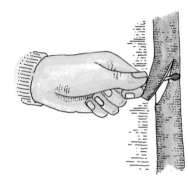

1 Water the plant the day before. Use a sharp knife to make an upward-slanting cut, two-thirds through the stem and 8–10cm (3–4in) below the lowest leaf. Take care that the top of the plant does not bend and snap. Use a matchstick to keep the surfaces of the cut apart. If they are allowed to close, the wound heals and does not readily develop roots. Trim off the ends of the matchstick and use a small brush to coat the plant's cut surfaces with hormone rooting powder and push powder into the cut.

2 Wind a piece of polythene around the stem with the cut area in the centre. Use strong string to tie it about 5cm (2in) below the cut, winding the string around several times to hold it.

3 Carefully fill the polythene with moist peat. Fill the tube to within 8cm (3in) of the top, then tie it off. Place the plant in gentle warmth and light shade. Check that the peat is moist fortnightly.

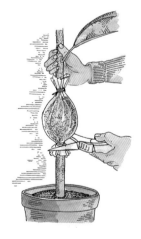

4 Within two months roots show through the polythene. While they are still white, cut the stem below the the tube. Remove the polythene and string and retain as much peat as possible. Pot up.

Left: Place cactus cuttings in gentle warmth and light shade. Rooting should occur in a few weeks in spring and early summer.

propagating cacti & other succulents

There are various ways of taking cuttings of succulent plants. One method is to cut a leaf into sections; sometimes whole leaves are rooted; and cacti are grown from short stubs. Take

care when detaching leaves that the mother plant's shape is not ruined; a few leaves removed from the back of a plant usually does no harm and passes unnoticed.

LEAF DIVISION

Some large plants, such as *Sansevieria trifasciata*, can be increased by cutting stems or leaves into pieces.

1 Water the plant well a few days before severing the leaves because flaccid leaves do not readily root. Use a sharp knife to sever one or two leaves at their base. Do not take all of them from one side, as this will mar the plant's shape.

2 Place the leaf on a flat surface and use a sharp knife to cut it into pieces about 5cm (2in) deep. Cut cleanly because torn surfaces do not root readily.

3 Fill and firm a shallow but wide pot with equal parts moist peat and sharp sand. Form a slit with a knife, then push a cutting about 2cm (¾in) into it. Make sure that the cutting is the right way up. Lightly water the compost and place in gentle warmth.

SMALL AND CIRCULAR LEAVES

Several succulents have small, circular and flat leaves. These include *Sedum sieboldii* and *S. s.* 'Mediovariegatum'. These are easily increased in spring and early summer by pressing leaves into the surface of well-drained compost formed of equal parts moist peat and sharp sand. Cut off entire stems, rather than removing a few leaves from several shoots.

Snap off the leaves, taking care not to squash them. Leave them to dry for a couple of days. Press individual leaves on the compost's surface, then lightly water them. Place the pot in gentle warmth and light shade.

WHOLE-LEAF CUTTINGS

The leaves of some succulents, such as *Crassula ovata* (jade plant), can be removed and inserted vertically into well-drained compost in spring and early summer. High temperatures are not necessary. Select a healthy, well-watered plant and gently bend the leaves down so they snap off close to the main stem. Leave them to dry for a couple of days. Fill a clean pot with equal parts moist peat and sharp sand and firm it to about 1cm (½in) below the rim. Form a hole 20mm (¾in) deep and insert a cutting in it. Firm compost around it. Water and put the pot in light shade and gentle warmth.

CACTUS CUTTINGS

Most cacti are known for their spines, but this should not stop cuttings being taken. If necessary, wear a pair of thin rubber kitchen gloves. Cacti that create a mass of small stems from around their base are easily increased from cuttings. Mammillarias and *Echinopsis* spp. can be increased in this way.

1 Use a sharp knife to remove well-formed young stems from around the outside of the clump. Sever the stems directly at their base so that unsightly short stubs of growth are not left on the mother plant. Do not take them all from the same position to avoid spoiling the plant's appearance.

2 Leave the cuttings for a couple of days so that their ends can dry before inserting in cactus compost. This allows them to root much more quickly than if inserted immediately after being severed.

3 Fill a small pot with equal parts moist peat and sharp sand and firm it to 1cm (½in) below the rim. Sprinkle a thin layer of sharp sand on the surface and use a small dibber to make a hole about 2.5cm (1in) deep, into which a cutting can be inserted. Firm compost around its base. Lightly water the compost. Place cuttings in gentle warmth and light shade. Rooting takes a few weeks in spring and early summer.

9 TROUBLESHOOTING

Unlike plants grown outdoors, houseplants are in artificial surroundings: their roots are confined in a small amount of compost that can be easily excessively watered or underwatered; they are frequently exposed to high temperatures even though the intensity of light is poor; and the temperature may fluctuate rapidly throughout the day and, in winter, be cold at night when heating systems are turned down or off. It is remarkable, therefore, that so many houseplants succeed and this is invariably due to the enthusiasm and vigilance of houseplant growers.

Opposite: Many problems with plants can be avoided by putting them in the right situation. For example, *Cissus rhombifolia* (grape ivy) will tolerate light shade that would be too dark for *Philodendron scandens* (sweetheart plant).
Left: Hoyas, such as *H. carnosa* 'Tricolor' might be suitable for a bathroom in summer as they like humidity during the growing season. In the winter, however, they may need a drier atmosphere with a more even temperature.

Pests and diseases soon devastate houseplants if they remain undetected or neglected. Leaves, stems, shoots and flowers can all be affected, as well as roots. Prevention is easier than trying to eliminate an established colony of pests or a severe infection of a disease. Buying only clean and healthy plants reduces the risk of most pests or diseases infecting your plants. If you are doubtful about the health of a plant, isolate it for a couple of weeks before introducing it into a room where there are other plants. When watering plants, cleaning leaves or removing dead flowers, thoroughly inspect the plants to ensure they are clean and healthy. If a problem is noticed, treat it immediately, before other plants become affected. Use only clean potting composts and never take cuttings from infected plants.

Some of the cultural problems affecting houseplants are outlined below, and the pests and diseases most often seen are described on pages 122–3. Most houseplants underachieve and this is because they are not regularly fed. Those that are given a balanced diet have a better chance of surviving an infestation of pests or diseases than if undernourished and struggling for life. On the other hand, do not feed plants excessively, because this may make the compost toxic, which will retard growth or even kill them. Nor should you feed summer-flowering or foliage plants after late summer, because this will encourage the lush growth that is susceptible to pests and diseases, just when the plants are preparing to take a winter rest.

Left: Plants that might be more suited to a conservatory or cool greenhouse are best kept near a window in the home, where they can be used to provide welcome shade.

APPLYING CHEMICALS

There are several ways in which to apply chemicals to plants: spraying with a concentrated insecticide diluted in clean water is the most popular method. Some liquid sprays are ready to use. Dusting plants is also effective, but may leave an unattractive residue. Watering compost with a systemic insecticide and using insecticidal sticks are other methods.

Inserting an insecticidal stick into compost is a quick, clean and effective way to control pests. Each stick contains a systemic insecticide that makes a plant toxic to insects.

Dusting plants with a powder is not a popular way to apply insecticides to houseplants, but it is quick and effective. When you use powder distribute it evenly and take the plant outdoors to avoid inhaling it and to protect furniture and soft furnishings.

When you apply a liquid spray put the plant inside a clean dustbin or large plastic bag. Then, apply the spray and leave the container closed for an hour.

Remove the plant and allow the fumes to disperse before replacing it indoors.

CULTURAL PROBLEMS

In addition to being damaged by pests and diseases, plants can become unhealthy through incorrect conditions, such as too little or too much water, excessive shade or strong sunlight, inappropriate temperatures, excessive humidity or insufficient food. Some common cultural problems are detailed opposite.

CULTURAL PROBLEMS

Variegated leaves become green if the plant is not in good light; reposition the plant near a window.

Leaves sometimes develop holes in their centre or along the outer edge. This is because they either have been knocked by people or pets, or are infested with pests such as caterpillars.

Flowers become dry and rapidly fade if compost becomes dry, the temperature is too high, the air too dry or if the plant is in dense shade.

Flower buds fall off if the compost or air is dry, the plant is in poor light or, in the case of some cacti, if the plant is moved and knocked.

Leaves curl at their edges, then fall off, if the plant is in a cold draught, the temperature is low or the compost has been excessively watered.

Leaves wilt if compost is either very wet or dry. Excessively dry air and too much heat also causes wilting. On hot days plants may temporarily wilt in the early afternoon but recover by evening.

Leaves wilt and decay if the compost is too wet. This especially applies to foliage plants in winter.

Lower leaves become dry and crisp and eventually fall off if the compost is too dry, temperatures are too high or there is too little light.

Blemishes occur on leaves for a number of reasons: burned areas appear after leaves with water droplets on their surfaces are left in strong sunlight; diseases such as leaf spot also produce holes.

A white, powdery coating on a clay pot usually indicates that the plant has been excessively fed. It also means that the water may contain a great deal of chalk.

Green slime appears on clay pots if the compost has been excessively watered. The slime may also appear on the surface of compost.

pests & diseases

Aphids

These soft-bodied insects, usually green, suck sap from leaves and petals, causing mottling and distortion. They excrete honeydew, which attracts sooty mould. Spray plants regularly, especially in summer.

Caterpillars

Although they are seldom seen indoors, caterpillars do occasionally crop up in sun rooms and conservatories. They chew holes in leaves. Pick off and destroy them and spray with an insecticide. Repeat the spray as necessary.

Cyclamen mites

These minute, spider-like pests infest plants such as cyclamen, saintpaulias and pelargoniums. They cause stunting; leaves curl and become wrinkled, and flowers become distorted and fall off. Burn infested plants.

Earwigs

Outdoor as well as indoor plants can be affected. They are rarely seen in daytime but at night they chew leaves and flowers, causing ragged holes and edges. Check for them at night – they hide under leaves and flowers – pick off and destroy them.

Eelworms

There are several different types of these microscopic worms, including some that infest chrysanthemums or bulbs and some that cause irregular, corky swellings on roots (root-knot eelworm). If these worms are seen on the plant, it must be burned.

Mealy bugs

These insects resemble small woodlice but are covered in white, woolly wax. They cluster on the stems and under leaves of subtropical and tropical plants, sucking sap and causing leaves to yellow. Wipe off with cotton buds dipped in methylated spirits or alcohol.

Red spider mites

The minute, spider-like pests that infest the undersides of leaves and suck sap, causing speckling and yellow blotches. Daily misting of leaves helps to prevent an attack. Use a systemic insecticide. Burn seriously infected plants.

Root mealy bugs

Like mealy bugs, these resemble small woodlice, but live on the outer roots of plants in pots. They eat roots, especially of cacti and other succulents. Inspect roots, especially when plants are repotted. Drench the compost in an insecticide.

Scale insects

The first sign of an infestation is usually when plants become sticky. Swollen, protective, waxy-brown discs appear and female scale insects produce their young under them. Wipe off with cotton buds dipped in methylated spirits or alcohol. Burn seriously infected plants.

Thrips

These tiny, dark brown, fly-like pests have light coloured legs and wings. They jump from plant to plant, sucking leaves and flowers, causing silvery streaks and mottling. Flowers become distorted. Plants with dry compost suffer most. Spray several times with insecticide.

Whitefly

These are small, white and moth-like and when disturbed flutter around their host plant. Their young are green, suck sap and excrete honeydew, encouraging the presence of sooty mould. Eradication is not easy; spray repeatedly with insecticide.

Black leg

This is a disease mainly of cuttings and especially pelargoniums. The bases of stems become soft and turn black. Wet, cold, compacted and airless compost encourages it. Destroy seriously infected cuttings.

Botrytis

Also known as grey mould, this forms a grey, furry mould on soft parts of plants, especially flowers, young leaves and shoots. It is encouraged by still, damp air. Cut off infected parts, remove dead flowers and spray with a fungicide. Create better air circulation around plants.

Leaf spot

Especially prone to this disease are dieffenbachias, dracaenas and citrus plants. It causes black spots that enlarge and merge. Remove and burn infected leaves and spray infected plants with a fungicide.

Powdery mildew

This produces a white, powdery coating over leaves – often on both sides. It also infects flowers and stems. Remove badly infected parts, increase ventilation and keep the surrounding air drier.

Root rot

Sometimes known as tuber rot, this occurs on palms, cacti and other succulents, begonias and African violets. Plants wilt and leaves become yellow. It is caused by continuously waterlogged compost.

Rust

This is uncommon on indoor plants, except for pelargoniums. Carnations and chrysanthemums in sun rooms and conservatories are sometimes infected. Raised rings of black or brown spores appear on leaves. Remove and burn infected leaves, increase ventilation and spray with a fungicide.

Sooty mould

The black, powdery, soot-like mould lives on honeydew excreted by aphids and other sap-sucking pests. It coats leaves, stems and flowers. Spray against aphids and use a damp cloth to wipe away light infestations.

Viruses

Microscopic particles invade plants, causing disorder but seldom killing their host. Deformed growth, mottling and streaking in leaves and colour changes in flowers are the most usual results. No treatment is possible, except to control sap-sucking insects that spread viruses.

Safety First with Chemicals

All chemicals used to control pests and diseases must be handled with care.

- *Keep all chemicals out of the reach of children, and never transfer them to bottles that youngsters might believe to hold a refreshing drink.*
- *Always follow the manufacturer's instructions. Using a chemical at a higher concentration does not improve its effectiveness and may even damage plants.*
- *Some plants are allergic to certain chemicals, so check with the label, especially when spraying palms, ferns, cacti and other succulents.*
- *Never mix chemicals, unless recommended.*
- *Whenever possible, take houseplants outdoors to spray them and never use sprays in rooms where birds, fish and other pets are present.*
- *Never use chemical sprays near to food and fruit, and avoid spraying wallpaper and fabrics.*
- *Do not assume that insecticides derived from natural plant extracts are not dangerous.*

GLOSSARY

Acaricide A chemical used to kill parasitic spider mites, such as red spider mites.

Acid Compost or soil with a pH below 7.0. Most plants grow best in slightly acid conditions, about pH 6.5.

Adventitious roots Roots that develop from unusual positions, such as on leaves and stems.

Aerial roots These are roots that appear from a stem and above soil level, as with the Swiss cheese plants (*Monstera deliciosa*), some ivies and orchids. Their prime task is to gain support for stems.

Air layering A method of propagating plants by encouraging roots to form on stems. The rubber plant (*Ficus elastica*) is often increased in this way.

Alkaline Compost or soil with a pH above 7.0.

Alternate Buds or leaves that grow on opposite sides of a stem or shoot.

Annual A plant that completes its life-cycle within a year; seeds germinate, the plant grows, and flowers and seeds are produced within one growing season.

Anther Part of a stamen, the male reproductive part of a flower. A stamen is formed of a stalk (filament), with an anther at its top. Pollen grains form within anthers.

Aphids Perhaps the main pest of house and garden plants and also known as greenfly. They breed rapidly in spring and summer, clustering around the soft parts of the flowers, shoots, stems and leaves. They suck sap, causing debilitation as well as spreading viruses.

Apical The tip of a shoot or branch.

Areole A modified sideshoot, resembling a tiny hump, unique to cacti. It bears spines, hairs, bristles or wool.

Asexual A non-sexual way to increase plants, such as by cuttings, layering and division rather than seed.

Axil The junction between a leaf and stem, from where sideshoots or flowers may develop.

Bigeneric hybrid A plant produced by crossing two plants from different genera. This is indicated by a cross positioned in front of the plant's name. For instance, the ivy tree (x *Fatshedera lizei*) is a cross between a form of the false castor oil plant (*Fatsia japonica* 'Moderi' – also known as the Japanese fatsia), and the Irish ivy (*Hedera helix* 'Hibernica').

Bloom This has two meanings, either flowers or a powdery coating on flowers, stems or leaves.

Bottle gardening Growing plants in environments created by carboys and other large glass jars. Sometimes the container is stoppered and the air inside recycled by plants, while in other cases, the container is left open.

Bract A modified leaf; some provide protection for a flower while others assume the role of petals and are the main attraction. Poinsettia (*Euphorbia pulcherrima*) has brightly coloured bracts.

Bromeliad A member of the Bromeliaceae family. Many have rosettes of leaves that form urns. A few of them are epiphytes.

Bulb A storage organ with a bud-like structure. It is formed of fleshy scales attached at their base to a flattened stem called the basal plate.

Bulbil An immature and miniature bulb that usually grows at the base of another bulb. However, some plants, such as the mother fern (*Asplenium bulbiferum*), develop plantlets on their leaves which are also known as bulbils. These can be detached carefully using tweezers and encouraged to form roots.

Cactus A succulent plant belonging to the Cactaceae family. All cacti are characterized by having areoles.

Capillary action The passage of water upwards through potting compost ro soil. The finer the soil particles, the higher the rise of moisture. The same principle is used in self-watering systems for plants in pots in sun rooms, conservatories and greenhouses.

Chlorophyll Green pigment in plants that captures the energy in sunlight and allow the process of photosynthesis.

Clone A plant raised vegetatively from another plant, so ensuring that it is identical in every particular to the parent.

Columnar Describes a plant that rises vertically; usually used to refer to trees and conifers but also to describe some cacti.

Compost In the context of houseplants refers to the medium in which plants grow when in pots or other containers, and in North America is known as potting compost. It is formed of a mixture of loam, sharp sand and peat, plus fertilizers, or peat and fertilizers.

Corolla The ring of petals in a flower that create the main display.

Corona Petals in certain plants that form a cup or trumpet, as in daffodils.

Cristate Crested, used to describe some ferns and cacti, as well as a few forms of houseplants.

Crock A piece of broken clay pot put in the base of a clay pot to prevent compost blocking the drainage hole.

Cultivar A variety raised in cultivation by selective breeding.

Cutting A vegetative method of propagating plants by which a severed piece of a plant is encouraged to develop roots.

Damping down Increasing the humidity in a sun room, conservatory or greenhouse by using a fine-rosed watering-can to spray water on the floor and around plants. It is best carried out early in the day so that excess moisture dries by nightfall.

Dead-heading The removal of faded and dead flowers to encourage the development of further flowers. It also helps to prevent deseases infecting decaying flowers.

Dibber A rounded, blunt-pointed tool for making planting holes in compost.

Division A vegetative method of propagation, involving dividing the stems and roots of plants.

Dormancy The resting period of a plant or seed.

Double flowers Flowers with more than the normal number of petals.

Drawn Describes thin and spindly shoots or plants, after having been grown in crowded or dark conditions.

Epiphyte A plant that grows above ground level, attached to trees, rocks and, sometimes, other plants. Epiphytes do not take nourishment from their hosts, but just use them for support. Many orchids and bromeliads are epiphytes.

Ericaceous compost Acidic potting medium, suitable for such plants as azaleas.

Etiolated Blanched and spindly, the result of being grown in poor light.

F1 The first filial generation and the result of a cross between two pure-bred and unrelated parents. F1 hybrids are large, strong and uniform, but their seeds will not produce replicas of the parents.

Fern A perennial, flowerless plant that produces spores.

Fertilization The sexual union of male (pollen) and female (ovule) parts.

Filament the slender stalk that supports the anthers of a flower.

Collectively, the anthers and filaments form the stamen.

Fimbriate Fringed and usually referring to a flower or petal.

Flore-pleno Refers to flowers with a larger than normal number of petals.

Floret A small flower that, with others, forms a flower head, such as in chrysanthemums and other members of the Compositae family.

Frond Leaf of a palm or fern.

Fungicide A chemical used to eradicate or deter fungal diseases.

Germination The process that occurs within a seed when given moisture, air and warmth. The seed's coat ruptures and a seed leaf (or seed leaves) grows towards the light, while a root grows downwards.

Glaucous Greyish-green or bluish-green and usually applied to describe stems, leaves or fruits.

Glochid Describes a small, hooked hair growing on some cacti.

Inflorescence Part of a plant that bears flowers.

Insectivorous Describes plants that are adapted to trap, kill and digest insects such as small flies. In this way they are able to supplement food that their environment is not able to provide.

Joint The junction of a shoot and stem, or a leaf and a leaf-stalk. These are also known as nodes.

Juvenile leaf Several houseplants have, when young, differently shaped leaves from those on mature plants.

Layering A vegetative way to increase plants, involving lowering stems and slightly burying them in soil or compost. By creating a kind, twist, bend or slit in the part of the stem that is buried, the flow of sap is restricted and roots are encouraged to develop.

Leaflet Some leaves are formed of several small leaves, each known as a leaflet. A leaflet is characterized by not having a bud in its axil.

Leggy Describes plants that have become tall and spindly, often through being kept in dark places.

Neutral Compost that is neither acid nor alkaline and with a pH of 7.0. Horticultural neutral is considered to be between 6.5 and 7.0.

Node A leaf-joint or position where a shoot grows from a stem or branch.

Ovary The female part of a flower where fertilization takes place and seeds grow.

Peat Partly decomposed vegetable material, usually with an acid nature.

Because of its capacity to retain water it is used in seed and potting composts. Substitutes are now preferred because of the rapid destruction of peat bogs.

Perennial Usually used when referring to herbaceous perennials, but also applied to plants that live for several years, such as trees and shrubs.

Petiole A leaf-stalk.

Photosynthesis The food-building process when chlorophyll in leaves is activated by sunlight and, together with moisture absorbed by roots and carbon dioxide absorbed through stomata from the atmosphere, creates growth.

pH A logarithmic scale used to define the acidity or alkalinity of a soil/water solution. The scale ranges from 0 to 14: neutral is 7.0, with figures above indicating increasing alkalinity and, below, increasing acidity.

Pinching out Removing the tip of a shoot to encourage the development of sideshoots.

Plantlet An offset produced on a plant's leaves or stem.

Pot-bound Describes a plant that completely fills its pot with roots and needs repotting.

Potting on Transferring an established plant from one pot to another.

Potting up Transferring a young plant from a seed tray into a pot.

Pricking oou Transferring seedlings from the seed tray in which they were sown into other seed trays and giving them wider spacing.

Propagation The raising of new plants.

Pseudobulb The thickened stem of some orchids.

Rhizome A thick underground stem that enables a plant to spread through the soil. It may also be used for food storage.

Root-ball The packed ball of roots and compost in which a houseplant grows.

Root hair The fine, feeding roots that develop on roots to absorb nutrients.

Seed leaf The first leaf (sometimes two) that appears after germination.

Seedling A young plant produced after a seed germinates.

Self-coloured Flowers with just one colour, in contrast to bicoloured (two colours) and multicoloured (several shades).

Sessile Leaves and flowers that do not have a stalk or stem attaching them to the plant.

Softwood cutting A cutting formed of a non-woody shoot.

Spadix A dense spike of tiny flowers, usually enclosed in a spathe.

Spathe A large bract or pair of bracts, often brightly coloured, surrounding a spadix.

Spores The reproductive cells of non-flowering plants.

Stamen The male part of a flower.

Stigma The female part of a flower.

Stipule Leaf-like sheaths at the base of some flower stalks.

Stolon Horizontally growing stem that roots at the nodes, as in *Saxifraga stolonifera*.

Stomata Minute holes – usually in the underside of a leaf – that enable an exchange of gases between the plant and the surrounding air.

Stop The removal of a growing tip to encourage the development of sideshoots.

Style Part of the female reproductive element of a flower, linking the stigma to the ovary.

Succulent Any plant with thick and fleshy leaves. Cacti are succulent plants, but not all succulents are cacti.

Systemic pesticide Describes chemicals that enter a plant's tissue, killing sucking and biting insects.

Tendril A thread-like growth that enables some climbers to cling to their supports.

Terrarium A glass container, partly or wholly enclosed, used to house plants.

Terrestrial Describes plants that grow in soil at ground level.

Top dressing Replacing the surface soil of plants in large containers with fresh potting compost, rather than transferring them into an even larger container.

Turgid Describes a leaf or plant that is firm and full of moisture.

Variegated Describes leaves of more than one colour.

Variety A natural occurring variation within a species. The term is also commonly used to include both true varieties and variations created by people, which are correctly termed cultivars.

Vegetative propagation Methods of increasing plants, including the division of roots, layering, air-layering and taking cuttings.

Xerophytic Describes plants adapted for living in dry climates, such as desert cacti; they are commonly characterized by slow growth, swollen storage tissues and spines.

INDEX

Stroudsburg
Cedar Grove
Paterson
Montclair State Univ.
23
3
B Garfield
Clifton
Passaic
Wallington
Paterson
80 95 Fair
Ridgefield Park
46
Leonia
Palisades Park
21
Wood Ridge
17
Teterboro Airport
Moonachie
Ridgefield
Nutly
Rutherford
Meadowlands Sport Complex
North Bergen
1 9
Edg
Montclair
3
120
Hackensack River
Fairv
Montclair Art Museum
Glenn Ridge
Lyndhurst
95
3
Gutten berg
Belleville
North Arlington
Secaucus
West New York
Edison Nat'l. Historic Site
Stroudsburg
Bloomfield
95
Weehawken
506
Kearney
7
95
280
Harrison
Union City
2
East Orange
NJ Perf. Arts Ctr.
21
7
Hoboken
124
1 9
Allenton
Newark Museum
Newark
JERSEY CITY
440
3
Union
78
95
Roosevelt Stadium
Ellis I.
Hudson River
22
27
Newark Int'l. Airport
78
Statue of Liberty Nat'l. Mon.
4
5
6
Hillside
New Brunswick
81
Newark Bay
Bayonne
NEW JERSEY
NEW YORK
278
The B Mus
1 9
Elizabeth
169
Upper Bay
27
Br. (Toll)
Kill van Kull
B R
95
278
440
The Narrows
278
Philadelphia
(Toll)
(Toll)
Lower Bay
Cartere
440
S T A T E N ISLAND
Norton Point
Coney
A
Richmondtown Restoration
Keyspan Park
Perth Ambay

Gateway National Recreation Area

1 George Washington Br. (Toll)   6 Ma
2 Lincoln Tunnel (Toll)   7 Qu
3 Holland Tunnel (Toll)   8 Qu
4 Brooklyn-Battery Tunnel (Toll) 9 Atu
5 Brooklyn Br.

3 miles
3 km

146

Map Labels

Row 1 (top):
- Street East
- 127 th
- 126 th
- St
- East
- Street
- BRONX CO
- NEW YORK CO
- 19
- Harlem River Station (Freight)
- Street

Left / East Harlem area:
- cus Garvey
- emorial
- Park
- Morris
- chtower
- East
- North Gen. Hosp.
- 125 th St (M.L.K.) St
- M
- East
- 124 th
- 123 rd St
- Ronald E. McNair Pl
- 121 st St
- EAST HARLEM
- 122 nd St
- 120 th
- 119 th
- 118 th
- 117 th
- 116 th
- 115 th
- Jefferson
- E 113 th St
- Houses
- 112 th St
- E 114 th St
- Jefferson Park
- 111 th
- 110 th Street
- 109 th
- Benjamin
- Franklin
- Plaza
- Woodrow Wilson Houses
- East River Housing
- Recreation Pier
- Foot Bridge (Pedestrian)
- Park
- Lexington
- Third
- Second Avenue
- First Avenue
- Avenue
- Drive
- East River Drive
- Harlem River
- East River

Center / Avenue area:
- M. Luther King Jr. Blvd
- Avenue
- Louis Guvillier Park
- Paladino
- First Street
- Pleasant Avenue
- Avenue
- Street
- 18
- 17
- 16
- 15
- Willis Ave Bridge
- Triborough Bridge (Toll)
- 278

Right / Wards Island:
- Wards
- Island
- Little Hell Gate
- Manhattan Psychiatric Center
- H
- Triborough Bridge (Toll)
- 278
- 5
- Kirby-Forensic Psychiatric Center
- H
- Manhattan Children's Psychiatric Center
- H
- Wards Island Park
- Wards Island
- Wards Island Park

Bottom:
- 14
- Mill Rock Park
- Hell Gate
- 145
- 200 yd
- 250 m
- Blvd

Grid references: D, E, F, 1, 3, 4, 5, 6

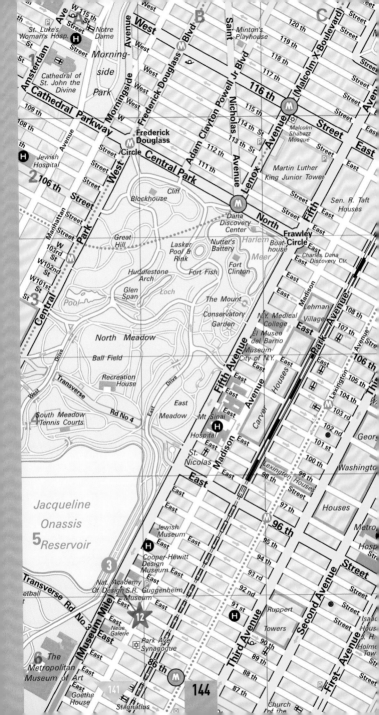

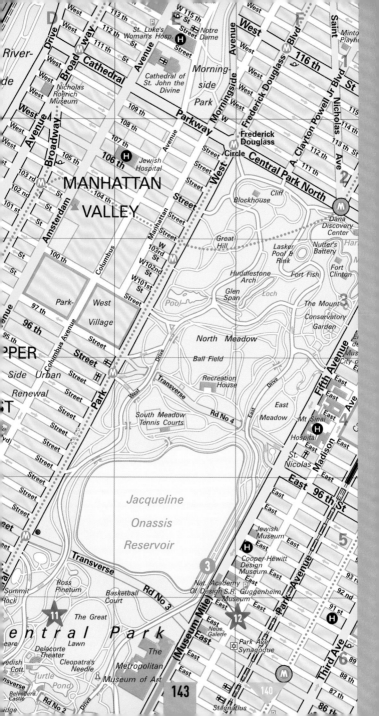

D

West 113th St
W 115th St
St. Luke's Woman's Hosp. H
Notre Dame
West 112th St
Broadway
Cathedral
West 111th St
West
West
Avenue
West 116th St
Saint
Minto
Playh
West
116th St
Frederick Douglass Blvd
Nicholas Ave

River- de
Drive
West
Nicholas Roerich Museum
Cathedral of St. John the Divine
Morning- side Park
West
West
West
West
A. Clayton Powell Jr Blvd
115
114th

West Avenue
West
109th
Parkway
Morningside
W
113th St
112th St

Broadway
108th
Avenue
Frederick Douglass Circle
111th

Amsterdam
107th
Street
West
Central Park North
2

105th
106th H
Jewish Hospital
Street
Street

103 rd St
MANHATTAN
104th St
Street
Cliff Blockhouse
Dana Discovery Center
Har

102 nd St
VALLEY
Street
Street
Nutter's Battery

101 st St
103rd St
Great Hill
Lasker Pool & Rink
Fort Clinton
Fort Fish

Columbus Avenue
W102nd St
Street
Huddlestone Arch
Glen Span
Loch
The Mount
3

UPPER
100th
Park- Village
West Village
West Street
Pool
Conservatory Garden
E
de Mus City E

97th
96th
Street
North Meadow
Fifth Avenue
East

95 th
Columbus Avenue
Street
Ball Field
Drive
East
Ave

PER
Street
Transverse
Recreation House
East

Side Urban
Street
West
Rd No 4
East Meadow
Madison
East

Renewal
Street
South Meadow Tennis Courts
Drive
Mt Sinai H
East

Street
Hospital
St. Nicolas
East

vd)
Street
East
96th St
East

Street
Jacqueline
East
East
5

Onassis
Jewish Museum
East

et
Reservoir
Cooper-Hewitt Design Museum
East

Transverse
3
Nat. Academy Of Design S.R. Guggenheim Museum
92 nd

Summit Rock
Rd No 3
East
91 st

Ross Pinetum
Basketball Court
Museum Mile
Neue Galerie
12
East
East
H

11
The Great Lawn
East
Park Ave Synagogue
Third Ave

entral
Delacorte Theater
Cleopatra's Needle
The Metropolitan Museum of Art
East
88th

edish Cott
Turtle Pond
Park
143
140
M
87th

sverse
Belvedere Castle
Rd No 2
Stignatius
86th

idge

EDGEWATER

200 yd
250 m

Hudson

BERGEN CO
HUDSON CO

NEW JERSEY
NEW YORK
NEW YORK
NEW YORK CO

River

11

Circle Line Boat Tour

Hudson

West End

West

West

West

West

Riverside

West

West

Avenue

94 th

93 rd

Soldiers & Sailors Monument

Riverside Park

West

West

West

West

9a

West

90 th

91 st

Amsterdam

B'nai Jeshurun

89 th

(H.J. Bro

Tower

West

88 th

West

Riverside

West

Amsterdam

West

Houses

87 th

86 th

Jewish

SIDE

West

West

West

West

End

Broadway

Childrens Museum of Manhattan

84 th (Edgar Allen Poe St)

85 th

Boat Basin

West

10

West

79th Street Marina

West

First Baptist Church

West

H

83 rd

82 nd

Jesus Christ R. Sh

St Con

81 st

80 th

St

West

79 th

St

Henry

West

Hayden Planetarium

Rose Ctr. for Earth & Space

Riverside

West

78 th

St

77 th

St

Street

West

West

American Museum of Natural History

9

76 th

10

Highway

West

West

West 72 nd St

Ansonia Hotel

Rutgers

75 th

Street

142

74 th

N.Y. Hist. Society

139

Blvd

West

73 rd

Street

D East
87 th Street
Ignatius
85 th Street
84 th Street
83 rd Street
YORKVILLE
82 nd Street
81 st Street
80 th Street
79 th Temple
Shaaray Tefila
78 th
77 th
76 th
75 th

Church
of the
Holy Trinity
86 th

Beth Israel
Hosp. North
Gracie
Mansion Carl
Schurz

Fire Boat
Station

Gracie
Sq.

Park
East River Prom

200 yd
250 m

CIRCLE LINE BOAT TOUR

Lighthouse
Park

Bird S. Coler
Mem. Hospital

BIDE

Hellenic
Cathedral
Light Opera
of Manhattan

Gracie Sq.
Hospital

Cherokee

Street

Jhon
Jay
Park

End

Gracie
Ter.

East

Drive

The
Noguchi
Museum

Rainey
Park

Street

Roosevelt

West

Road

River

Island

Street

East

Channel

Boulevard

Street

N.Y. Hospital
Cornell Medical
Center

13

West Channel

Channel

35 th

Mem. Sloan Ketter.
Cancer Ctr. Rockefeller

University Dr.

Franklin Dr.

Roosevelt

Main

Roosevelt Island
Bridge

36 th

York

Correction
Hospital

37 th

38 th

12

East
60th Street
Heliport

NEW YORK CO
QUEENS CO

40 th
9 th

LONGISLAND
CITY

Aerial Tramway

Queensboro

West

East

Road

Road

Franklin

Queens
Bridge
Park

Vernon

Queensbridge
Houses

11 th

13 th
Street

Goldwater
Memorial

West

Bridge (2 Levels)

10 th
41 st

41 st Road

12 th

Hospital

Queens

Street

25

21 th

22 nd

23 rd

East

Hospital

43 rd

137 Queens Plaz

CONTENTS

Shopping → p. 72

Entertainment → p. 82

Where to stay → p. 94

Street atlas → p. 128

MAPS IN THE GUIDEBOOK
(130 A1) Page numbers
and coordinates refer to the
street atlas
(0) Site/address located off
the map
Coordinates are also given for
places that are not marked on
the street atlas
A public transportation route
map can be found inside the
back cover

**INSIDE BACK COVER:
PULL-OUT MAP →**

PULL-OUT MAP 📖
(📖 A–B 2–3) Refers to the
removable pull-out map

The best MARCO POLO Insider Tips

Our top 15 Insider Tips

INSIDER TIP Humble beginnings

The Tenement Museum is a faithful reproduction of the way immigrants experienced New York way back in the 19th century → **p. 40**

INSIDER TIP Starry ceiling

Grand Central Station is the city's cathedral-like rail traffic hub. Take a free guided tour of the world's largest station and be sure to look up at the ceiling mural with its 2500 stars depicting the winter skies → **p. 43**

INSIDER TIP Club par excellence

Live concerts, dancing, karaoke and ping-pong are all on offer at The Bell House, Brooklyn's trendy new club → **p. 88**

INSIDER TIP World affairs lunch

The United Nations canteen is open to the general public so you can rub shoulders with politicians while you enjoy your lunch with a view of the East River → **p. 69**

INSIDER TIP Asian delight

The hip MomofukU Ssäm Bar in East Village – regrettably not for vegetarians – offers its guests delicious meat dishes → **p. 66**

INSIDER TIP A street vendor worth hunting down

Before you can eat you need to check Facebook, twitter or the Schnitzel & Things website: this gourmet vendor is parked in a different venue every day but the hunt is worth it → **p. 71**

INSIDER TIP Eccentric eatery

Inspired by the cult film *The Big Lebowski* the owner of the Little Lebowski family eatery in Greenwich will serve you your meal clad in his dressing gown → **p. 77**

INSIDER TIP Oasis in the sky

Spectacular views – especially after sunset – from the rooftop terrace of 230 Fifth high above Midtown Manhattan's sparkling sea of lights (photo right) → **p. 84**

INSIDER TIP Dose with a difference

The waiters at Apothéke wear white lab coats to present you with your specialty cocktail. Here it is all about the location and the drama of the experience! → **p. 84**

INSIDER TIP Party beneath chandeliers

The Warsaw Club is the meeting place for the Polish community but it plays host to contemporary rock and indie bands in its imposing 1950s ballroom (photo left) → **p. 90**

INSIDER TIP Drinks overlooking the park

Get an amazing view of Central Park from the Metropolitan Museum of Art's rooftop bar – open until sunset on Fridays in summer → **p. 53**

INSIDER TIP Sea sensation

The rooms in the historical Jane Hotel are called cabins and are decorated like berths on a ship. It has a marvellous view of the Hudson River → **p. 100**

INSIDER TIP Flying high

The Trapeze School in Hudson River Park gives you the opportunity to fulfill a childhood dream and become a circus performer for the day as a juggler, a trampolinist or a trapeze artist. Learn to 'fly' fearlessly with a safety net → **p. 113**

INSIDER TIP Ode to joy

Not to be missed are the many open air concerts of the world renowned Metropolitan Opera held in various parks all over the city. They are among the most impressive New York experiences to be had (for free) → **p. 91**

INSIDER TIP What's on

For some reliable tips go to *www.flavorpill.com/newyork*. Every Tuesday the site posts a must-see selection of current cultural events. Everything from festivals and music to films, documentaries, art, literature and poetry → **p. 120**

BEST OF ...

FOR FREE

● *Bastion of contemporary art*
Entry to The Museum of Modern Art (*MoMA)* is free every Friday afternoon. The museum's collection of contemporary art is phenomenal and its special exhibitions are outstanding (photo) → p. 44

● *The ferry not to be missed*
When the *Staten Island Ferry* pulls away from the shore you get to see the full sweep of the Manhattan skyline from the Statue of Liberty, Ellis Island and on to New Jersey. On the other side of the ferry the view is of Brooklyn, New York City's biggest borough → p. 33

● *Row upon row of art*
The 20 or so streets between Tenth and Eleventh Avenue are home to the city's art district with countless small, large, famous or lesser known *galleries* showcasing a variety of art genres. Exhibition openings are usually at 6pm on Thursdays and wine is served → p. 37

● *Newfound friends*
Big Apple Greeters are enthusiastic New Yorkers who volunteer themselves as guides for visitors to their city. See the city through the eyes of a local and make a friend at the same time → p. 36

● *Gospel songs that strike a cord*
The voices of the Baptist Church *gospel singers* – clad in their Sunday best with their flamboyant hats – are guaranteed to give you goose pimples! → p. 44

● *Where robots roam*
At the *Sony Wonder Technology Lab* you can see how robots are programmed, animation characters created and how remote controlled gadgets work→ p. 46

● *Mini-stage with maxi-music*
An excellent repertoire of jazz, world and eastern European music is on offer on the tiny stage at *Barbes* jazz club and bar in Brooklyn's Park Slope – admission is free → p. 88

●●●● Dots in guidebook refer to 'Best of ...' tips

ONLY IN NEW YORK
Unique experiences

● *A new lease on life after 9/11*

Construction work at *Ground Zero* is finally in full swing. The highest skyscraper is expected to measure 541 m (1776 ft) on completion. Tours recount 9/11 and explain the new structures being built → p. 31

● *Front row seats on the square*

With 42nd Street on *Times Square* having been declared a pedestrian precinct visitors can now take in the world-famous neon lights from the comfort of a chair or seated on a stair → p. 21, 27

● *Department store of superlatives*

Macy's is a world-famous department store and a New York institution. Its Thanksgiving parade is an extravagant spectacle with gigantic balloons and dancing cheerleaders → p. 76

● *A bird's eye view of the Big Apple*

The view from the viewing platform of the *Rockefeller Center* is breathtaking. Before you is the vast of Central Park, a forest of skyscrapers and the Empire State Building. Seen from above the city seems surprisingly calm and serene → p. 45

● *A feast for the senses*

SoHo is known for its large lofts belonging to stars like Madonna, its superb galleries and boutiques and its gourmet grocery stores. The most famous is *Dean & DeLuca* who have been sourcing delicacies from around the world for more than 30 years – delicious but pricey! → p. 75

● *A breath of fresh air*

Extensive *Central Park* with its trees, rock features and waterfalls was established more than a century ago. Today this green belt is a rollerbladers', joggers', rowers', dog-lovers', concertgoers' and sun-worshippers' paradise. Whether lazing on the lawns, rowing on the lakes or listening to a concert – New Yorkers flock here (photo) → p. 50

● *Donut delight*

The *Doughnut Plant* steps it up a notch when it comes to the stereotypical donut. Their decadent donuts come in a selection of unusual flavours (like pistachio, peanut butter or blueberry) and shapes → p. 62

ONLY IN

BEST OF ...

● *Egyptian temples, American paintings*
You could easily spend a whole week in the *Metropolitan Museum.* The remarkable collection is one of the finest in the world → p. 53

● *Parlor jazz in Harlem*
Marjorie Eliot entertains guests from around the world with live jazz in her *parlor* while she waxes lyrical about Martin Luther King and civil rights. An excellent afternoon's entertainment! → p. 90

● *Haven for book lovers*
At the *Strand Book Store* you can find rare books, out of print books, second-hand and current bestsellers straight off the press → p. 74

● *Gateway to the world's highest mountain range*
The *Rubin Museum of Art* in Chelsea is dedicated to Himalayan art and the stylish building also houses a small restaurant, bar and souvenir shop → p. 38

● *Shopping and eating in an old factory*
Feel like a brownie straight from the oven or a delicious fresh lobster? Then head to the *Chelsea Market* to experience the industrial charm of this renovated factory and its gourmet delights (photo) → p. 75

● *Fitness by the river*
Chelsea Piers is a massive sports and entertainment complex on the Hudson River in Chelsea. Dancing, bowling, basketball, climbing, swimming and golf are some of the activities on offer → p. 54

● *A relaxing coffee break*
The lattes and baked treats at *Amy's Bread* are excellent and the glass frontage means you can relax and enjoy the views of Greenwich Village with its charming cobbled streets and houses → p. 62

RAIN

RELAX AND CHILL OUT
Take it easy and spoil yourself

● *New energy for tired limbs*
In *Chinatown* there is a masseuse on every corner, just what you need to ease your stiff shoulders and tired feet. There is a lot to be said for the 2000-year-old Chinese therapies on offer → **p. 32**

● *Water under the bridge*
Relax and let yourself be gently rocked as you float to the strains of the classical music on the *Bargemusic*, an old barge docked beneath Brooklyn Bridge which is an unusual concert venue with a spectacular view of the Manhattan skyline → **p. 92**

● *Manhattan sights by boat*
The *Circle Line* boat takes you around the island. The relaxing three hour tour is full of interesting *facts* and is an excellent way to familiarise yourself with Uptown, Downtown and Eastside and Westside (photo) → **p. 118**

● *Garden on railway tracks*
The elevated *High Line Park* is not only a landscape of greenery and plants. You can also stretch out on one of the wooden loungers and watch cruise ships, ferries and sailing boats go by → **p. 21**

● *Wellness the traditional way*
East Village boasts the famous *Russian & Turkish Baths* that have been offering steam baths, saunas, and mud and aromatherapies for over a century → **p. 32**

● *Balance and harmony Asian style*
With crossed legs and seated on cushions visitors to the *Shambhala Meditation Center* are taught meditation and total relaxation though the traditional Asian way → **p. 32**

● *Cocktails under the stars*
Sip a cocktail at sunset and enjoy the views across the city from Ink48 hotel's rooftop bar *Press*. Its glistening sky-high swimming and views will leave an indelible impression of your New York experience → **p. 18, 86**

INTRODUCTION

DISCOVER
NEW YORK!

New York City is synonymous with the American dream and the only way to understand this massive, adrenaline-fuelled, influential and nerve-racking metropolis is to come and see it for yourself. Wake up to the sounds of the city that never sleeps – cars hooting, sirens howling and screeching brakes and then get up close and personal with the city!

The city has made a full recovery after the 11 September 2001 terror attacks and is once again a proud and vibrant global capital of commerce – hectic, loud, provocative, immense and powerful. Almost too powerful when you consider the dramatic impact the Wall Street financial crisis of 2008 has had on the whole world! New York has also retained its position as the world's entertainment capital. Every evening it plays host to a diverse array of film premiers, musicals, ballets, gala theatre events, rock and pop concerts, jazz sessions and high-end opera and its multitude of cutting-edge

Photo: Manhattan and Central Park

clubs perfectly encapsulate the current zeitgeist. The New York audiences are varied, enthusiastic, discerning and above all, critical. If you can make it here you can make it anywhere, as Frank Sinatra says in his famous hit *New York, New York*.

Downtown Manhattan (in other words everything south of 14th Street) is where it all happens. The restaurant and bar scene here is far more exciting than in Midtown Manhattan or in northern Manhattan. Trendy new hotels, hip nightclubs and daring architecture such as the Cooper Union building and the New Museum draw locals and tourists alike to the south of the city. Here the visitor will find old run-down buildings next to stylish bars, the historical next to the modern and it is these contrasts that lure the visitor. Robert de Niro also helped make the area popular with his TriBeCa Film Festival that was launched in 2003. Every year in May international filmmakers and Hollywood movie stars descend on the city. The event is a magnet for movie buffs, celebrity hunters and everyone who is fan of the glitz and glamour of red carpet events.

> **Manhattan south of 14th Street exudes its own particular charm**

In the hustle and bustle of the night Manhattan feels as if it is one single, massive party and that impression continues even as the day begins when the subway buskers and musicians (possibly the stars of tomorrow) ply their trade. Skateboarders turn street squares into sports arenas and just about every street corner has its own *stand-up comedian*. The pace, the drama and the theatre of the city are unrivalled and as

The iconic yellow cabs are an enduring symbol of the vibrant hustle and bustle of New York

Simone de Beauvoir commented 'there is something in the New York air that makes sleep useless'. As the media hub of the United States, everything cultural this city has to offer tends to be amplified. Key global television broadcasters, major news magazines and the *New York Times* – arguably the world's most important daily newspaper – are all based here. All the leading publishing houses and much record companies are based in the city and use it as their platform to the world market. The city also attracts creative people like no other: actors, artists, authors, designers and even software developers. For centuries New York has thrived on, and drawn its energy from, the constantly changing cycle of boom and bust.

Today around eight million people live the city. Once the world's largest, it can no longer lay claim to that title as it has been overtaken by other megacities. Metropolitan New York also includes areas such as Long Island, Westchester County, New Jersey and Connecticut has 24 million inhabitants and most work in Manhattan, the city centre.

On the go in the city that sweeps you off your feet!

Added to this figure are all the tourists who join the throng on the fast paced pavements. The speed of life here may well be one of the reasons why New York does not have a strong political history. Before 9/11 its most memorable event took place in April 1776, when George Washington relocated his headquarters to the banks of the Hudson River during the war of independence against the British. After World War II

the United Nations set up their headquarters in New York. After the shocking events of 9/11, New York became a political focal point for American politics and the UN headquarters were the world's focus point for the Gulf War. Today the importance attributed to New York cannot be ascribed to politics. Politics remains the domain of Washington, D.C.

Mayor Michael Bloomberg has spearheaded a drive to turn New York into an environmentally friendly city. Times Square is now a pedestrian precinct, there are new cycle paths everywhere, traffic islands in Manhattan are going green and the umbrellas of outdoor bistros are a common sight. A disused elevated subway railway line has been transformed into an urban park. The lengths of Manhattan Island along the Hudson River are now parkland and beneath Brooklyn Bridge

miles of river frontage have also been reclaimed and boast an urban beach, boat trips and playgrounds. Even the Empire State Building has undergone extensive renovations to optimise its energy consumption. To ease traffic congestion, new bus lanes and cycle lanes have been introduced albeit with strong criticism from the powerful car lobby. In amongst all of this are the sounds of the bells of the bicycle rickshaws that will get you around quickly and safely without leaving an environmental footprint. However, at times it is still easiest to get around on foot.

New York has for some time now prided itself for being one of America's most pedestrian-friendly cities. Many of the city's attractions are located in close proximity to one another and the grid layout and numerical street numbers are easy to follow so you should find your way around with ease. As always when travelling in a big city it is a good idea to follow the usual travel rules especially if you suddenly find yourself in unfamiliar surrounds.

Parks, playgrounds and bicycles – the city has gone green

New York is a city of contrasts. Winters are dry with freezing temperatures. In summer the mercury can easily rise into the 80s (over 30 degrees Celsius) and it can be very, very humid. The endless grey concrete jungle is juxtaposed by the expansive green belt of Central Park. Skyscrapers dwarf church spires. There is a constant dichotomy between large and small, rich and poor, old and new. Every race and nation is represented here. Driven by the hope for a better future many have turned their backs on their countries of origin for political or economic reasons. All have brought with them a touch of home, be it cuisine from Ethiopia, samba dancing from Brazil, festive parades from Italy or the dragon dance from China all contributing to making this a city of unimaginable diversity.

The mix of immigrant nations is constantly changing. In the 19th century the first wave of immigrants from Ireland, Germany, Austria and Russia all made their influence on the English society and also assimilated themselves well. At the beginning of the 20th century Italian and Polish immigrants joined them and later New York also became a safe haven for the persecuted Jews of Europe. This melting pot or fusion of diverse cultures is unique to New York and is unrivalled in the United States. It is for this reason that New Yorkers also consider themselves as a distinct breed, culturally aware, abreast of the economic situation, enquiring, tolerant and even arrogant at times. In more recent years the waves of immigrants have included millions of people from central and South America, hundreds of thousands of Chinese, Koreans and Vietnamese, as well as many Afro-Americans from the southern states. Their arrival has once again changed the dynamics of the city. The recent influx has been so great that the city has almost lost one of its most important attributes: the ease with which it is able to merge, mix and integrate many diverse cultures. This has completely changed its character. In 1989 the first African American mayor of New York, David Dinkins described it best in his acceptance speech when he said, 'New York is not a melting pot. It is a gorgeous mosaic of people'.

Once a traffic jam, now a social space: relax in the pedestrian precinct on Times Square

Sadly the 'gorgeous mosaic' symbolising equality is showing flaws. The immigrants are invariably poor and often illegal while those working on Wall Street have had their earnings skyrocket to dizzying heights once again after the 2008 financial crisis. Although the occasional broker may have lost their job, those remaining have once again been able to make huge profits in a short space of time. After the American public bailed out the banks, in October 2011 everything came to a head with the Occupy Wall Street protests against corporate dominance of politics. New York's real flaws are discernible if you simply examine its five *boroughs*. Independently they could each be an entire city. This was indeed the case up until 1898 before

Between Harlem and the Statue of Liberty

Greater New York was formed by merging Manhattan, Brooklyn, Queens, Staten Island and the Bronx. Today Brooklyn is gaining in popularity thanks to its museums, architecture, massive Prospect Park, designer boutiques and sophisticated restaurants. Williamsburg in northern Brooklyn has become the perfect quarter for a night out on the town. Here young artists and designers have created a network of galleries, restaurants and interesting small shops that are well worth a visit. Queens, Staten Island and the Bronx tend to attract fewer visitors. They are residential areas with a more suburban flair. Tourists usually make Manhattan – between the Statue of Liberty and Harlem – their ultimate destination. It is after all the heart of the city!

WHAT'S HOT

1

Flowers and more

Multifunctional You would be forgiven for thinking you had just stepped into a florist at the *Sycamore Flower Shop & Bar*. A trendy new watering hole in Brooklyn that is indeed a flower shop but it doubles up as a bar that serves tasty snacks and good cocktails at night *(118 Cortelyou Rd, photo)*. Multifunctional is also how you could describe Sarah Tallman's floral and interior design store *(99 Warren St)* as is the case with Florist Zezé selling flowers, furniture and home décor *(938 First Ave)*. Just around the corner you will find his charming French bistro, in the studio space that was previously his florist shop *(Zé Café, 398 E 52nd St)*.

2

Goodnight story

Curl up with a good book at the *Library Hotel* and you will not run out of reading matter. There are books in the lobby, the suites and the corridors *(299 Madison Av, www.libraryhotel.com, photo)*. The *Cooper Square Hotel (25 Cooper Square, www.thecoopersquarehotel. com)* and *Roger Smith Hotel* are also for book lovers, the latter specialises in plays and the classics *(501 Lexington Av, www.rogersmith.com)*.

3

Urban jungle

Green Apple In a surprise move the city's parks have begun opening their doors to campers. Guided excursion with park rangers have transformed the *New York State Parks* into adventure parks for adults and children and you get to camp in one of the parks over-night. There are canoe trips for those into adventure sport, also lectures on herbal medicine and survival skills *(www.nycgovparks.org)*.

Food on the go

Too Good to Go Mouth-watering veal cutlets on a carrot bun instead of the usual *hot dogs* with sauerkraut relish? There are stands selling gourmet fare on every street corner of the Big Apple and busy pedestrians are always spoilt for choice. You can for example indulge in Korean tacos from Korilla BBQ *(www.korillabbq.com)* on one street corner then grab a delicious dessert on the next. *Waffles & Dinges* serve mouth-watering sweet and savoury Belgian waffles, try one with strawberry and syrup or the pulled pork with coleslaw *(www.wafelsanddinges. com)*. Some very unlikely combinations can also be had at the *Big Gay Ice Cream Truck* and their chocolate ice cream with caramelised bacon sandwiched between two waffles is an absolute hit *(www.biggayice creamtruck.com, photo)*.

Soul of the city

Harlem The Harlem district has a wealth of history to its name and is as hip and happening today as it was in the 1970s. A recent hotel addition *Aloft* is an excellent choice of a place to stay, its lobby was designed by local artists and it attracts a younger clientele and prices for the trendy rooms are reasonable *(2296 Frederick Douglass Blvd)*. Not to be missed is *Melba's Restaurant* where traditional southern *soul food* is on the menu. Try the ribs, which are outstanding *(300 W 114th St)*! The *Red Rooster* is a true tribute to yesteryear with its walls decorated with works by up-and-coming artists *(312 Lenox Ave)*. It is a good idea to take a tour of the district to get a good overall impression. *Harlem Heritage (104 Malcolm X Blvd)* offers the widest selection.

IN A NUTSHELL

BIG APPLE

The expression has its beginnings in the jazz scene of World War II. If your performance made it to New York you were getting a bite from the Big Apple. Not only were musicians' earnings in New York much better but the city also held the promise of a career stepping stone. In the 1970s a clever advertising campaign by the tourism industry adapted and used the slogan, establishing it as a catch phrase.

BIRD'S EYE VIEW

See the city from above: bars are opening their doors high above New York's streets on high-rise rooftops and terraces. Manhattan is densely populated, the pace of life hectic and its visitors discerning. Necessity is the mother of invention and today a skyscrapers' architecture will invariably incorporate a roof terrace. Many hotels offer their guests the option of enjoying a lofty cocktail in their rooftop bars. The most impressive of these with captivating views of the lit-up concrete and steel jungle that is New York by night are the *Salon de Ning* at the Peninsula Hotel, ● *Press* at Ink48, *Le Bain* at The Standard Hotel and of course there is the renowned *230 Fifth* on Fifth Avenue. Enjoy your classic Martini a little closer to the sky.

Photo: Brooklyn Bridge

Welcome to the Big Apple – skyscrapers, island hopping, musicals and much more – this dynamic city has its own unique atmosphere

DIZZYING HEIGHTS

New York's first skyscrapers made their appearance in the 19th century. All things considered a shortage of real estate is hardly a satisfactory explanation for the enthusiasm with which they were built. Some attribute their coming into being to the status that having the world's highest buildings would give the city. First there was the World Building (1890), then came the Metropolitan Life Tower (1909), the Woolworth Building (1913), the 319 m (1046 ft) high Chrysler Building (1930) and of course the Empire State Building (1931) beating its precursors with a height of 443 m (1454 ft) to the top of the lightning conductor. Eventually the brilliantly executed art deco style of the Chrysler Building would be replaced by Ludwig Mies van der Rohes' Bauhaus style (Lever House and Seagram

years, it is intended to remind us of those who died in the 9/11 attack and send out the signal that terrorism cannot subjugate peace.

The new architecture of the city seems more modest and is no longer all about the quest for the world's highest building. The new architecture has a design language all of its own. The impressive Cooper Union University building opened in 2009 is a structure with a vertical section that looks like a massive tear. Next to the Brooklyn Bridge and completed in 2011 is the Beekman Tower by Frank Gehry. Its 76 floors make it the city's highest apartment block. The remarkable and stylish building has a façade of stainless steel that reflects light and gives the illusion that it ripples and undulates. Critics are hailing this as the advent of a new era in architecture.

The rippling skyscraper –
Frank Gehry's Beekman Tower

Building) and scrollwork gave way to glass, simplicity and functionality. The twin towers of the World Trade Center completed in 1971 and 1973 became the city's ultimate record holder with the highest standing 419,7 m (1368 ft) tall. They collapsed on 11 September 2001 in the worst terror attack in the history of the United States, when two passenger aircraft were flown into them. The World Trade Center will be replaced by the new 541 m (1776 ft) high One World Trade Center which is earmarked for completion in the next few

DOORMEN

Uniformed doormen are part and parcel of elite areas like the Upper East and Upper West Side. There are 100,000 or more of them in New York and they are the status symbols of the wealthy elite. The television series *Gossip Girl* popular among American teenagers describes this privileged world of the Manhattan elite. A world where people have spacious, luxury homes in huge apartment blocks and have a doorman at their beck and call. The doormen assist residents by holding open doors, carrying shopping parcels, signing in couriered items, flagging down cabs as well as by screening and announcing visitors. Of course it is all done attentively and with a polite smile. Being a doorman is a well-paid and sought after job.

DOWNTOWN

The term 'downtown' has a fairly broad meaning in the rest of the United States and usually denotes the city centre,

however in New York its meaning is very specific. Take a quick glance at a city map and you will see why. Downtown is the southern half of Manhattan and is synonymous with young up-and-coming and creative New Yorkers. In contrast, Uptown is the northern part west and east of Central Park which has immaculate and glamorous apartments with their own libraries, servants' rooms, large dining halls, thick walls, high ceilings and fireplaces all of which shape the image of the chic lifestyle its residents enjoy. All this and the money that goes with it is what makes the Uptown image. People residing here are considered part of the establishment, which means anyone wanting to be seen as being part of the creative, hip and in-crowd will want to have an address in TriBeCa or the East and West Village.

GOING GREEN

☺ Above the city on a section of disused railway is an urban park with wooden deck chairs: the perfect spot to relax. ★ ● *High Line in Chelsea (www. thehighline.org* (134 B6–C1) (*ᗕ BC 139)*) even has wild flowers growing on it and it has become symbolic for an environmentally friendly New York. In Manhattan, traffic calming measures are being introduced to the streets and ● Times Square is already a pedestrian precinct and cycling lanes are making their appearance on Manhattan's West Side. *Hudson River Park* that stretches from the southernmost point to George Washington Bridge in the north makes an excellent urban retreat with its lawns, tennis courts and paddleboats. New York also has 46 weekly markets. The very successful health food chain Whole Foods is gaining in popularity – one of its many branches can be found on Union Square. Organic is the buzzword and New Yorkers are discovering the benefits of eating healthier.

ISLAND HOPPING

New York City is made up of a whole series of islands – a fact that is easy to forget. Manhattan itself is one, the Statue of Liberty stands tall on *Liberty Island* and *Ellis Island* is where arriving immigrants were received until 1954. The city's shore is 577 miles long. A ferry will take you from the southernmost tip of Manhattan across to *Governors Island* which has lawns and old military buildings that are ideal for a picnic. The ferry to *Staten Island* is invariably accompanied by people on kayaks and sailing boats and at the Brooklyn, Queens and Manhattan water taxi stations you will see commuters, on their way to work or out shopping, embarking and disembarking from the bright yellow taxi boats.

Swinging high up on the east end of 60th Street is the aerial tramway that takes you to ⚡ *Roosevelt Island* in East River. The island itself is not a real attraction but the view from the cable car is what makes the ride worthwhile. *Randall Island* can be reached on foot via the bridge on 103rd Street and the subway and bus will take you to *City Island* which is a sailor's paradise. The newly renovated *Coney Island* in the south of Brooklyn is once again attracting many visitors. Amusement parks and rollercoasters, the beach and an aquarium and the prospect of a Russian meal all draw visitors to this seaside peninsula. People from around the world come here to enjoy a stroll along the wide promenade and to enjoy its holiday atmosphere.

NEIGHBOURHOODS THEY ARE A CHANGING

New York's residents are often on the run, not from the IRS or the law, but from rising rentals, the loud music of new neighbours or from the bars and clubs that never sleep. This has always been the case:

Greenwich Village used to be busy with the coming and going of authors and artists but its narrow streets and quaint houses were turned into lucrative rental cash cows. The creative minds and free spirits have now had to make way for the movers and shakers. In *Little Italy* you will find very few genuine *Italian-Americans. Chinatown* is the culprit. With its cheap labour and great variety of shops and restaurants it is bursting at the seams. It is a phenomenon that is causing it to spread northwards slowly encroaching on the Italian quarter. The *Lower East Side* has historically always been a working class neighbourhood. Jewish families from Eastern Europe came here to start their American dream. Today the district is a haven of designer boutiques, high-end restaurants, trendy bars and small art galleries. Its nightlife draws visitors from all over New York. In the hip district of *Williamsburg* prices of lofts apartments are skyrocketing. Its young residents are being forced to look to other parts of Brooklyn for alternatives. Especially *Greenpoint* and *Bushwick* are benefiting from the influx of ambitious young people.

SINGLES SCENE

New York is a singles' city. The television series *Sex and the City* showed the world the unique New York dating scene. The women in the series are constantly on the lookout, either for a casual adventure or a long-term relationship. They seek a partnership that has a balance between independence and dependency but find that their ideal is seldom the reality. This is not unique to New York. However, what is unique here is the ambition and dedication is greater as here than elsewhere, as is the choice. Statistics say that around 60 per cent of all New Yorkers are on the lookout for a partner. There is an entire industry built up around singles; speed dating services, online dating services,

matchmakers and even psychotherapists. Most New Yorkers will have tried at least one of them at some stage or other. So what is it that makes it so difficult for New Yorkers to find love? Perhaps it is the notion that they deserve only the best or that they have too little time for a relationship or that their careers take precedence over love?

SUMMERTIME

In the summer months many New Yorkers choose to leave behind the buzz of the city. East of the metropolis lies *Long Island* with its legendary villages and hamlets know as the Hamptons with its very inviting 62-mile stretch of fine sandy beaches. These Atlantic beaches were once the domain of whalers and smugglers but are now where the East Coast in-crowd and Hollywood big names spend their summers feasting on lobsters and scallops.

Long Island is in the shape of a crocodile with its jaw open. The *Hamptons* are located in its lower 'jaw'. These picture-perfect old villages lie one after another along the coast like a string of pearls: South Hampton, Bridgehampton, East Hampton and Amagansett. Montauk with its distinctive red and white lighthouse forms the most eastern point of Long Island. Charming villages with whitewashed, clapboard and wooden houses, narrow streets, small boutiques and cafés all lend character to this exclusive and very pricey area. The narrow barrier sandbar of *Fire Island* is located at Long Island's southernmost point. It to get there you takes a boat across and once there you have to get about on foot. There are no cars and bicycles are restricted so you have to carry daypacks for your food, towels and reading material. With conservation high on the agenda the island is full of deer and perfect for bird watching.

Spring in the Hamptons – perfect city escape

THEATRELAND

New York is the epicentre of the theatre genre that has become synonymous with it – the Broadway musical. These productions attract some ten million visitors a year, many of them come from all over the world. However this success story belies the fact that local composers and authors are being forced to take the back seat as many musical productions are either imports from London or revivals of all-time classics.

The risk of producing a new musical or theatre production on Broadway is huge. Potential investors are nervous of the high costs involved in developing and advertising as well as the constantly changing tastes of audiences spoilt for choice by what the film industry has to offer. The benchmark for a successful production keeps getting higher. A prime example is the plight of the musical *Spider-Man: Turn off the Dark* developed by U2 singer Bono and his guitarist The Edge. The production was marred by a number of issues: an extended pre-production stage, countless accidents, a weak script and then the dismissal of the director. The most expensive musical of all times was declared a flop even before it opened.

It is worth taking a chance and seeing an Off-Off-Broadway piece. With smaller budgets and less glitz and glamour they tend to be more imaginative and provocative. Incidentally a theatre's proximity to the famous avenue has absolutely nothing to do with it being classed Broadway or not. It is an on Broadway theatre if it has more than 500 seats and if it has 100 seats it is an Off-Broadway theatre and any theatre with fewer seats is Off-Off-Broadway.

THE PERFECT DAY
New York in 24 hours

08:00am **BREAKFAST THEN A STROLL ACROSS THE BRIDGE**

Given the time difference you will no doubt wake up in New York feeling ravenous. At *Eisenberg's* → p. 62 – a traditional diner in Chelsea – they serve sizzling bacon and eggs pretty much around the clock. The eatery has been serving sandwiches and their fries since 1929. Sit at the counter and watch in awe at the speed with which the chefs and waiters go about their work. After a good breakfast take the subway to Brooklyn for a stroll across *Brooklyn Bridge* → p. 29. Incidentally crossing it in the direction of the Manhattan skyline is far more exciting than the other way round! Beekman Tower – the new Frank Gehry architectural masterpiece – glistens invitingly at the other end while the Statue of Liberty seems to be waving to passers-by. Ships and ferries of every size chug through the waters beneath the famous bridge.

11:00am **A BIRD'S EYE VIEW**

Now head to the *Rockefeller Center* → p. 45 (photo left) for a bird's eye view of the city. Some rate the view from here superior to that from the Empire State Building the reason being that looking down at the city from a height of 67 floors gives you the feeling of being closer the action. Back on the ground it is decision time. You could settle opt for *MoMA* → p. 44, the Museum of Modern Art close by or alternatively walk north up *Madison Avenue* → p. 43 and take in its exclusive boutiques.

12:00pm **ART SPIRAL**

At the end of your walk is the *Guggenheim Museum* → p. 52. The building itself – a brilliant piece of architecture by Frank Lloyd Wright – is the main attraction. Walk up its internal spiral ramp, admiring the artworks to your right while to your left you can glance over the balustrade into the central void. If by now you can do with a break then look no further than *Central Park* → p. 50 right on the museum's doorstep.

02:15pm **SANDWICHES FIT FOR A KING**

If hunger pangs are getting the better of you take the subway south instead. In the Lower East Side go to *Katz's Deli* → p. 70 (photo right) and try a hearty sandwich something that a number of American presidents have also done. The pastrami sandwich is its claim to fame as is a scene in the classic movie *When Harry met Sally*. In the

Discover the best of New York – the very essence of the city – in a relaxed way in just one day

mood for shopping? Head north up First Avenue until you reach scenic *St. Marks Place → p. 39* a street that will have you spoilt for choice when it comes to second-hand boutiques.

03:00pm TRULY ASIA

You would be forgiven for thinking you are in Asia when you take a stroll through the exotic, busy and crowded streets of nearby *Chinatown → p. 34*. The area is packed with small restaurants, street markets, tourist shops, grocery stores and bric-a-brac. All the signage is in Chinese and a melange of Asian languages can be heard wherever you go. A very unique experience! In *Canal Street → p. 36* you can buy just about everything. Why not try a Chinese *massage→ p. 32* to relieve your tired aching feet.

05:00pm HIGH UP ON THE HIGH LINE

Further west you will come across the charming *High Line Park → p. 21* (photo right) established a few years ago along a stretch of disused elevated railroad tracks. The old tracks have been conserved and lawns and grasses grow between them while wooden loungers invite you to while away the time. From here you get great views of Greenwich with its old *brownstone* houses and new modern buildings, with the Hudson River in the backdrop. Then go on to *Malatesta → p. 71*, a lovely Italian restaurant south of the High Line and try its delicious homemade gnocchi.

09:00pm JAZZ, ROCK, POP AND A GLASS OF WINE

If you are up to it after your busy day then visit the *Village Vanguard → p. 91* a well established jazz club and enjoy some first class jazz. If rock or pop are more your scene hail a cab and go to the Lower East Side's *Living Room → p. 89* or the *Rockwood Music Hall → p. 90*. Here the local musicians may not be well known but the relaxed settings in these smaller clubs may be just the right ambiance in which to end your adventure-filled day as you sip your glass of wine.

Subway to point of departure: N, R
Subway station: 23rd Street – Broadway
The Metrocard, a magnetic bus and subway card, offers benefits and discounts

SIGHTSEEING

CITY **WHERE TO START?**
The best overview of the city is from the centrally located **Empire State Building (135 E2)** *(⬚ E9)* in Midtown. On Fifth Ave head north to get to the major museums and Central Park and in the south Broadway is only a block away. The best option is to take the bus, perfect for your first sightseeing tour (bus M34 to Fifth Ave and 34th St or Sixth Ave and 34th St; buses M1, M2, M3, M4, M5 will take you to 34th St). Subway: 34th St, B, D, F, M, N, Q, R.

Discovering a city like New York is both exciting and difficult at the same time. Exciting because there is so much to see and difficult because, at a first glance, the choice may seem quite overwhelming. What to see first and what are the absolute must-sees?

New York City is made up of bold and daring architecture concentrated over a relatively small area. Imposing skyscrapers, expansive bridges and statuesque churches make up its rich tapestry and in the middle of it all there is a park just over a third of the size of London's Richmond Park. The subway is the best way to get around or of course – on foot. Outside Grand Central

The Empire State Building, SoHo, Staten Island Ferry, Central Park and Broadway – the constant hustle and bustle of the city that never sleeps

shoe shiners await their customers so why not have your shoes polished before you set out to discover this amazing city. From Grand Central go to ● 🕐 Times Square and stroll around and experience firsthand this iconic hub with its massive flashing billboards and advertisements. Here hooting cars and screeching taxis are replaced by tables and chairs that invite you to sit down and take a break – welcome to a more environmentally aware green New York! The perfect way to get an overview is a round trip by boat or a rather more expensive helicopter ride. Depending on your budget the rides last anything from six to 20 minutes.

New York with its excellent museums, creative artists and its extremely discerning general public is the world's art metropolis. Anything you need to know

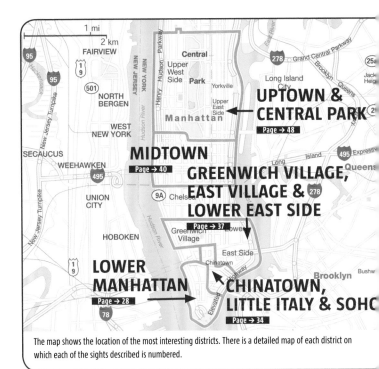

The map shows the location of the most interesting districts. There is a detailed map of each district on which each of the sights described is numbered.

about new exhibitions that are worth a visit can be found in the *New York Times (Fri and Sat)*, in the weekly magazines *New York Magazine*, *Time Out* and *The New Yorker* or on the INSIDER TIP excellent website *dks.thing.net*.

For a small fee most museums offer audio tours that you can hire at the entrance and which will guide you through the exhibition. Some museums do not charge a set entrance fee but expect a small donation (amount specified at entrance). Americans in a position to do so are generally keen to pay, but donating what you can afford is not frowned upon. Most museums in New York are closed on a Monday. Plan ahead and buy your tickets for the Empire State Building, the Statue of Liberty and the Museum of Modern Art online. This will save you a lot of time valuable time that would be wasted in long queues.

LOWER MANHATTAN

Versatile and interesting – Lower Manhattan has it all, from stylish restaurants to historical sites and impressive skyscrapers.

Take a long walk around the gigantic buildings and along the narrow cobbled streets in this southernmost tip of Manhattan. It is home to New York's world famous

financial centre – Wall Street. This is also where the two towers of the Word Trade Center stood before 9/11, where the new One World Trade Center is being built and where the immigrants arrived – right up until the middle of the last century – to seek their fortune in the new world. For an impressive view from the water of the southern Manhattan skyline take a ferry ride out to Staten Island. Walk along the Hudson River through Battery Park to reach TriBeCa, a neighbourhood whose pricey restaurants are very popular with celebrities. You may even find yourself sitting next to Woody Allen!

■1 BROOKLYN BRIDGE ★
(131 D5) (*∅ D17*)

The first bridge to connect Manhattan with Brooklyn was completed in 1883 after 13 years of construction by engineers John A. Roebling and son. Its two pylons, standing nearly 292 feet high, support hundreds of steel cables. The structure spans just over 1738 feet above the East River and has been lauded as the eighth wonder of the world. The centre walkway that runs under its neo-Gothic arches gives you a stunning view of the Manhattan skyline. It is most striking when you INSIDER TIP walk towards Manhattan. For this, take subway line A or C to High St Station or set out from Manhattan starting from Park Row/ Centre Street. *Subway: Brooklyn Bridge/ City Hall, 4–6*

■2 CITY HALL (130 C3–4) (*∅ B16*)

Originally the southern façade of the mayoral office (completed in 1812) was covered in marble, the northern façade in brick. At the time the city fathers assumed that New York would not expand further north. East of City Hall Park is the *Municipal Building*, where tourists keen

MARCO POLO HIGHLIGHTS

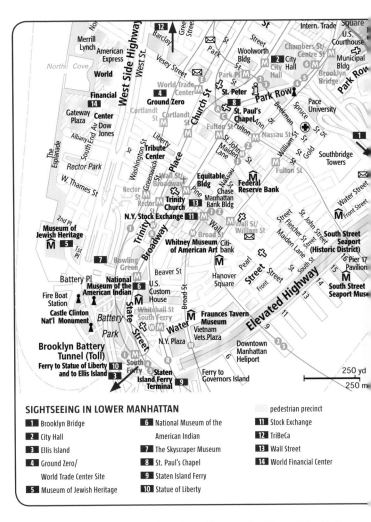

SIGHTSEEING IN LOWER MANHATTAN

- **1** Brooklyn Bridge
- **2** City Hall
- **3** Ellis Island
- **4** Ground Zero/
  World Trade Center Site
- **5** Museum of Jewish Heritage
- **6** National Museum of the
  American Indian
- **7** The Skyscraper Museum
- **8** St. Paul's Chapel
- **9** Staten Island Ferry
- **10** Statue of Liberty

░░░ pedestrian precinct

- **11** Stock Exchange
- **12** TriBeCa
- **13** Wall Street
- **14** World Financial Center

to tie the knot can pay $35 by credit card for a *marriage license (www.cityclerk. nyc.gov). Mon–Fri 8.30am–3.45pm | 141 Worth St | subway: City Hall, R*

3 ELLIS ISLAND (146 C3) *(ଡ଼ O)*
Around 12 million immigrants first stepped onto American soil at this transit centre.

It all happened on this small island in New York Bay over period of over 60 years between 1892 and 1954. To date only the main building has been restored. There is also an interesting museum on the topic of immigration. The future of the remaining 32 buildings is uncertain. *Daily 9am–5pm | Statue of Liberty Line, Battery*

Park point of departure, ferry every 30 minutes | entrance fee $12, audio tour $8 | expect delays up to one hour for security reasons; no large bags permitted | ww wellisisland.org | subway: South Ferry, 1 (only board the front five carriages!)

to replace the old. The design concept by Daniel Libeskind forms the template of the project with architect David Childs holding the reigns. Britain's most prolific architect Lord Norman Foster is building Tower Two and the Spanish architect

Ellis Island – the gateway to the new world for new immigrants until 1954

■4■ GROUND ZERO/WORLD TRADE CENTER SITE ★ (130 B4) (*∅ B16*)

After 11 September 2001 the term Ground Zero became the expression that would epitomise the horror of that day that would forever change the face of history. The World Trade Center – the city's landmark since its completion in 1973 and work-place to some 50,000 people – was completely levelled to the ground. Only 16 people survived the 10.28am collapse of the North Tower. It took until the end of May 2002 to clear the area of the 1.6 million tons of debris. Reconstruction is in full swing and a handful of renowned architects are involved in the massive new One World Trade Center building project

Santiago Calatrava has been awarded the final design for the Word Trade Center Transportation Hub. The highest tower is expected to be 541 m (1776 ft) in height. An observation platform at 415 m (1362 ft) will make for spectacular views.
● Tours of the site are conducted by the fire brigade, survivors, relatives of the victims and local residents. Additionally the *Tribute WTC Visitor Center* provides extensive information on 9/11 and its aftermath. *Mon, Wed–Sat 10am–6pm, Tue noon–6pm, Sun noon–5pm | 120 Liberty St | guided tours: Sun–Fri hourly from 11am–1pm and 3pm, Sat hourly from 11am–4pm | price $10 | www.tributewtc. org | subway: Chambers St, A, C, 1–3*

5 MUSEUM OF JEWISH HERITAGE
(130 A5) (m A17)

Subtitled *A Living Memorial to those who perished during the Holocaust* this museum's hexagonally shaped granite building – representative of the Star of David and as a tribute to the six million Jews who lost their lives in the Holocaust – is located in Manhattan's south end. The exhibits include items from everyday concentration camp life as well as video presentations and documentaries. *Sun–Tue, Thu 10am–5.45pm, Wed 10am–8pm, Fri and before Jewish holidays 10am–3pm | 36 Battery Place | entrance fee $12 | www.mjhnyc.org | subway: South Ferry, 1, Bowling Green, 4, 5*

6 NATIONAL MUSEUM OF THE AMERICAN INDIAN
(130 B5) (m A18)

Displays some three million items from New York banker George Gustav's American Indian heritage collection (including carpets, baskets, pottery and photos) over two floors of the former U.S. Custom House near the southern tip of Manhattan. Also has changing exhibitions showcasing young Indian artists as well as a souvenir shop. *Fri–Wed 10am–5pm, Thu 10am–8pm | One Bowling Green | entrance free of charge | www.nmai.si.edu | subway: South Ferry, 1, Bowling Green, 4, 5*

7 INSIDER TIP THE SKYSCRAPER MUSEUM (130 A5) (m A17)

Showcasing the rich architectural history of Manhattan's famous skyline, the museum's polished steel floors and ceilings spectacularly illuminate the photographs and models of its skyscrapers. The last existing original architectural model of the World Trade Center is also housed here. *Wed–Sun noon–6pm | 39 Battery Place | entrance fee $5 | www.skyscraper.org | subway: Rector St, R, 1, Bowling Green, 4, 5*

8 ST. PAUL'S CHAPEL
(134 B4) (m B16)

This small Episcopal chapel was built in a field near the harbour in 1766 and was a beacon of hope for new immigrants but also attracted the famous. George Washington prayed here on the day of his inauguration in 1789. It remained completely unscathed although it is directly across from the World Trade Center. Its exhibition *Unwavering Spirit: Hope and Healing at Ground Zero* documents the work of the church after the attack. *Church St | between Vesey St and Fulton St | www.*

RELAX & ENJOY

Being a tourist in New York can be quite exhausting so allow yourself some time out between sightseeing to treat yourself. Why not enjoy a pedicure? Always a welcome relief for tired feet and there are salons all over because New Yorkers – both men and women – love to be pampered. Another good option is a massage in ● Chinatown where there are no shortages of salons offering reflexology, facials and shoulder and neck massages. The Buddhist ● Shambhala Center offers an introduction into meditation on Sundays *(noon)* and Wednesdays *(6pm)* for $10 *(118 W 22nd St, sixth floor | www.ny.shambhala.org)*. Or how about a ● Turkish bath in the East Village for only $30 *(268 E 10th St | www.russianturkishbaths.com)*?

saintpaulschapel.org | subway: Broadway Nassau/Fulton St, A, C, 1, 2, 3, 4, 5

9 STATEN ISLAND FERRY ★ ●

(130 B6) (*B18*)

Perhaps the most inexpensive experience you can have in New York is the round trip on the ferry that takes in the Manhattan skyline past the Statue of Liberty and Ellis Island – all for free. *Every 30 minutes during the day (every 15 minutes in rush hour), hourly 11.30pm–6.30am | South St/State St | subway: South Ferry, 1 (only the first five front carriages of the train)*

10 STATUE OF LIBERTY ★

(146 C4) (*0*)

Erected by French sculptor Frédéric-Auguste Bartholdi together with Gustave Eiffel in 1886 as a symbol of the political ideals of the United States, 'Lady Liberty' stands 151 ft tall and weighs 221 t. A limited number of day tickets are issued. Expect delays of around an hour. A good alternative is to hop on a ferry to Ellis Island which passes close by the statue. *Ferries to Liberty Island 9am–5pm every 30 minutes from the office of the Circle Line in Castle Clinton in Battery Park | tel. 1866 782 88 34 | www.statuecruises.com | ticket $13 (including Ellis Island) | subway: South Ferry, 1, Bowling Green, 4, 5*

11 STOCK EXCHANGE

(130 B5) (*B17*)

Constituting the hub of the financial district is the landmark NYSE with its neoclassical architecture. The visitors' gallery is closed for security reasons. *20 Broad St | www.nyse.com | subway: Rector St, R, Wall St, 2–5*

12 TRIBECA

130 B1–3) (*B–C 15–16*)

South of Canal Street (*Tri*angle *Be*low *Ca*nal) was once the city's market district – Washington Market. Today its renovated warehouses have become stylish residential lofts. The TriBeCa district was the hardest hit by 9/11 but thanks in part to Robert De Niro's TriBeCa Film Festival the

National landmark – the Statue of Liberty

nightlife has since returned. There is a good chance of *celebrity* spotting if you have a meal at hot spots *Nobu* and *Next Door Nobu (p. 64) subway: Franklin St, 1*

13 WALL STREET
(130 B–C5) (*B17*)

This small street may not be quite so famous if it wasn't the scene of the infamous stock exchange disaster: the Wall Street Crash in October 1929. 'Black Thursday' ('Black Friday' in Europe because of the time difference) saw the *New York Stock Exchange* become both a symbol of might and misery for the speculator. Nothing in the financial district with its banks and investment firms visually conveys the authority and power of international money as the NYSE. *Subway: Wall St, 2–5*

14 WORLD FINANCIAL CENTER
(130 A3–4) (*A16*)

This complex of buildings on the southern-most tip of Manhattan across from Wall Street comprises office blocks, shops, apartments *(Battery Park City)*, an imposing conservatory *(Winter Garden)*, yacht harbour and green areas. The Winter Garden has a variety of restaurants and shops not to mention INSIDER TIP free concerts and exhibitions. *Information: 'events calendar' of www.worldfinancial center.com | West St | between Vesey St and Liberty St | subway: Chambers St, A, C, J, M, Z, 1, 2, 3*

CHINATOWN, LITTLE ITALY & SOHO

New York's ethnic diversity is particularly conspicuous in these districts. The unfamiliar smells, exotic foods and colourful buzz in the streets are so authentic that will feel as though you have travelled to another continent without ever leaving the city.

A host of Chinese grocery stores, pizzerias, high-end boutiques, pricey galleries, Vietnamese restaurants and Italian cafés all capture the imagination and tempt you to try all there is on offer.

Vibrant and colourful Chinatown

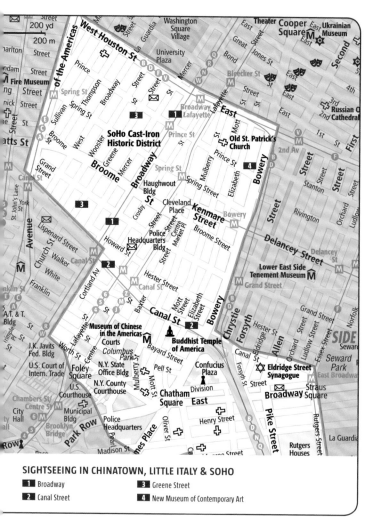

SIGHTSEEING IN CHINATOWN, LITTLE ITALY & SOHO

1 Broadway

2 Canal Street

3 Greene Street

4 New Museum of Contemporary Art

Almost half of New York's 300,000 or so Chinese inhabitants live in *Chinatown* and many do not speak a word of English. Everything is signposted in Chinese. For as little as the price of a subway ticket you could get to explore Asia. When eating out in Chinatown bear in mind that many of its restaurants do not have a *liquor license* – but you can bring along your own beer or wine for a nominal corkage fee of around $3.

The Italian immigrants who settled in *Little Italy* at the beginning of the 20th century are having a hard time of it today.

ergetic and its galleries, quaint designer shops and unconventional bars all draw in the visitor.

■1■ CHRISTOPHER STREET
(134 B–C5) (🕮 B–C 12)

In the heart of Greenwich Village lies the hub of New York's gay community. Christopher Street was the scene of the gay rights movement and in the area around Christopher and Gay Street are all the pubs, bars, bookstores and restaurants that draw New York's homosexual community. *Subway: Christopher St, 1*

■2■ FIFTH AVENUE ★
(135 D5–144 C1) (🕮 D–K 12–1)

It is here where all of New York's large parades take place (e.g. the Thanksgiving Parade and the Saint Patrick's Day Parade). It is also where New York showcases its crème de la crème of glamorous boutiques and department stores (e.g. Tiffany and Bergdorf Goodman), superb museums (e.g. Metropolitan Museum and Guggenheim Museum) and architectural innovations (e.g. the Rockefeller Center and the Empire State Building). You will soon notice that Fifth Avenue, which begins in the south on Washington Square, serves as an important orientation point in this concrete jungle. It halves Manhattan's numbered streets into West (W) and East (E).

■3■ OLD MERCHANT'S HOUSE
(135 D6) (🕮 D 13)

The house of an affluent ironmonger dating back to 1832 is the city's only one from the 19th century whose interior has survived. *Thu–Mon noon–5pm | 29 E 4th St | between Lafayette St and Bowery | entrance fee $10 | www.merchantshouse. com | subway: Astor Place, 6*

■4■ RUBIN MUSEUM OF ART ●
(134 C3) (🕮 D11)

This small jewel of a museum displays the Buddhist art, mainly from the Himalayas, which New Yorkers Shelley and Donald

Fifth Avenue – synonymous with Manhattan's best addresses

One Fifth Avenue

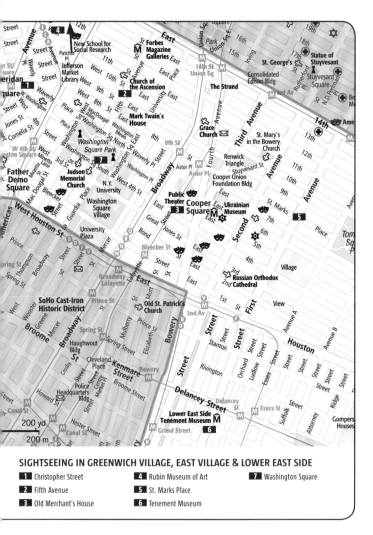

SIGHTSEEING IN GREENWICH VILLAGE, EAST VILLAGE & LOWER EAST SIDE

1 Christopher Street
2 Fifth Avenue
3 Old Merchant's House
4 Rubin Museum of Art
5 St. Marks Place
6 Tenement Museum
7 Washington Square

Rubin have been collecting for three decades – mandalas, meditation material and exhibits by contemporary Asian artists. Round off your visit with a visit to the trendy bar. *Mon, Tue 11am–5pm, Wed 11am–7pm, Fri 11am–10pm, Sat, Sun 11am–6pm | 150 W 17th St | between Sixth Ave* *and Seventh Ave | entrance fee $10 | www. rmanyc.org | subway: 14th St, F, L, M*

5 ST. MARKS PLACE
(135 E–F6) *(Ø E13)*

Saint Marks Place is the section of 8th Street where Polish and Ukrainian immi-

Washington Square with its triumphant arch – the perfect spot to take time out

grants have been settling for decades. Plenty of second-hand clothing and cheeky T-shirt shops can be found here alongside authentic eastern European restaurants and cafés. Try *Ukrainian (140 Second Ave, E)* or the 24-hour night owl favourite *Veselka (144 Second Ave, E. Subway: Second Ave, F)*

6 INSIDER TIP TENEMENT MUSEUM
(131 E2) (*Ш E15*)

A guided tour gives you a feel for the way of life of poor, immigrant New Yorkers in the 19th century. *Daily 10am–5pm | 90 Orchard St | entrance fee $20 | bookings essential tel. 1212 4 31 02 33 | www.tene ment.org | subway: Delancey St, F*

7 WASHINGTON SQUARE
(134–135 C–D5) (*Ш D 13*)

The landmark Washington Arch forms the focal point of this square that was built to commemorate the centennial of the inauguration of the first American president George Washington. The ground

had previously been used as a public burial ground and for public hangings. No hint of these remains today as street musicians, children, joggers and students from New York University all vie for a spot in the sun on the lawns. *Subway: W 4 St, A–F, M*

MIDTOWN

A pedestrian rush best describes the daily activity in Midtown's high-rise jungle. The splendours of the art deco Chrysler Building and the renovated Grand Central Station go by unnoticed as workers throng to and from their offices.

Take time out to admire the magnificent skyscrapers, the stylish luxury apartment blocks and impressive museums and watch the parade of life that is New York go by in the knowledge that you need not be anywhere in a hurry. At nightfall take in a musical, jazz concert or the opera in the Theater District or the Lincoln Center.

1 AMERICAN FOLK ART MUSEUM
(139 E4–5) (*𝄞 F7*)

An interesting collection of folk art and crafts are on display in this award-winning cultural building. Among them the saddlecloths used by American Indian chiefs and intricate cotton quilts made by the early settlers and much more. *Tue–Thu, Sat, Sun 10.30am–5.30pm, Fri 10.30am–7.30pm | 45 W 53rd St | between Fifth Ave and Sixth Ave | entrance free of charge Fri from 5.30pm otherwise $12 entrance fee | www.folkartmuseum.org | subway: Rockefeller Center, B, D, F, M*

2 CHRYSLER BUILDING
(136 A1) (*𝄞 G9*)

An all time favourite skyscraper among New Yorkers themselves, this magnificent art deco building dates back to 1930. Even though the rooftop area is off limits, a visit to its lobby with its marble floors, murals and 18 lifts – with doors manufactured from a variety of woods – is well worth it. Built by architect William van Alen for the Chrysler motor vehicle group, its elegant and distinctive exterior was a play on the chrome-laden features of the Chrysler cars like the radiator grill and bonnet or hood. *405 Lexington Ave | between 42nd and 43rd St | subway: Grand Central, 4–7, S*

3 EMPIRE STATE BUILDING ★ ⋇
(135 E2) (*𝄞 E9*)

102 floors high and built of concrete, limestone and granite with a steel frame, the Empire State Building stands 1454 ft tall (to the end of its lightning conductor) and is one of the city's key landmarks. At night it is floodlit – on the fourth of July in red, white and blue to mark Independence Day. Take a closer look at the beautiful marble and bronze inlays in the lobby on your way to the *Ticket Office (entrance in 34th St)*. The view from the *observatory*

on the 86th floor reached by high-speed lifts will make for an absolutely memorable experience. If the sky is clear you can see for miles. Come prepared for lengthy delays because of security checks! 😊 The building has been converted to fulfil stringent ecological criteria which resulted in

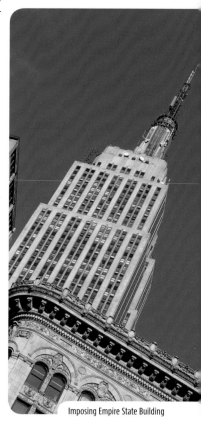

Imposing Empire State Building

a 40 per cent energy saving. *Daily 365 days a year 8am–2am | 350 Fifth Ave/34th St | entrance fee $20 or buy the $42 combo ticket that includes the NY Skyride simulator | www.esbnyc.com | subway: 34 St–Herald Square, B, D, F, M, N, Q, R*

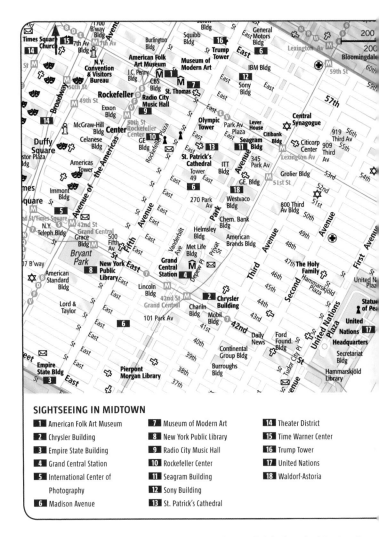

SIGHTSEEING IN MIDTOWN

4 GRAND CENTRAL STATION
(136 A1) (ω F9)

Some 88 million cubic feet of soil had to be excavated, 25 km (15 mi) of railway tracks repositioned and around 18,000 tons of steel processed to build this massive train station in 1913. More than 150,000 people attended the launch of the Grand Central Terminal as it is officially called nearly a century ago. Today the terminal only serves commuter trains from the suburbs. Its cavernous main concourse area is bigger than the nave of the Notre Dame cathedral in Paris, its façade em-

bellished with Beaux Arts. Above the up to 25 m (82 ft) high windows is a ceiling painted with 2500 stars. Gracing its gallery level are a number of restaurants and bars and like *Michael Jordan's Steakhouse* and *Harry Cipriani* – which offer 🔅 great views of the station – and there is also the impressive Food Court in the basement.

Aside from the free INSIDERTIP Municipal Art Society's tour of Grand Central *(Tue 12.30pm | meet at the information point E 42nd St, between Vanderbilt Ave and Lexington Ave | recommended donation $10 | tel. 1212 9 35 39 60 | www.mas.org)* there is also the free 90 minute INSIDERTIP Tour of Grand Central and the Surrounding Neighbourhood *(Fri 12.30pm | meet at Altria in the sculpture court of the Whitney Museum, E 42nd St, Ecke Park Ave | tel. 1212 8 83 24 20 | www.grandcentralpartner ship.org)*. Subway: Grand Central, 4–7, S

5 INTERNATIONAL CENTER OF PHOTOGRAPHY (139 D6) (*Ø F8*)

This relatively new art form is brought under the spotlight here with exhibitions by both celebrated and up-and-coming photographers. It is a museum and a photography school and aside from its changing exhibitions the museum houses more than 100,000 photographs. An adjoining bookstore sells a wide selection of books on photography. *Tue–Thu, Sat, Sun 10am–6pm, Fri 10am–8pm | 1133 Avenue of the Americas (43rd St) | entrance fee $12 | www.icp.org | subway: 42 St, B, D, F, M*

6 MADISON AVENUE

(135 E3–145 D1) (*Ø E–K 1–11*)
Madison Avenue is the name that is still identified with the advertising industry that had its start here in the 1920s although today many leading US agencies have long since moved from here. The award winning television series *Mad Men* brought its golden era in the 1960s to our screens. Madison Avenue between 44th St and 86th St is also the domain of Europe's top haute couture designers and the United States' best fashion houses.

Cavernous main concourse at Grand Central Station

■7 MUSEUM OF MODERN ART ★
(140 A4–5) (*QQ G7*)

After having been redesigned by architect Yoshio Taniguchi, Manhattan's bastion of art now covers an area of 650,000 ft². The foyer alone stretches across an entire block from 53rd Street to 54th Street. It has a view across the sculpture garden that is now the size that noted architect Philip Johnson had originally intended for it in 1953. Many regard the museum as the worlds best because it gives the visitor a conclusive overview of 20th century art thanks to masterpieces such as Henri Matisse's *Dance*, Vincent Van Gogh's *Starry Night*, Frida Kahlo's *Self-Portrait with Cropped Hair* and Pablo Picasso's *Les Demoiselles d'Avignon*.

The museum owns 100,000 works among them 3500 paintings and sculptures, 2200 design objects, 40,000 prints, 20,000 photographs and 9000 big screen films. It offers an excellent cross section of the art epochs: cubism, expressionism, Futurism, post-Impressionism, constructivism and surrealism. Big names like Monet, Mondrian, Kandinsky, Klee and Miró are also on display as well as outstanding contemporary exhibitions. *The Modern (www.themodern nyc.com)* housed in the museum is a restaurant with an excellent reputation although somewhat pricey. *Sat–Mon, Wed, Thu 10.30am–5.30pm, Fri 10.30am–6pm | 11 W 53 St | between Fifth Ave and Sixth Av | ● entrance free Fri 4pm–8pm otherwise $20 entrance fee | www.moma.org | subway: 47–50 St, B, D, F, M*

■8 NEW YORK PUBLIC LIBRARY
(139 E6) (*QQ F9*)

Two impressive landmark stone lions flank the entrance to this 1911 Beaux Arts building on Fifth Avenue. Its neoclassical marble façade, wood panelled reading room (with computers and internet access) and exhibitions are most impressive. It is an important research and reference library and houses some national treasures including a handwritten annotated version of the Declaration of Independence, a Gutenberg bible and manuscripts by Galileo Galilei. *Mon, Thu, Fri, Sat 10am–6pm, Tue, Wed 10am–8pm, Sun 1pm–5pm, guided tours Tue–Sat 11am and 2pm, Sun 2pm | Fifth Ave | be-*

GOSPEL SERVICES

● Joyful, powerful and energised: the singing that takes place in New York's gospel churches on Sunday mornings is something special. Take in a gospel service and be swept up in the marvellous experience of one of these 'live concerts'. Listening to the gospel turned into music is free of charge – although the parishes always welcome a donation. Organised tours will take you to some of the bigger churches but you can quite happily turn up at any of these impressive services your own.

The communities are exceptionally welcoming and you can of course join in the singing. In Harlem the service that stands out is that of the *Abyssinian Baptist Church (Sun 9am and 11am | 132 Odell Clark Place (W 138 St) | tel. 1212 8 62 74 74 | www.abyssinian.org | subway 135th St, 2, 3)*. In Brooklyn there is the *Brooklyn Tabernacle (Sun 9am and noon | 17 Smith St (Fulton St) | tel. 1718 2 90 20 00 | www.brooklyn tabernacle.org | subway: Jay St-Borough Hall, A, C, F)*.

80 years of entertainment – Manhattan's Radio City Music Hall

tween 40th St and 42nd St | www.nypl.org | subway: 42nd St, B, D, F, M

9 RADIO CITY MUSIC HALL
(139 E5) (ω F7)

Art deco is what defines the character of this concert hall in the Rockefeller Center. When it first opened its doors in 1932 it was the worlds biggest, seating an audience of 6000. Aside from the rock concerts that take place here today, its massive movie screen draws in the crowds as do the special shows put on by its own dance team, the Rockettes, during Easter and Christmas. *Viewing daily 11am–3pm | 1260 | Avenue of the Americas | between 50th St and 51st St | entrance fee $22.50 | tickets tel. 1 800 7 45 30 00 | www.radiocity.com | subway: 47–50 St, B, D, F, M*

10 ROCKEFELLER CENTER ★ ●
(139 E5) (ω F7)

In the 1930s oil tycoon John D. Rockefeller Jr had 228 houses torn down in New York to build a city within a city. Forming part of the complex are 14 skyscrapers – among them the 70 storey high *General Electric (GE) Building* – squares, gardens, the *Radio City Music Hall, Christie's* auction house and broadcaster *NBC*. The *Top of the Rock* ☼ viewing platform on the 70th floor offers spectacular views across midtown Manhattan and Central Park *(entrance fee $22 | www.topoftherocknyc.com)*.

At the heart of the complex lies the world-famous ice rink that doubles up as a café on the square in the summer. In December this is where New York's iconic 20 m (50 ft) illuminated Christmas tree stands tall. Check the internet *at the end of November* for the grand lighting of the tree. If you are interested in old plans, models and photos then head to the *Rockefeller Center Museum* in the basement. Maps to tour the whole Rockefeller Center are available in the lobby. *30 Rockefeller Plaza | between 49th and 50th St | www.rockefellercenter.com | subway: 47–50 St, B, D, F, M*

Saint Patrick's Cathedral – a quiet oasis amid the hustle and bustle of Fifth Avenue

🔟 SEAGRAM BUILDING
(140 A–B5) *(📖 G8)*

The black metal building with bronze-coloured windows dating back to 1958 is New York's only building by architect Mies van der Rohe and is exemplary of the US dominated International style of corporate modernism. It is also home to the renowned *Four Seasons (www.fourseasons restaurant.com) restaurant 375 Park Ave | between 52nd and 53rd St | subway: 51st St, 6*

1️⃣2️⃣ SONY BUILDING
(140 A4) *(📖 G7)*

Built by the influential New York architect Philip Johnson, this building clad in pink granite once housed the AT&T exchange. Today it belongs to the Sony Group. Thanks to a semi-circular incision in its pediment the post-modern skyscraper has landed itself the nickname 'Chippendale' after

the English furniture design style used for bookcases and cabinets.

The lobby is a haven for electronics buffs with the latest technical innovations on display at ● *Sony Style.* The *Sony Wonder Technology Lab* has four floors of interactive displays that tell the history of technical communications. *Tue–Sat 9.30am–5.30pm | 560 Madison Ave | between 55th St and 56th St | entrance free of charge | wondertechlab.sony.com | subway: Fifth Ave, N, R*

1️⃣3️⃣ ST. PATRICK'S CATHEDRAL
(139 F5) *(📖 G8)*

The neo-Gothic cathedral built from stone and marble was dedicated to the Irish saint in 1879 and is the seat of New York's Catholic archdiocese. It is the world's eleventh largest church with room for 2500 people. A tranquil spot to seek solace from the hustle and bustle of Fifth Avenue

at any time of day! *Fifth Ave/50th St | subway: 47th–50th St, B, D, F, M*

🔳 THEATER DISTRICT
(139 D–E5) (𝄞 E7)

During the day, the area north of Times Square draws visitors with attractions like *Disney Store, 42nd St/Seventh Ave* and at night the flashing neon lights form the world-famous backdrop for theatregoers making their way to a show. Restaurant Row in 46th Street (between Eighth and Ninth Avenue) is where everyone heads to for a meal afterwards. On 31 December every year Times Square becomes the site for New Yorkers and visitors alike to see in the New Year. *Subway: 42nd St/Times Square, N, R, S, 1–3, 7, Q*

🔳 TIME WARNER CENTER
(139 D–E3) (𝄞 F6)

Construction work on the 229 m (751 ft) high twin towers of the Time Warner Center began with in 2000 and was completed in 2003. The Time Warner Group has its headquarters in this 2.8 million sq ft luxury city within a city by architects Mustafa Abadan and David Childs. The building includes the *Hotel Mandarin Oriental*, exclusive apartments, a penthouse worth $45 million, high-end stores, broadcasts of the Lincoln Center's jazz concerts and *Per Se (p. 64)*, the most sought after restaurant in the city. *10 Columbus Circle | subway: 59th St–Columbus Circle, A–D, 1*

🔳 TRUMP TOWER
(140 A4) (𝄞 G7)

Built by the scandal-plagued billionaire property developer Donald Trump in 1983, this 200 m (663 ft) tall building has 68 floors and is renowned for its bold foyer. Five floors lined with unique orange marble, bronze ornaments, gold escalators, mirrors and an illuminated waterfall and a bridge. The five floors of the foyer make up a vertical shopping area and the boutiques and speciality shops are all very exclusive and expensive. *725 Fifth Ave | between 56th and 57th St | subway: Fifth Ave, N, R*

United Nations Headquarters on the East River

🔳 UNITED NATIONS
(136 B–C1) (𝄞 H9)

Built between 1949 and 1953 and made up of a complex of four skyscrapers this is the United Nations headquarters as well as the seat of several of its organisations such as Unesco and Unicef. Join a guided tour of the art, photographic and

multimedia exhibitions from around the world in the foyer and the imposing hall where the General Assembly meets once a year. There is also a bookshop, coffee shop and gift store. *Tours Mon–Fri 9.45am–4.45pm | United Nations Plaza, First Ave (46th St) | entrance fee $16 | www.un.org/tours | subway: 51st St, 6*

🔟 WALDORF-ASTORIA
(139 F5) *(🕮 G8)*
This luxury hotel built in the art deco style of the 1930s stretches across an entire block. The well-to-do guests of yester-year staying in its 1380 rooms had a very unusual special service made available to them: the hotel had its own platform as part of Grand Central Terminal. Traces of the hotel's splendour of yore only really remain in its opulent ballrooms. *301 Park Ave | between 49th and 50th St | www.waldorfastoria.com | subway: 51st St, 6*

UPTOWN & CENTRAL PARK

Uptown is for the affluent, elegant and well-educated in New York – it is for those who have succeeded in life.

This is probably an oversimplification and increasingly no longer valid because of the number of successful people who are now moving south. Usually into one of the expansive trendy lofts that are all the rage in TriBeCa. Nevertheless you will find that the Upper East and Upper West Side with their impressive architecture, large museums and sense of affluence still makes for an exciting outing. Here it is a common sight to see the *nanny* taking the baby for a stroll while Mum and Dad

If buildings could tell a story – the historic Hotel Waldorf Astoria

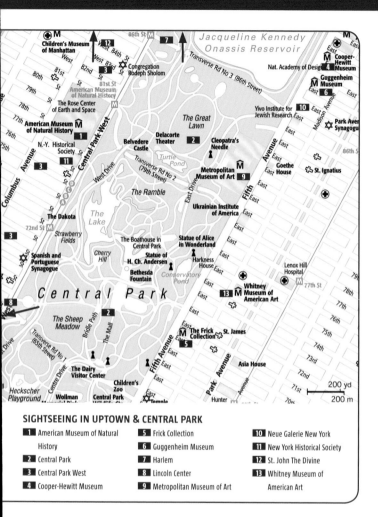

SIGHTSEEING IN UPTOWN & CENTRAL PARK

1 American Museum of Natural History

2 Central Park

3 Central Park West

4 Cooper-Hewitt Museum

5 Frick Collection

6 Guggenheim Museum

7 Harlem

8 Lincoln Center

9 Metropolitan Museum of Art

10 Neue Galerie New York

11 New York Historical Society

12 St. John The Divine

13 Whitney Museum of American Art

dedicate their days to pursuing a career somewhere in the city.

The area between the Hudson and Central Park is called *Upper West Side*. Young people and families for whom money is no object are the residents of this district. Columbus Avenue has one exclusive boutique up next to another, while Amsterdam Avenue is a lively restaurant mile. On Broadway you will come across gourmet shops like *Zabar's*. The Museum of Natural History and the Lincoln Center housing the Metropolitan Opera are the cultural havens here. *Upper East Side* is traditionally even more well to do than its western counterpart. The district between Central Park and East River has to a large extent been upmarket in character since the

end of the 19th century. The renowned Metropolitan Museum and the Guggenheim Museum are located here, as are expensive boutiques and several high-end hotels.

◾1 AMERICAN MUSEUM OF NATURAL HISTORY ★ (142 C6) (*ω G 3*)

Located alongside Central Park it houses 36 million objects among them a 30 m (98 ft) long blue whale skeleton, the biggest sapphire (563 carat), the largest meteorite and the most comprehensive collection of dinosaur skeletons (fourth floor). The third floor will give you an insight into the way the original inhabitants of the American continent lived. The *Hall of Biodiversity* covers the topic of how different organisms came into being, while *Habitats of the World* introduces the visitor to new ecosystems. The first two floors are devoted to different cultures and the Imax cinema – New York's biggest big screen.

An absolute must is the computerised lightning-speed space flight through our vast universe in the *Rose Center for Earth and Space.* The *Journey to the Stars* takes you through the Milky Way with commentary by film star Whoopi Goldberg. In the *Big Bang Theater* you will be able to observe the dawn of the universe through the glass floor and the *Hayden Planetarium* regularly screens films about space. *Daily 10am–5.45pm | Central Park West/79th St | admission with a voluntary donation of $16, $24 for a combination ticket to include special exhibition or IMAX film | www.amnh.org | subway: 81st St, B, C*

◾2 CENTRAL PARK ★ ●
(139 E3–144 B2) (*ω F–K 6–1*)

After a planning phase that lasted two decades under Frederick Law Olmsted, the park was finally completed in 1873. Almost twice the size of the principality

of Monaco, it stretches 843 acres from 59th Street to 110th Street. New Yorkers take full advantage of it from sunrise to sunset. They jog around the reservoir and row on the lake *(from $12 with $20 in cash as a security deposit)*, hire bicycles *(The Boathouse | in the vicinity of E 72nd St | prices $9–15/hour, credit card or passport as deposit)*, go inline skating *(Wollman Rink | in the east of the park between 62nd and 63rd St | price $15/day, $100 security deposit)* go ice-skating in *Wollman Rink* in winter *(entrance fee $10–15, skate hire $6.25)*, take a walk in *Central Park Zoo* or meet for coffee at the *Boathouse Café*. In summer the park stages a whole variety of concerts – anything from classical music to rock. They are free of charge but you must still get yourself a ticket: *Shakespeare in the Park (tel. 1 212 5 39 87 50 | www. publictheater.org).* 🍴 Dinner al fresco at

Park View at the Boathouse can be very romantic *(Loeb Boathouse | April–Oct | tel. 1212 5 17 22 33 | Moderate). www.central park.com | subway: 59th St–Columbus Circle, 1, A–D, 72nd St, B, C and buses*

■ CENTRAL PARK WEST
(139 E3–143 E2) *(ⁿ F–J 5–1)*

In 1884 enterprising developers had to come up with a way to lure tenants from Fifth Avenue to their vacant properties in the unfashionable area west of the park. They decorated the interiors and came up with the innovative concept that instead of living in a home with servants the rich would rent fully serviced flats instead.

One of the most notable of these was the *Dakota* on the north side of 72nd Street – the building where Beatles singer and guitarist John Lennon was shot dead by a deranged fan in 1980. Similar properties were the *Beresford (81st St)*, the *San Remo (74th/75th St)* and the *Hotel Des Artistes (1 W 67th St)*. *Subway: 72nd St, B, C*

■ COOPER-HEWITT MUSEUM
(144 A–B5) *(ⁿ J3)*

Today this 64-room town house built by industrialist Andrew Carnegie in 1901 houses New York's National Design Museum with an impressive collection of textiles, furniture, glass, ceramics and metal ornaments. INSIDER TIP DJs appear here in the summer – both amateurs and stars of New York's nightlife *(July, Aug Fri 6pm–9pm | tel. 1 212 8 49 83 49)*. Only parts of the collection can be seen at a time and there are also temporary exhibitions. *Mon–Fri 10am–5pm, Sat 10am–6pm, Sun 11am–6pm | 2 E 91st St(Fifth Ave) | entrance fee $15 | www.cooperhewitt.org | subway: 86th St, 4–6*

Mirroring the metropolis that is New York – Central Park's idyllic lake

Architectural landmark – the world-famous Guggenheim Museum with its internal spiral

5 FRICK COLLECTION
(140 B2) (𝕸 H5)

Industrialist Henry Clay Frick's small collection of art housed in his Beaux Arts palace will give you an insight into the obsession that rich Americans have with art. On display are paintings by Rembrandt, Holbein, Vermeer, Fragonard and Renoir as well as furniture from the epochs of Louis XV and XVI. The building that became a museum in 1935, with its tranquil garden, is well worth a visit. More on its changing exhibitions and classical concerts *(Sun 5pm)* can be found on their homepage. *Tue–Sat 10am–6pm, Sun 11am–5pm | 1 E 70th St (Fifth Ave) | entrance fee $18 including audio tour, Sun 11am–1pm admission with a voluntary donation | www.frick.org | subway: 68th St, 6*

6 GUGGENHEIM MUSEUM ⭐
(144 A5–6) (𝕸 J3)

The Guggenheim's extraordinary building by famous architect Lloyd Wright – at times described as a giant white cement tea cup by its critics – is one of New York's iconic buildings. Temporary exhibitions of modern art are on display along its 400 m (1300 ft) upward spiralling ramp that goes up four floors from street level. Exhibits include big names like Mondrian, Brancusi and Matthew Barney. A permanent exhibition is devoted to the collection of American copper magnate Solomon Guggenheim with works by van Gogh, Monet, Degas and Picasso as the main attractions. The museum shop sells a beautiful selection of art books. *Sun–Wed 10am–5.45pm, Fri 10am–5.45pm, Sat 10am–7.45pm | 1071 Fifth Ave | between 88th St and 89th St | entrance fee $18, Sat 5.45–7.45pm admission with a voluntary donation | www.guggenheim.org | subway: 86th St, 4–6*

7 HARLEM (144–145 C–E 1–2) (𝕸 0)

Nieuw Haarlem was founded by Dutch settlers in 1658. When slaves later built a road to New York – Broadway – many of

them stayed on. In the 1920s and 1930s Harlem became the nucleus for black artists and musicians and it became chic to listen to jazz musicians like Duke Ellington and Count Basie at the *Sugar Cane* or *Cotton Club (today the Cotton Club is dedicated to Gospel Brunch on a Sat and Sun | 656 W 125th St | tel. 1212 6 63 79 80 | www.cottonclub-newyork.com)*. Harlem is now a perfectly safe area and the small shops on 125th Street are a browser's paradise. You may even bump into former president Bill Clinton who has his offices there. For a tour of the district with its unique wood-frame houses contact *Harlem Spirituals (tel. 1212 3 91 09 00)* or *Harlem Your Way! (tel. 1212 6 90 16 87)*. *Subway 125th St, 2, 3, A–D*

⑧ LINCOLN CENTER ⭐
(139 D–E2) (*𝄞 E–F 5*)
New York's cultural hub is huge with its seven concert halls and theatres stretching across eight blocks and seating an audience of 15,000 at one time. The focal point is the plaza where open air performances are staged in the summer. The theatre foyers are open to the public and you will be able to admire a magnificent tapestry by Marc Chagall in the foyer of the *Metropolitan Opera House (backstage tours Oct–June, Mon–Fri 3.30pm, Sun 10.30am and 1.30pm | entrance fee $16 | tel. 1212 7 69 70 20)*. Jazz at Lincoln Center (JALC)'s *Frederick P. Rose Hall*, is now housed south of the main Lincoln Center inside the Time Warner Center. (*Broadway/ 60th St* (143 E3) (*𝄞 F 6) | www.jalc.org). Between W 62nd St and 65th St and Columbus Ave and Amsterdam Ave | www. lincolncenter.org | subway: 66th St, 1*

⑨ METROPOLITAN MUSEUM OF ART
● (143 E6) (*𝄞 H–J 3–4*)
Founded in 1870 the Met's imposing grey sandstone façade was designed by Richard

Morris Hunt in 1902. The huge flight of stairs leading up to its entrance is one of the city's most popular spots. There is little to see of the original structure as the museum has had numerous additions and its extensions have encroached into Central Park. Only a quarter of its 3.2 million items can be exhibited in its two million sq ft in floor space and the space problem is further exacerbated by the display of temporary exhibitions.

Devote at least two two-hour sessions to the permanent exhibitions. On your first visit head straight to the Egyptian wing (ground floor to the right) which has the original Temple of Dendur. The structure was going to be submerged by the floodwaters of the Aswan Dam but was rescued and completely rebuilt here. Then go on to the Charles Engelhard Court in the *American Wing* with its glassed in atrium featuring leaded glass windows, lamps and metalwork by the acclaimed American artist Louis Comfort Tiffany. There are also 20 period rooms chronicling the history of American decorative arts. Among them is the Frank Lloyd Wright Room, a living room designed and decorated by the famous architect as well as the grand ballroom where George Washington attended his last birthday in 1799 that was moved from Virginia and rebuilt here.

On your second visit take in the ethnic art collection in the *Michael C. Rockefeller Wing* and the contemporary American sculptures in the *Sculpture Garden* on the roof. The ⚘ garden is open between April and October and should not be missed – not only for its artwork but for its stunning views of Central Park and the Midtown Manhattan skyline INSIDER TIP During summer the bar is open until sunset on Fridays.

The museum is also home to Roman, Greek, European, Middle Eastern and Islamic paintings and art. Sections are

also devoted to musical instruments, weapons, sketches, prints, photos and fashion – 40,000 garments from five centuries and all the continents. On a Friday and Saturday from September to May visitors are treated to `INSIDER TIP` chamber music and drinks in the gallery from 5pm. *Tue–Thu, Sun 9.30am–5.30pm, Fri, Sat 9.30am–9pm | Fifth Ave/82nd St | entrance fee of $20) | www.metmuseum. org | subway: 86 St, 4–6*

🔟 NEUE GALERIE NEW YORK
(144 A6) (*m J3*)

Meaning 'New Gallery' it houses works by German and Austrian artists such as Gustav Klimt and Egon Schiele as well as by designers of the Bauhaus school whose works all had an important impact on modern American architecture and design. The Viennese-style coffee shop *Café Sabarsky* adjoining it serves breakfast, lunch and light snacks throughout the day as well as the occasional *cabaret dinner*. *Sat–Mon, Thu, Fri 11am–6pm | 1048 Fifth Ave (86th St) | entrance fee $15 | www.neuegalerie.org | subway: 86th St, 4–6*

1️⃣1️⃣ NEW YORK HISTORICAL SOCIETY
(142 C6) (*m G4*)

Dating back to 1804 this is the city's oldest museum. Among the displays are some 500,000 photos from 1850 to the present day, a multitude of everyday items, newspapers, letters and an impressive collection of glass lamps by Louis Comfort Tiffany. *Tue–Thu and Sat 10am–6pm, Fri 10am–8pm, Sun 11am–5.45pm | 170 Central Park West | entrance fee $12 | www.nyhistory.org | subway: 81st St, B, C*

KEEP FIT!

Even though you find yourself in the concrete jungle you can still keep fit – just remember to pack your trainers! Jogging around the reservoir running track in Central Park or through Prospect Park in Brooklyn is an experience in itself. There is also the new Hudson River Park located on Manhattan's West Side where you can either jog, cycle or rollerblade along the waterfront all the way from the southernmost point to far north of the island. Other fitness opportunities along this route include a trapeze school, kayaking, tennis, rock climbing and bowling. If golf is your thing then why not practise your swing at the massive sports complex, the ● *Chelsea Piers* *(Opening times vary | day pass $50 | (134 B2) (m B 9) www.chelseapiers. com)* (in line with 23rd Street) where there is a huge choice of keep fit options available. In summer you can swim for free in the municipal pools in Brooklyn, Queens and Manhattan *(www.nycgovparks.org/facilities/pools)* and in winter you can go ice skating in Central and Bryant Parks and at the Rockefeller Center. Many of the parks offer free t'ai chi and yoga courses in summer *(www.bbpc.net | www. bryantpark.org)*. One of the most unusual ways to keep fit is to dance in rollerblades to disco music in Central Park. The group meets on weekends (in line with 72nd St) – just follow the music!

12 ST. JOHN THE DIVINE
(143 E1) *(Ⓜ 0)*

As is the case with many of New York's buildings Saint John the Divine, one of the world's largest cathedrals, is a blend of various architectural styles. It started off in 1892 in a Byzantine and Roman style only to be continued in a neo-Gothic style in 1911. The project is expected to be completed sometime in this century. In the evenings the church hosts poetry readings and concerts and at the end of October one of New York's most INSIDER TIP offbeat Halloween celebrations *(7pm and 10pm | entrance fee $8–15)*. Animal lovers can witness the blessing of animals on the first Sunday in October. Some 5000 people and their pets arrive for the service and on occasion the zoo may even send along a camel! *Tours Tue–Sat 11am and 1pm, Sun 2pm | Amsterdam Ave/112th St | entrance fee $10 | tickets tel. 1 212 6 62 21 33 | www.stjohndivine.org | subway: 110th St, 1*

13 WHITNEY MUSEUM OF
AMERICAN ART (140 C2) *(Ⓜ H5)*

This minimalist granite block-like structure was designed by Bauhaus disciple Marcel Breuer in the 1960s. You will need a few hours to go through all the exhibits on its four floors. The focus is on 20th and 21st century American art and it includes excellent works by Georgia O'Keefe, Edward Hopper, Roy Lichtenstein, Andy Warhol and Jasper John as well as the occasional Alexander Calder exhibit. Every two years during May it hosts the INSIDER TIP *Whitney Biennale of American Art* which showcases lesser-known contemporary artists.

A good selection of art books and exhibition catalogues and gifts are sold in the museum shop. *Wed, Thu, Sat, Sun 11am–6pm, Fri 1pm–9pm | 945 Madison Ave (75th St) | entrance fee $18, Fri 6pm–9pm*

Nestled below the skyscrapers –
Saint John the Divine

admission with a voluntary donation | www.whitney.org | subway: 77 St, 6

OTHER DISTRICTS

BROOKLYN HEIGHTS ☼
(131 D–E6) *(Ⓜ D18)*

In Brooklyn's most beautiful residential area you feel like you have stepped back into the 19th century. Located on the other end of the Brooklyn Bridge it is

characterised by well preserved *brown-stone* tenement building made of sandstone. Some of the buildings are listed. Follow Pierrepoint Street through to the Brooklyn Heights promenade which is an excellent spot for some wonderful views of Manhattan. *Subway: Clark St, 2, 3*

CARROLL GARDENS (146 C4) (*∅ 0*)

Young families, hip couples and singles with a healthy cash flow are the kind of residents who have moved into the *brownstones* in Carroll Gardens and Park Slope *over* the past few years. American novelists like Jonathan Lethem have written about this old Italian neighbourhood which was previously popular with African-Americans and Puerto Rican families. Today this once seedy part of Brooklyn is a sought after area with charming restaurants, delightful designer boutiques and small cafés which are all well worth a visit. *Subway: Carroll St, F, G*

CONEY ISLAND (146–147 C–D5) (*∅ 0*)

The price of a subway ticket will get you to this beach known for its amusement park, boardwalk and listed Ferris (which has are great views from the top). Coney Island is supposedly the birthplace of the *hot dog*. Up to half-a-million people head here on weekends. Directly next to it is the *New York Aquarium (p. 112)* with its shark enclosures. *Surf Ave Brooklyn | subway: Coney Island, Brighton Beach, D, F, Q, N*

GREENPOINT (147 D3) (*∅ K 4*)

The district north of Brooklyn's Williamsburg has been nicknamed Little Poland, although nowadays you will also find immigrants from Puerto Rico living alongside those from Eastern Europe. It is also

SPECTATOR SPORTS

New Yorkers love sports events and it doesn't matter if they watch them in the pub with a cold beer or live at a stadium. The baseball season runs from April to September so go and see the *New York Yankees (Yankee Stadium | Bronx* **(147 D1)** (*∅ 0*) *| tickets via Ticket Master: tel. 1800 745 30 00 | www.yankee.com)* or the *New York Mets (Shea Stadium | Queens* **(147 E3)** (*∅ 0*) *| tickets tel. 1718 5 07 84 99 | www.newyorkmets.com)* hit some home runs.

Basketball fans can watch the *New York Knicks (tickets via Ticket Master: tel. 1800 7 45 30 00 | www.nba.com/knicks)* in *Madison Square Garden* **(135 D1)** (*∅ D9*) from April to October.

The *Giants Stadium* **(146 B2)** (*∅ 0*) is home turf to American football's *New York Jets* and *New York Giants (Sept–Dec Meadowlands | New Jersey | www. newyorkjets.com | www.giants.com)*. While the players in their pads and helmets clash on the field you can and enjoy the razzmatazz of the cheerleaders.

Things are a little more elegant at *Flushing Meadows Park* for annual *U.S. Open Tennis Championships (Aug/ Sept tickets: tel. 1718 7 60 62 00 | www. usopen.org)* **(147 E3)** (*∅ 0*) while *Belmont Park* is New York's horse racing hot spot. June is when the prestigious Belmont Stakes is held so remember to place your bets *(second Saturday in June | Belmont Stakes | Belmont Park Race Track | Long Island* **(147 F3)** (*∅ 0*) *| www.nyra.com)*.

Life is a beach – summer fun on Coney Island

attracting young couples, artists and students escaping Williamsburg's rising rentals. This new mix of people has created quite a vibe. The catchy sounds of salsa, the inviting smells of Polish kielbasa sausages and a growing number of beer gardens with BBQs along the East River characterise the district. So many beer gardens have sprung up in Brooklyn that the New York Times has jokingly written in an article that parts of Brooklyn now feel like Bavaria. Imagine listening to a live pop or rock concert with Manhattan's iconic skyline as the backdrop. *McCarren Park (www.mccarrenpark.com)* – in what was formerly farmland – is where you can do just that.

INSIDER TIP **DUMBO** ☆
(131 E–F6) *(₥ E18)*
The acronym stands for *D*own *U*nder the *M*anhattan *B*ridge *O*verpass. It is an area

that has undergone dramatic change. Factories have been converted into apartments with idyllic views of Manhattan and it has the *Brooklyn Bridge Park* on the East River which is New York's longest waterfront park. There are theatres, galleries and an outdoor cinema *(www.dumboartscenter.org)* and hip bars like *Superfine (126 Front St | tel. 1 718 2 43 90 05 | subway: York St, F)* where on Sundays you can enjoy brunch to music. If you are in the mood for an ice cream then look no further than the *Brooklyn Ice Cream Factory (Fulton Ferry Landing). Subway: High Street, A, C or water taxi (www.nywatertaxi.com)*

RED HOOK (146 C4) *(₥ 0)*
This district right on the water's edge is one of New York's *final frontiers*. The film classic *On the Waterfront* – for which Marlon Brando received an Oscar in

(391 Van Brunt St | tel. 1 718 6 43 66 36 | www.goodfork.com | *Budget–Moderate*).
Subway: Jay St, A, C, F, G then Bus B61 to the terminal

WILLIAMSBURG
(133 D–F 3–4) (*ⵏⵏ H–L 16–17*)
This Brooklyn neighbourhood has seen its third incarnation. Once upon a time it was the domain of the prestigious Whitney und Vanderbilt entrepreneurial families, it then became an industrial area and today it is inhabited by hip artists and intellectuals as well as being home a 30,000-strong Jewish community.

The Metropolitan Avenue and Grand Street areas are home to an array of eclectic restaurants and galleries with quirky, off-beat names like *Momenta Art* and *Fish Tank*, as well as small book and record dealers with interesting and unusual selections. Bedford Avenue with its many small shops, cafés and galleries is where it is at. *Subway: Marcy Ave, Bedford Ave, L*

FURTHER AFIELD

BROOKLYN MUSEUM
(146 C4) (*ⵏⵏ 0*)
The United States' seventh largest art collection – comprising more than two million items – is housed in this 1897 building belonging to New York architect group McKim, Mead & White. The Egyptian (third floor) and pre-Columbian (first floor) are must-see collections. The *Period Rooms* (fourth floor) showcase more than 20 New England living and dining rooms from 1675 to 1830. The American Collection (fifth floor) offers an overview of American art. On display at the *Iris and Gerald Cantor Gallery* are 58 sculptures by Rodin and the *Sculpture Garden* behind the museum

Williamsburg – the neighbourhood for the young and hip

1955 – put this working class neighbourhood on the map. Then it was discovered by artists on the hunt for cheap rents and now property speculators are moving in and its face may change forever. In summer, weekends are the best time for outings here or come in October when the *Brooklyn Waterfront Artist Coalition (www. bwac.org)* is held in Van Brunt Street. Before heading back, indulge in some chocolate cake from *Baked (359 | Van Brunt St | tel. 1 718 2 22 03 45 | Budget)* or if hunger pangs have gotten the better of you order steak & eggs at *The Good Fork*

showcases architectural pieces and ornamentations from the 20th century.

Controversial exhibitions of contemporary art have pushed the museum into the spotlight in more recent times. Members of the public are invited to participate in a INSIDER TIP changing programme (free of charge!) every first Saturday of the month until 11pm. It may entail anything from swing dancing lessons and portrait painting, to movie screenings, world music concerts and hip hop DJ sets. *Wed 11am–6pm, Thu/Fri 11am–10pm, Sat/Sun 11am–6pm | 200 Eastern Parkway | Brooklyn | entrance fee $10 | www.brooklynmuseum.org | subway: Eastern Parkway, 2, 3*

THE CLOISTERS (147 D1) (*Ø 0*)

Displaying French and Spanish medieval architectural influences this museum complex was built between 1934 and 1938. It is located inside Fort Tryon Park and has some amazing view of the steep forested banks of the Hudson and the George Washington Bridge opposite it. The Metropolitan Museum's medieval art collection is housed here. *Tue–Sun 9.30am–4.45pm, March–Oct until 5.15pm | Fort Tryon Park | admission with a voluntary donation of $20 – it includes admission to the museum on the same day | www.metmuseum.org | subway: 190th St, A; Bus: M 4, Cloisters/Fort Tryon Park, hop on the bus in Madison Ave, between 32nd St and 110th St*

HUDSON RIVER VALLEY (0) (*Ø 0*)

A day trip north along the Hudson River is highly recommended. Hire a car and head in the direction of the Rockefeller Estate and enjoy the impressive hilly, green and forested landscape through which the river flows.

Follow Route 9 north to *Kykuit* and the imposing *Rockefeller Estate* where the 41st American Vice President, Nelson B. Rockefeller's amazing art collection awaits you *(May–Nov Wed–Mon | entrance fee $23)*. Further north in *Hyde Park*, you can take in the 54-room Renaissance mansion of renowned 19th century railroad magnate Frederick W. Vanderbilt *(9am–5pm daily | www.nps.gov/vama)* along with the stately home of ex-President Franklin D. Roosevelt which is also located in Hyde Park *(9am–5pm daily | www.nps.gov/hofr)*. From Manhattan it takes just under two hours to reach Hyde Park, which is also home to the *Culinary Institute of America.* Here the United States' talented up-and-coming chefs prepare gourmet menus in four restaurants housed in a former Jesuit seminary *(Reservations essential tel. 1 845 4 71 66 08 | www.ciachef.edu | Budget–Expensive)*. Viticulture also thrives in the Hudson Valley, its warm humid climate is ideal for excellent white wines *(Millbrock Vineyards in Millbrock: noon–5pm daily | tel. 1 845 6 77 83 83 | www.millbrookwine.com)*. To end your day, pop into the picture-perfect town of *Rhinebeck* that dates back to 1686.

P. S. 1 CONTEMPORARY ART CENTER

☼ (147 D3) (*Ø L10*)

Housed in an old school, its innovative curators have given the museum its creative, avant-garde and offbeat feel. Just before sunset take a seat in the James Turrell installation – a room with an opening cut through ceiling and the roof – and watch the play of light that unfolds before you when you look up. Another stunning view is from the roof – this time of Manhattan. On Saturday evenings in summer the courtyard is where one of INSIDER TIP New York's most popular parties is held *(2pm–9pm | entrance fee $15)*. *Thu–Mon noon–6pm | 22–25 Jackson Ave (46th Ave), Queens | entrance fee $10 | www.ps1.org | subway: 23rd St (Ely Ave), E, M*

FOOD & DRINK

New Yorkers are always on the go and rarely find the time to sit down and enjoy a meal. Many will simply grab a sandwich and they will eat it standing or on the go. For many a home cooked meal after work is not necessarily the norm.

Heating a ready meal the convenient way to get around mealtimes for many New Yorkers but by far the most popular choice is eating out. For those who want to get their fill quickly, there are the omnipresent fast-food outlets. Inexpensive Chinese restaurants and pizza stands are where to head for your takeout or food to go. Then of course there are the typical coffee shops or diners which are a uniquely American phenomenon. They will serve you a bottomless coffee (albeit not the strongest) where for the price of a cup you can have as many refills as you can drink. Some outlets of this typically American way of eating out will even offer you a full breakfast for under $5. Most coffee shops serve lunch and dinner the whole day and many are open 24/7. In contrast to this, plenty of restaurants, especially the expensive ones are closed between lunch and dinner. It is standard practice in the United States to have a maître de table to show you to your table.

A *tip* is also standard and in the United States is regarded as more than just a

Multinational cuisine – the sky is the limit in this melting pot of nations – New York will take you on a culinary journey around the world

gesture, as the tip forms part of your waiter's wage and the argument is that if left solely to the discretion of the patron it will not necessarily suffice. Generally speaking Americans tip an amount equating to double that of the sales tax which is 8.875 per cent in New York. However, in some touristy places the gratuity may be included in the final amount. If you are paying by credit card simply enter the amount in the space provided.

If not otherwise indicated, the restaurants mentioned in the travel guide are open daily for lunch and dinner. Lunchtime is usually between noon and 2pm and dinner from 7.30pm to 9pm.

INSIDER TIP Restaurant Week in New York takes place at the end of January and in summer and is a real attraction. For a very

CAFÉS

reasonable fixed price you will be able to enjoy a three-course lunch *($24.07)* or dinner *($35)* excluding tax and tip. Information on participating restaurants from *NYC Visitor Information (tel. 1212 4 84 12 22)* or at *www.nycvisit.com/restaurantweek)*.

A Voce – pasta in style

CAFÉS

AMY'S BREAD ● (134 C5) *(ᐱ C13)*

A bakery that produces wonderful breads, excellent cakes and delicious gourmet sandwiches. Sweet and savoury for breakfast or lunch – or how about a particularly decadent devil's food cupcake for dessert? *Daily | 250 Bleecker St (Leroy St) | tel. 1212 675 78 02 | www.amysbread.com | subway: W 4 St, A, B, C, D, E, F, M*

DOUGHNUT PLANT ● (135 D2) *(ᐱ D 0)*

Doughnut connoisseurs swear that this is where you will get the best *donuts* in town. The delicious and colourful doughnuts are echoed in the décor which has ring-shaped cushions adorning its walls. It is situated in the former foyer of the legendary Chelsea Hotel. *Daily | 220 W 23rd St | tel. 1212 675 9100 | www.doughnutplant. com | subway: 23rd St, 1, C, E*

EISENBERG'S (135 E3) *(ᐱ E11)*

This *sandwich shop* has been serving its soups, burgers, salads and range of hearty meals for more than 80 years. There are more than 40 different sandwiches to choose from and celebs like Cynthia Nixon, Bono and Jeff Goldblum are keen patrons. *Daily | 174 Fifth Ave corner 22nd St | www.eisenbergsnyc.com | subway: 23rd St, N, R*

CAFÉ KINSKI (131 F2) *(ᐱ E15)*

This café on the Lower East Side is a worth a visit for its traditional Austrian fare like its signature sweet *knodel* or dumpling dishes, the *kaiserschmarren* (Austrian pancakes) and their Viennese iced coffee. *Daily | 128 Rivington St | subway: Delancey St, F*

CAFÉ PICK ME UP (135 F6) *(ᐱ F13)*

The ideal spot to people watch – order a delectable pecan pie from the buffet for tea in the afternoon or a sumptuous quiche at dinnertime – and enjoy them as you watch the passing parade. *Daily 7am–11.30pm | 145th Ave A | between 9th St and 10th St | subway: First Ave, L, Astor Place, 6*

SWEET MELISSA (146 C4) *(ᐱ 0)*

This delightful garden café is worth the trip to Brooklyn. *Sun–Thu 8am–10pm, Fri, Sat 8am–midnight | 276 Court St | between Butler St and Douglass St | subway: Bergen St, F, G*

VENIERO'S (135 E6) *(𝄞 E13)*

Vibrant, loud and crowded – this café and pastry shop has a selection of delicious Italian *dolci* and has been going since 1894. *Daily 8am–midnight | 342 E 11th St | between First Ave and Second Ave | subway: First Ave, L*

RESTAURANTS: EXPENSIVE

A VOCE (135 E3) *(𝄞 E10)*

A modern interior and delectable Italian cuisine make for a winning combination on Madison Square Park. *Closed Sun | 41 Madison Ave | tel. 1 212 545 85 55 | www. avocerestaurant.com | subway: 23rd St, 6*

CASA LEVER (139 F5) *(𝄞 G7)*

In the 1960s this glass and steel design was considered the epitome of modernism. Enjoy its design while sampling some classic Italian dishes like their signature Veal Milanese. *Closed Sun | 390 Park Ave, entrance E 53rd St | tel. 1 212 888 27 00 | www.casalever.com | subway: Lexington Ave/53rd St, E*

CHURRASCARIA PLATAFORMA ★ (139 D4) *(𝄞 E7)*

Meat – and plenty of it – grilled to perfection on a skewer. Easy to get derailed by the salad bar so be sure to leave space for your sumptuous main. *Belvedere Hotel: 316 W 49th St | between Eighth Ave and Ninth Ave | tel. 1 212 245 05 05 | www. churrascariaplataforma.com | subway: 50th St, C*

ELEVEN MADISON (135 E3) *(𝄞 E11)*

Top class French cuisine on offer – a three-course set menu for $56 for dinner and half price at lunchtime. *Sat evenings only, closed Sun | 11 Madison Ave | tel. 1 212 889 09 05 | www.elevenmadisonpark.com | subway: 23rd St, R, 6*

PETER LUGER (130 B4) *(𝄞 J17)*

To this day this 120 year old steakhouse entices its guests with its charm and large portions. Credit cards not accepted. *178 Broadway | between Driggs St and Bedford St | tel. 1 718 387 74 00 | www.peterluger. com | subway: Marcy Ave, J*

★ **Churrascaria Plataforma**
A Brazilian feast in the heart of New York → p. 63

★ **Matsugen**
Japanese cuisine by master chef Jean-Georges Vongerichten → p. 64

★ **Buddakan**
Stylish décor and excellent Asian cuisine → p. 65

★ **Pastis**
Parisian-style bistro popular with celebrities → p. 67

★ **Prune**
Brunch here is amazing – nine Bloody Mary variations to choose from → p. 67

★ **Schiller's Liquor Bar**
Great location in the hip Lower East Side → p. 67

★ **Spice Market**
Thai-Malay fusion food in the hot and happening Meatpacking District → p. 67

★ **Malatesta**
Enjoy authentic Italian cuisine at affordable prices → p. 71

MARCO POLO HIGHLIGHTS

MATSUGEN ★ (130 B–C2) (🕮 B 15)

Jean-Georges Vongerichten's new restaurant has become an immediate hit with New York's in-crowd. The finest Japanese cuisine is complemented by very friendly service. *241 Church St/Leonard St | tel. 1212 925 02 02 | www.jean-georges.com | subway: Franklin St, 1*

INSIDER TIP ▶ TELEPAN (139 E1) (🕮 F 4)

A little pricey but worth it for a taste of Bill Telepan's new American cuisine. *Mon, Tue evenings only | 72 W 69th St | tel. 1212 580 43 00 | www.telepan-ny.com | subway: 66th St–Lincoln Center, 1*

TOCQUEVILLE (135 D4) (🕮 D 12)

Contemporary American cuisine at its best! The prix fixe menu of four courses never disappoints with fare like elk carpaccio, wild boar served with sweet chestnuts and forest mushrooms in a red wine reduction – always at a fixed price of $125. *Closed Sun | 1 E 15th St | tel. 1212 647 15 15 | www.tocquevillerestaurant.com | subway: 14th St–Union Square, L, N, Q, R, 4, 5, 6*

WALLSÉ (134 B4) (🕮 B 12)

Austro-Hungarian cuisine by chef/owner Kurt Gutenbrunner served in a restaurant decorated with neo-expressionist

GOURMET RESTAURANTS

Le Bernardin (139 E4) (🕮 F7)

Pure luxury! This is one of the best restaurants in the United States. Famous for its seafood dishes and its steep prices. *Closed Sun | 155 W 51 St | tel. 1212 5 54 15 15 | www.le-bernardin.com | subway: 50th St, 1, 49th St, N, R*

Daniel (140 B3) (🕮 H6)

Upper East Side restaurant that has three Michelin stars to its name! A sea bass roulade in a potato crust served with leeks are among its signatures dishes. Excellent wine list. Three course prix fixe menu for $110 (Mon–Tue 5.30pm– 6pm). *Mon–Sat evenings only | 60 E 65th St | tel. 1212 2 88 00 33 | www.danielnyc.com | subway: 66th St, 6*

La Grenouille (140 A5) (🕮 G7)

An eclectic mix of traditional and contemporary cuisine makes this one of New York's most stylish restaurants and has the critics waxing lyrical over the pièce de résistance – the sole. *3 E 52nd St |* tel. 1212 752 14 95 | www.la-grenouille. com | subway: 5th Ave–53rd St, E, M

Nobu (130 B2) (🕮 B15)

Order the *omakase* menu and leave your selection up to top chef Nobu himself. From $60 and only at lunchtime. Reservations a month in advance, but walk-ins need not despair as there is also *Next Door Nobu*. *105 Hudson St (Franklin St) | tel. 1212 2 19 05 00 | www.noburestaurants.com | subway: Franklin St, 1*

Per Se (139 E3) (🕮 F6)

Thomas Keller, top chef and owner of some the world's finest restaurants, will take you on the ultimate culinary journey in Per Se. Reservations two months in advance. The nine-course tasting menu for $295 changes daily. *Evenings daily, also open for lunch Fri–Sun | 10 Columbus Circle (60th St), 4th floor | tel. 1212 8 23 93 35 | www. perseny.com | subway: 59th St– Columbus Circle, A–D, 1*

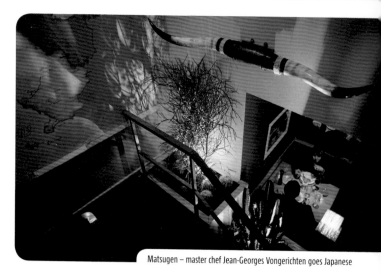

Matsugen – master chef Jean-Georges Vongerichten goes Japanese

artworks from Julian Schnabel's private collection. *Daily from 5.30pm | 344 W 11th St (Washington St) | tel. 1212 352 23 00 | www.wallserestaurant.com | subway: Christopher St, 1, 14 St, A, C, E, L*

WD-50 (131 F2) (*m̠ E15*)

Michelin star chef Wylie Dufresne is a fan of molecular cuisine and likes to mix unusual combinations: duck breast with cheddar and Korean kimchi couscous. His nine-course tasting menu will set you back $140 but is very much in vogue. *Daily from 6pm | 50 Clinton St | tel. 1212 477 29 00 | www.wd-50.com | subway: Delancey St, F, M*

RESTAURANTS: MODERATE

BRYANT PARK GRILL (139 D–E6) (*m̠ F8*)

This restaurant behind the New York Public Library is where the fashionistas congregate in the *open air* – a hit are its seafood and barbecue dishes. *Sat, Sun brunch | 25 W 40th St | between Fifth Ave and Sixth Ave | tel. 1212 840 65 00 | www. arkrestaurants.com | subway: 42nd St, B, D, F, M*

BUDDAKAN ⭐ (134 B3) (*m̠ C11*)

An elaborate restaurant with banquet tables, stylish Chinese cuisine and great ambiance. *75 Ninth Ave, corner 16th St | tel. 1212 989 66 99 | www.buddakannyc. com | subway: 14th St, A, C, E, L*

CHEZ JOSEPHINE (137 C5) (*m̠ D7*)

In the Theater District the son of the legendary Josephine Baker welcomes diners into his bistro. Smoking permitted in the outdoor area. *Tue–Sun evenings only | 414 W 42nd St | tel. 1212 594 19 25 | www.chez josephine.com | subway: 42nd St, A, C, E*

CRAFT (135 D3) (*m̠ D11*)

Chef Tom Colicchio who developed the concept for this stylish restaurant is a huge favourite among the critics. Excellent quality comes with prices on the expensive side! *Daily from 5.30pm | 43 E 19 St | tel. 1212 780 08 80 | www.craftrestaurant. com | subway: 23rd St, R, 6*

INSIDER TIP ▶ FETTE SAU

(133 D–E3) (ጠ J16)

Barbecue – ribs, sausages and lamb – is the speciality of this restaurant in the hip Williamsburg district. The name translates as 'Fat Pig'. *Daily from 5pm | 354 Metropolitan Ave | tel. 1718 963 34 04 | www. fettesaublog.com | subway: Bedford Ave, L*

THE GROCERY (146 C4) (ጠ 0)

Rated among New York's best by the *Zagat* restaurant guide this stylish restaurant serves new American cuisine. It also has a garden. *Tue–Sat from 5.30pm | 288 Smith St | between Sackett St and Union St | tel. 1718 596 33 35 | www.thegrocery restaurant.com | subway: Carroll St, F, G*

Easy to let the Oyster Bar in Grand Central Station derail you

LES HALLES (135 F3) (ጠ F10)

Anthony Bourdain conjures up beautiful French cuisine at this brasserie, many of its recipes are available in his Les Halles cookbook. *411 Park Ave S | between 28th St and 29th St | tel. 1212 679 41 11 | www. leshalles.net | subway: 28th St, 6*

HAN BAT (135 E1) (ጠ E9)

Authentic Korean food like the rice dish *bi bim bab* is available around the clock here along with meat and vegetables served on the hot stone grill that is typical of this cuisine. The area around the Empire State Building is also known as Koreatown. *53 W 35 St (Fifth Ave) | tel. 1212 629 55 88 | subway: 34th St, B, D, F, M, N, O, R*

CAFÉ KATJA (131 E2) (ጠ E15)

This Austrian restaurant's quark (similar to cream cheese) dumplings are its signature dish. The herring salad is also a favourite. A relaxing Lower East Side spot ideal for a candle-lit meal. *79 Orchard St (Broome St) | tel. 1212 219 95 45 | www.cafe-katja. com | subway: Delancy St, F*

MAREA (139 E3) (ጠ F6)

Seafood is celebrated in this excellent Italian restaurant serving delectable flounder, monkfish, muscles, lobsters and langoustine dishes. *Mon–Tue from 5.30pm, Fri–Sun from 5pm | 240 Central Park South (Broadway) | tel. 1212 582 51 00 | www.marea-nyc.com | subway: 59th St–Columbus Circle, A–D, 1*

INSIDER TIP ▶ MOMOFUKU SSÄM BAR

(135 E5) (ጠ E13)

Popular restaurant with a young and trendy vibe that offers a feast for meat fans: veal, lamb, ham and bacon all prepared Asian-style – does not cater for vegetarians. *207 2nd Ave | Corner 13th St | tel. 1212 254 35 00 | www.momofuku.com | subway: Third Ave, L*

OYSTER BAR (136 A1) (*⌂ F9*)
Grand Central Station's Oyster Bar offers dozens of varieties of oysters, *pan roasts*, lobster soup and fish fresh from the grill. *Closed Sun | Grand Central Station, Lower Level between Vanderbilt and Lexington Ave | tel. 1212 490 66 50 | www.oyster-barny.com | subway: Grand Central, 4–7*

PASTIS ★ (134 B3) (*⌂ B11*)
Treat yourself to *steak frites*, *crêpes Suzette* and *café au lait Parisien* any time of day at this French bistro in the Meatpacking District: open from 8am until well after midnight for those looking for a midnight snack. *9 Ninth Ave (Little West 12th St) | tel. 1212 929 48 44 | www.pastis ny.com | subway: 14th St, A, C, E, L*

PRUNE ★ (131 E1) (*⌂ E14*)
Its nine Bloody Mary variations are just one of the items on the menu that makes brunch *(Sat/Sun)* so popular here. *54 E 1st St | between First Ave and Second Ave | tel. 1212 677 62 21 | www.prunerestaurant. com | subway: Second Ave, F, M*

INSIDER TIP PURE FOOD AND WINE ☺ (135 E4) (*⌂ E12*)
No foods are heated to a temperature of more than 118° F (47.7° C) in this restaurant – in other words none of its dishes are cooked or baked. Its chefs produce mouth-watering organic vegan dishes using raw nuts, fruit and vegetables. Well worth a visit! *Daily | 54 Irving Place | tel. 1212 4 77 10 10 | www.purefoodandwine.com | subway: 14th St–Union Sq, L, N, Q, R, 4–6*

THE REDHEAD (135 F5) (*⌂ F13*)
This restaurant is a favourite meeting place for the residents of East Village and is always full. Its cuisine is inspired by the American southern states and has a warm atmosphere. *Mon–Sat from 5.30pm, Sun from 5pm | 349 E 13th St (First Ave) | tel.*

1212 533 62 12 | www.theredheadnyc.com | subway: First Ave, L

RESTO (135 F3) (*⌂ F10*)
This Belgian restaurant is famous for its hamburgers – which are served with home-made mayonnaise – and Belgian beers. *Daily lunch and dinner | 111 E 29th St | between Park Ave South and Lexington | tel. 1212 685 55 85 | www.restonyc.com | subway: 28th St, 6*

ROBATAYA (135 E6) (*⌂ E13*)
Here arriving guests are greeted loudly in Japanese by the staff. It is a good idea to sit right in front at the grill where you can watch the spectacle of two Kimono-clad men preparing the restaurant's dishes. *Daily from 6pm, Wed–Sun lunch also from noon | 231 E 9th St | tel. 1212 979 96 74 | www.robataya-ny.com | subway: Astor Place, 6th St, 8th St, R, N*

ROBERT ⌖ (139 E3) (*⌂ F6*)
What makes this restaurant in the Museum of Art and Design so inviting is the perfect view it affords of Columbus Circle and Central Park. Lounge on one of the comfortable couches or order a full meal. Try their tender *New York strip steak* and enjoy a memorable New York experience. *Daily | 2 Columbus Circle | tel. 1212 299 77 30 | www.robertnyc.com | subway: 59th St–Columbus Circle, A–D, 1*

SCHILLER'S LIQUOR BAR ★ (131 F2) (*⌂ E15*)
Located in the Lower East Side this is where the in-crowd meets for their weekend brunch. *Daily | 131 Rivington St corner Norfolk St | tel. 1212 260 45 55 | www. schillersny.com | subway: Delancey St, F*

SPICE MARKET ★ (134 B3) (*⌂ C11*)
In the Spice Market master chef Jean-Georges Vongerichten focuses on Thai

LOCAL SPECIALITIES

For those who are unfamiliar with what the names of certain dishes mean, here are some items found in New York's pubs, cafés and restaurants that visitors from other parts of the English-speaking world may find puzzling.

▶ **bagel** – the variations are countless anything from sesame to onions (photo right)

▶ **Caesar salad** – Cos lettuce with a dressing of vinegar, egg yolk, Worcestershire sauce and garlic and be sure to say *hold the anchovies* if you are not a fan

▶ **carpaccio** – in New York it is not the usual raw beef option but rather all kinds of raw fish

▶ **cheesecake** – New York's famous version is rich, creamy and indulgent. From plain to pistachio vanilla – the variations are endless

▶ **clam chowder** – clam soup – the New England version is white and the Manhattan version red (with tomatoes)

▶ **crab cakes** – sure beats traditional fish cakes!

▶ **typical American breakfast** – in New York it is a fry-up with eggs (in any variation) served with bacon (or Canadian bacon) and home fries – a must for any visitor

▶ **lobster** – in New York lobster is served in an endless variety of ways

▶ **New York strip steak** – a typical New York cut of loin (marbled with fat). Best cuts are prime rib or filet mignon

▶ **oyster** – served with vinegar and pink pepper or with ketchup (photo left)

▶ **roast turkey** – served for Thanksgiving with cranberries, gravy and sweet potatoes. Also popular as a cold meat.

▶ **sandwiches** – in New York the sandwich has a strong Jewish heritage. The *Reuben* (sauerkraut and soft cheese) and *pastrami* (a highly seasoned sliced smoked beef) are two classics. In the sandwich bars you choose the filling, the type of bread e.g. whole wheat or rye and your garnish e.g. lettuce, tomato, mayonnaise, mustard or onion.

and Malaysian fusion cuisine with unusual combinations and exotic presentations. *Daily | 403 W 13th St (Ninth Ave) |* *tel. 1212 675 23 22 | www.spicemarketnew york.com | subway: 14th St–Eighth Ave, A, C, E, L*

Amazing ambiance and Asian food make for the perfect recipe at the Spice Market

INSIDER TIP **UNITED NATIONS DINING ROOM** (136 B1) (*M H9*)

So you want to impress someone? Reserve a table in the United Nations' dining room. For $27 get you an opulent lunch buffet and included in the price is a fabulous view across the East River and the possibility of rubbing shoulders with famous politicians and celebrities from around the world. Remember to bring along ID (passport) and to observe the dress code: no jeans and trainers permitted and men must wear a jacket. *Lunch 11.30am–2.30pm | visitors' entrance: First Ave and 46th St | reservations the day before tel. 1212 963 76 25 | www.deligatesdiningroom.com | subway: Grand Central–42nd St, 4, 5, 6, 7, S*

RESTAURANTS: BUDGET

26 SEATS (135 F6) (*M F13*)

A small quaint French restaurant in the East Village and you guessed it – it seats exactly 26 patrons. *Tue–Sun evenings only | 168th Ave B (11th St) | tel. 1212 677 47 87 | www.26seatsonb.com | subway: Second Ave, F, M*

INSIDER TIP **CANDLE 79** (141 D2) (*M J5*)

Excellent vegetarian cuisine that may even have meat lovers converting once they have eaten here. Sunday brunch from noon to 4pm for $28. *1307 3rd Ave | between 14th St and 15th St | tel. 1212 472 09 70 | www.candlecafe.com | subway: 77th St, 6*

CITY BAKERY (135 D4) (*M D11*)

A good lunch venue with a fish, meat and vegetarian buffet with some innovative flavour combinations. *Daily 7.30am–7pm | 3 W 18th St | tel. 1212 3 66 14 14 | www.thecitybakery.com | subway: 14th St–Union Square, L, N, Q, R, 4–6*

DEGUSTATION (135 E6) (*M E10*)

Tapas at reasonable prices. *Mon–Sat evenings only | 239 E 5th St | tel. 1212 979 10 12 | www.degustationnyc.com | subway: Astor Place, 6, Second Ave, F, M*

DIM SUM GOGO (131 D3) (*M D16*)

A wide selection options from Chinese dumplings to hamburgers wrapped in pastry. *Daily | 5 East Broadway (Chatham*

RESTAURANTS: BUDGET

Square) | tel. 1212 7 32 07 97 | subway: Brooklyn Bridge, 4-6

DOGMATIC 😊 (135 E4) (*ш E11*)
With its wooden tables set against white tiles, this hip snack bar near Union Square serves hot dogs and hamburgers made from organic meat. Choose from turkey, pork, beef, chicken or lamb. 26 E 17th St (Union Square West) | tel. 1212 414 06 00 | www.eatdogmatic.com | subway: 14th St–Union Square, L, N, Q, R, 4, 5, 6

DOS TOROS TAQUERIA 😊
(135 E5) (*ш E12*)
Inexpensive, unpretentious and fast – this rustic snack bar serving tacos, burritos and quesadillas also recycles all its food waste and uses only locally sourced food. Daily | 137 Fourth Ave (13th St) | tel. 1212 677 73 00 | www.dostorosnyc.com | subway: 14th St–Union Square, L, N, Q, R, 4–6

LOW BUDGET

▶ The wine store Chelsea Wine Vault (134 B3) (*ш C10*) offers free wine tasting. Fri 4pm–7pm, Sat 2pm–5pm | 75 Ninth Ave | tel. 1212 4 62 42 44 | www.chelseawinevault.com | subway: 14th St, A, C, E

▶ For a free introduction to the art of beer brewing take the Brooklyn Brewery Tour (133 D2) (*ш J14*). Sat, Sun noon–6pm | 79 North 11th St | tel. 1718 4 86 74 22 | www.brooklyn brewery.com | subway: Bedford Ave, L

▶ Eating lunch instead of dinner at one of New York's stylish restaurants e.g. sushi at Nobu (page 64) can be a money saver.

ESPERANTO (132 A1) (*ш F14*)
Brazilian? Caribbean? Even if you cannot put a name to it you will be sure to enjoy excellent multicultural cuisine and live music. Lunch and dinner, Sat and Sun brunch | 145th Ave C (9th St) | tel. 1212 5 05 65 59 | www.esperantony.com | subway: Astor Place, 6

ESS-A-BAGEL (135 F4) (*ш F12*)
A vast selection of bagels and an even bigger selection of cream cheese. 359th First Ave (21st St) | tel. 1212 2 60 22 52 | www. ess-a-bagel.com | subway: First Ave, L

INSIDER TIP ▶ HAMPTON CHUTNEY
(135 E5) (*ш D14*)
Healthy fast food in the form of dosas – crispy Indian rice pancakes – is the speciality here. Try the classical masala dosa with an Indian spice and potato filling or a spinach dosa with grilled tomato and Portobello mushrooms and order a chai tea to accompany it. 68 Prince St | tel. 1212 226 99 96 | www.hamptonchutney. com | subway: Prince St, N, R

IPPUDO (135 E5) (*ш E13*)
Ramen – the Japanese noodle soup – is the speciality served here either with pork or vegetarian and the noodles are made on site. 65 Fourth Ave | between 9th and 10th St | tel. 1212 3 88 00 88 | www.ippudo. com/ny | subway: Astor Place/8th St–NYU, 6, N, Q

KATZ DELICATESSEN (131 F2) (*ш E14*)
Try this traditional Jewish deli's delicious sandwiches. 205 E | Houston St (Ludlow St) | tel. 1212 2 54 22 46 | www.katzdeli.com | subway: Second Ave, F

LORELEY (131 E2) (*ш D14*)
The imported beers are what make this German beer garden, run by renowned DJ Michael Momm, such a popular choice.

Daily | 7 Rivington St | between Bowery and Chrystie St | tel. 1212 2 53 70 77 | subway: Second Ave, F, M

MALATESTA ⭐ (134 B5) (*🗺 B12*)

This charming Italian restaurant serves homemade *gnocchi*, good wines and its meals are reasonably priced. *649 Washington St | tel. 1212 7 41 12 07 | subway: Christopher St, 1*

INSIDER TIP PORCHETTA ☺

(135 E–F6) (*🗺 E13*)

Pop in to this miniscule but elegant cafe with marble counters and enjoy one of their sandwiches. All the meats are organically produced. *Daily | 110 E 7th St | tel. 1212 7 77 21 51 | www.porchettanyc.com | subway: Astor Place/8th St–NYU, 6, N, Q*

Loreley – imported draft beer is its main attraction

PRETZEL SHOP (132 A2) (*🗺 F14*)

Charming and authentic little bakery with a wide selection of pretzels and a whole range of sauces – from mustard to their special beetroot horseradish mayonnaise – to choose from. *Closed Mon | 29th Ave B (3rd St) | tel. 1646 410 03 33 | www.sigmundnyc.com | subway: Second Ave, F*

RICE TO RICHES (131 D2) (*🗺 D14*)

There is only one item on offer here – rice pudding – but the selection is endless! *37 Spring St | between Mott and Mulberry St | www.ricetoriches.com | subway: Spring St, 6*

ROUGE TOMATE ☺

(140 B4) (*🗺 G6*)

Mouth-watering Belgian health food. *10 E 60th St | tel. 1646 2 37 89 77 | www.rougetomatenyc.com | subway: 59th St/Lexington Ave–59th St, 6, N, R*

INSIDER TIP SCHNITZEL & THINGS

This mobile food truck with its mustard coloured logo parks in a different New York street every day! For its sumptuous deep-fried cod, chicken and pork chops track it down at *www.schnitzelandthings.com* or on twitter. *Mon–Fri between 11.30am and 2pm | tel. 1347 7 72 73 41*

SMÖRGAS (134 C4) (*🗺 C11*)

Good service by friendly waiters, quirky design and Scandinavian food – ideal for brunch. *283 W 12th St (Eighth Ave) | tel. 1212 2 43 70 73 | www.smorgas.com | subway: 14th–St Eighth Ave, A, C, E, L*

SYLVIA'S RESTAURANT

(147 D2) (*🗺 0*)

A popular breakfast stop in Harlem that serves traditional southern soul food. *328 Lenox Ave | tel. 1212 9 96 06 60 | www.sylviasrestaurant.com | subway: 125 St, 2, 3*

TAI THAI (132 E–F1) (*🗺 E14*)

Authentic Thai food at Bangkok prices! *78 E 1st St | tel. 1212 7 77 25 52 | subway: Second Ave, F, M*

SHOPPING

(CITY) WHERE TO START?
Macy's (135 E1) *(M E9)* – one of the world's largest department stores – is where you should start. This emporium takes up an entire block in Herald Square and the subway takes you right there (34th St, B, D, F, M, N, Q, R). Also on Herald Square are stores like H&M and Gap. For high-end boutiques head straight to Madison Avenue in Midtown or go to the Upper East Side. For bargain hunting Broadway in the vicinity of Houston Street is your best bet.

There are many bargains to be had in New York – from trainers to electronic equipment – the list is endless. A shopping spree can be great retail therapy but bear in mind the 23 kg (51 lbs) luggage limit for when you fly back home.

There is always an excuse for the many *sales* you will come across in the Big Apple, be it Independence Day, Labor Day or simply clearance sales. Even books, CDs and DVDs are worth bargain hunting for, just be sure that the DVD country code coincides with your code back home. For some, a shopping trip in itself warrants a trip to New York. Madison and Fifth Avenue is where you will find rows of prestigious international and

The hottest trends, the latest craze, the coolest shops – New York has it all – this metropolis is a shoppers' paradise

American designers – *Calvin Klein, Donna Karans DKNY, Ralph Lauren* – as well as high-end department stores.

First came SoHo and then Chelsea, then hot on their heels the *Meatpacking District* (134 B–C 3–4) *(₪ B–C 10–11)* – Manhattan neighbourhoods that have undergone a transformation from shabby to chic. Districts like the *Lower East Side* (131 D–F 2–4) *(₪ D–F 15–16)* and *Park Slope*

(146 C4) *(₪ 0)* in Brooklyn are fast following suit. In the Manhattan neighbourhood of *NoLIta* (131 D1–2) *(₪ D–E 14–15)*, acronym for *N*orth of *Li*ttle *Ita*ly, a new generation of yuppies has moved into its maze of streets. On the Lower East Side, *LuSTO* (131 E–F 2–3) *(₪ E–F 15–16)* comprising *Lu*dlow, *St*anton and *O*rchard Streets, young designers are beginning to move into a neighbourhood that was

Dean & DeLuca – popular deli and coffee stop for New York's in-crowd

once dominated by the Jewish *shmatte* (clothing) trade.

Brooklyn is undergoing similar changes with Bedford Avenue drawing the younger crowd. The neighbourhoods on the *F Trains* (*Subway: Bergen St or Carroll Gardens*) – Boerum Hill, Cobble Hills and Carroll Gardens collectively known as *BoCoCa* (147 D4) (*⋔ O*) – have young fashion boutiques, cafés and bars.

It is worth noting that the price tags in stores generally only show the net price whereas food items, newspapers and books and for clothes and shoes costing less than $110, an extra 8.875 per cent in sales tax will be added on. Many stores are open on a Sunday and most stay open until 9pm.

BOOKS

BARNES & NOBLE

A well known chain with outlets spread across the city. Some New Yorkers will while away an entire day here so it hardly comes as a surprise that these bookstores have become meeting places for book loving singles. *e.g. 33 E 17th St* (135 E4) (*⋔ E12*) | *subway: 14th St–Union Square, L, N, Q, R, 4–6; 97 Warren St (Greenwich St)* (130 B3) (*⋔ B 16Y*) | *subway: Chambers St, 1, 2, 3*

PHAIDON STORE (130 C1) (*⋔ C14*)

A treasure trove of photography books in SoHo. *83 Wooster St | www.phaidon.com | subway: Prince St, R, Spring St, C, E*

INSIDER TIP ► POWERHOUSE ARENA (131 E6) (*⋔ E 18*)

A good place to go to for interesting books in Brooklyn, this shop belongs to the prestigious publishing house and specialises in art and photography books. Superb industrial building perfect for photo exhibitions – sometimes even hip-hop parties are held here. *37 Main St | www.power housearena.com | subway: York St, F, High St, A, C*

STRAND BOOK STORE ★ ● (135 D–E5) (*⋔ E12*)

This place is quite remarkable. It has an unrivalled 18 mile selection of used, rare

or out of print, art and photography books. This family business was founded in 1927 and is the sole survivor of the 47 other competitors that started out with it on New York's famous Book Row. *828 Broadway (12th St) | www.strandbooks.com | subway: 14th St–Union Square, L, N, Q, R, 4–6*

DELICATESSEN

DEAN & DELUCA ● ☺
(131 D1) (*D14*)

Gourmet deli whose espresso bar is the meeting place for New York's chic in-crowd. Organically grown foods. *560 Broadway (Prince St) | www.deandeluca.com | subway: Prince St, R*

INSIDER TIP DI PALO (131 E2) (*D15*)

There are Italian delicacies everywhere you look in this delightful Italian deli with prosciuttos hanging from the ceiling and huge wheels of Parmesan displayed on the counter along with salamis and mozzarella. A feast for the senses. *200 Grand St | www.dipaloselects.com | subway: Grand St, B, D, Spring St, 6*

CHELSEA MARKET ● (134 B3) (*C11*)

This market has an industrial feel with exposed pipes and red brick walls. Its stylish shops and gourmet restaurants selling all kinds of culinary delights have made it hugely popular. The building once belonged to the National Biscuit Company and it is here where the famous Oreo cookie was created. *75 Ninth Ave (15th St) | subway: 14 T, A, C, E*

DEPARTMENT STORES

BARNEYS NEW YORK ★
(140 B4) (*G6*)

Loved by the in-crowd both as a meeting place – especially at *Fred's* a restaurant on the ninth floor – and a rather expensive place buy their clothes. The range of luxury shoes, clothes and jewellery is endless. In the building alongside it, five floors are devoted exclusively to menswear. *660 Madison Ave (61st St) | www.barneys.com | subway: 59th St, 4–6*

BERGDORF GOODMAN
(140 A4) (*G7*)

Exclusive French, Italian and young American designers and what has to be the most attractive cosmetics department in New York. The men's store on the other side of Fifth Avenue also has a small restaurant. *754 Fifth Ave | between 57th St and 58th St | www.bergdorfgoodman.com | subway: Fifth Ave, N, R*

MARCO POLO HIGHLIGHTS

★ **Strand Book Store**
An endless selection of discounted books: paradise for book lovers'
→ p. 74

★ **Barneys New York**
Where New York's in-crowd and trendsetters meet and shop
→ p. 75

★ **Apple Store**
Showcase for all the latest Apple products open 24/7 → p. 77

★ **B+H Photo**
The world's largest photography shop → p. 78

★ **MoMA Design Store**
Modern art and design mementos to take home → p. 77

★ **F.A.O. Schwarz**
A massive toy emporium for children of the 21st century
→ p. 78

Macy's – the quintessential department store

exotic gifts. New York's best Japanese food emporium! *29 3rd Ave (9th St) | subway: Astor Place, 6*

MISCELLANEOUS

AJI ICHIBAN (131 D3) (*D15*)
Japanese confectionery and savoury snacks in the heart of Chinatown – colourful small bowls laid out so you can try before you buy. *167 Hester St | subway: Canal St, 6*

BEADS OF PARADISE (135 D4) (*D11*)
Smiling Buddhas, display cases bursting with jewellery, silk scarves and Indian pictures adorning the walls. All this and more, including beads galore at the back of the store where the creative can craft their own jewellery! *16 E 17th St (Fifth Ave) | www.beadsofparadisenyc.com | subway: 14th St–Union Square, L, N, Q, R, 4, 5, 6*

CONTAINER STORE (135 D3) (*D11*)
Packaging, storage, filing – every conceivable box, container or chest in any conceivable colour and shape for kitchen, office, garage usage or a gift is sold here. *629 Sixth Ave | www.containerstore.com | subway: 23rd St, F, M*

FISH'S EDDY ☺ (135 E4) (*E11*)
A crockery shop that sells anything from mugs with New York motifs and plates depicting the city's skyline, to T-Shirts made from organic cotton. Ideal for souvenirs. *889 Broadway (19th St) | www.fishseddy. com | subway: 23rd St, R, 6*

HAMMACHER SCHLEMMER (140 B4) (*H7*)
An eclectic mix of gifts – here you will find anything from a hi-tech futuristic noise neutraliser to your traditional pair of slippers. *Closed Sun | 147 E 57th St near Lexington Ave | www.hammacher.com | subway: Lexington Ave/59th St, N, R, 4–6*

BLOOMINGDALE'S (140 B4) (*H7*)
A visit to this famed store is an absolute must. *1000 Third Ave | between 59th St and 60th St | www.bloomingdales.com | subway: Lexington Ave/59th St, N, R, 4–6*

MACY'S ● (135 E1) (*E9*)
One of the world's largest department stores! Women can start their shopping spree with a make-up session downstairs before exploring its many floors for any item the heart desires. *151 W 34th St (Broadway) | www.macys.com | subway: 34th St–Herald Square, B, D, F, N, Q, R*

SUNRISE MART (135 E6) (*E13*)
The lift to Sunrise Mart is right next to St Mark's Bookshop. On the first floor is a supermarket whose beautifully packaged confectionery and odds and ends decorated with Japanese letters make ideal

INSIDER TIP LITTLE LEBOWSKI
(134 C6) (*C13*)

This small shop in the West Village draws its inspiration from the cult film *The Big Lebowski* with Jeff Bridges. Based on the 'Dude' the owner serves his customers wearing his pyjamas and dressing gown. Sells books, music, videos, magazines and T-Shirts. *215 Thompson St (3rd St) | subway: W 4th St, A, B, C, D, E, F, M*

MOMA DESIGN STORE ★
A great décor selection and a whole range of items for everyday use from the collection of the Museum of Modern Art. *Sat–Thu 9.30am–6.30pm, Fri 9.30am–9pm | 44 W 53rd St and 11 W 53rd St | between Fifth Ave and Sixth Ave (139 E–F 4–5) (*G7*) | subway: 47th St–50th St, B, D, F, M; Mon–Sat 11am–8pm, Sun 11am–7pm | 81 Spring St (Crosby St) (131 D1) (*D14*) | subway Spring St, 6 | www.momastore.org*

MUJI (130 C2) (*C15*)
Collapsible alarm clocks, waterproof speakers, New York skyscrapers made from wooden blocks – a wide variety of interesting household novelties. *455 Broadway | www.muji.us | subway: Canal St, N, Q, 6*

INSIDER TIP MXYPLYZYK
(134 B3) (*C11*)

Lamps, crockery, stationery and designer pieces – an excellent source for souvenirs. *125 Greenwich Ave (13th St) | www.mxyplyzyk.com | subway: 14th St, A, C, E, L*

WILLIAMS SONOMA (140 B4) (*H7*)
This department store specialising in kitchenware will leave you spoilt for choice when it comes to regional American ingredients – excellent consumable souvenirs. *Four branches, among them 121 E 59th St | between Park Ave and Lexington Ave | www.williams-sonoma.com | subway: Lexington Ave, B, Q*

ELECTRONICS

APPLE STORE ★
(131 D1) (*G 7*)

Be it the MacBook, the iPod, the iPad or Mac mini – Apple remains a design trendsetter. Workshops are run by experts are held daily. The store is open around the clock. *767 Fifth Ave (59th St) | www.apple.com/retail/fifthavenue | subway: 59th St, 4–6, 57th St, F*

LOW BUDGET

▶ The colourful *Pearl River Mart* **(131 D2)** (*C14*) is the ultimate gift shop with a massive selection of cheap, fun and outrageous items from Asia. *477 Broadway | between Broome and Grand St | www.pearlriver.com | subway: Prince St, R*

▶ ☺ *Whole Foods* is an organic supermarket also selling fresh produce and there are always tasters to be had – be it a guacamole dip or crackers with Brie and cranberries. *250 Seventh Ave/Corner 24th St* **(135 D2)** (*D10*) *| www.wholefoodsmarket.com | subway: 23rd St, 1 or 4 Union Square South, corner Broadway* **(135 E4)** (*E12*) *| subway: 14th St–Union Square, L, N, Q, R, 4, 5, 6*

▶ *Housing Works* **(131 D1)** (*D14*) is a charming bookstore reminiscent of an old library with its winding staircase and wooden floors. Inexpensive books – some second-hand – and a small café. *126 Crosby Street, corner Houston St | www.housingworks.org/social-enterprise | subway: Broadway–Lafayette, B, D, F, M*

FLEA MARKETS

B+H PHOTO ⭐ (135 D1) (📖 D9)
A shopping must for anyone with a passion for photography and film. *Mon–Tue 9am–7pm, Fri 9am–1pm, Sun 10am–6pm | 420 Ninth Ave (33rd St) | www.bhphotovideo.com | subway: 34th St, A, C, E*

J & R MUSIC WORLD (130 C4) (📖 B16)
Cameras, computers, CDs and other electronic equipment at bargain prices. *23 Park Row (Beekman St) | www.jr.com | subway: City Hall/Brooklyn Bridge, N, R, 4–6*

NINTENDO WORLD (139 E5) (📖 F8)
Game crazy? Be it Wii or Game Boy – you can try them all on more of the more than 50 consoles. *10 Rockefeller Plaza (48th St, 5th Ave) | www.nintendoworldstore.com | subway: Time Sq–42nd St, N, Q, R, S, 1, 2, 3, 7*

FLEA MARKETS

In New York Sunday is the day for flea markets, *street fairs* and *crafts fairs*. For more information or go to *www.fleausa.com*

GALLERIES

Opening hours generally 10am–6pm, often closed Sun/Mon

EXIT ART (138 B6) (📖 D8)
A gallery that encourages new and experimental forms of art and young emerging artists. *475 Tenth Ave (36th St) | www.exitart.com | subway: 34th St, A, C, E*

MATTHEW MARKS (134 B2) (📖 C–B 9–10)
Showcases big names like Ellsworth Kelly, Bryce Marden as well as American newcomers. *523 W 24th St and 522 W 22nd St | between Tenth Ave and Eleventh Ave | www.matthewmarks.com | subway: 23rd St, C, E*

DAVID ZWIRNER (134 B2) (📖 B10)
Exhibits influential artists like Neo Rauch and Marcel Dzamas and fosters the careers of future stars. *525 W 19th St | between Tenth Ave and West St | www.davidzwirner.com | subway: 23rd St, C, E*

TOYS & CHILDREN'S FASHION

BABY GAP (140 A4–5) (📖 G7)
This is the largest of Gap's 30 Manhattan stores and has clothing dedicated to children from newborn through to toddlers. *680 5th Ave (54th St) | www.gap.com | subway: 47th–50th St, B, D, F*

F.A.O. SCHWARZ ⭐ (140 A4) (📖 G7)
This New York institution is a toy paradise but not only for children – huge selection of nostalgic, contemporary and hi-tech toys. *767 Fifth Ave (58th St) | www.fao.com | subway: Fifth Ave, N, R*

FASHION & ACCESSORIES

AÉROPOSTALE
A chain that sells hip clothing at unbeatable prices. Young, fresh and cute fashion for *girls* and *guys*. Lots of special deals. *15 W 34th St (6th Ave)* (135 E6) *(📖 E9) | subway: 34th St, B, D, F, M, N, Q, R; 1515 Broadway (Times Square)* (139 D5) *(📖 E8) | subway: Times Square–42nd St, N, Q, R, S, 1, 2, 3, 7 | www.aeropostale.com*

AMERICAN APPAREL ☺ (134 C5) (📖 D9)
These T-Shirts are not only produced in LA on the West Coast but also have the LA feel: casual understatement coupled with social commitment (no sweatshops). LA cool available in no less than 20 New York outlets! *Among others 345 Seventh Ave (29th St) | www.americanapparel.net | subway: 28th St, 1*

AMERICAN EAGLE OUTFITTERS (139 D5) (🗺 E7)

This American clothing and accessories chain offers an enormous selection for both men and women. *1551–1555 Broadway (46th St) | www.ae.com | subway: 49th St, N, R*

INSIDER TIP ▶ BARNEYS WAREHOUSE (134 C3) (🗺 C11)

Barneys is an especially expensive and high-end designer fashion store and twice a year (February and August) it holds its famous *warehouse sale* to make room for its new range. The clothing items (prices reduced by 50–80 per cent) are highly sought after, so if you are planning on attending be prepared for some forceful behaviour by fellow bargain hunters and try to keep a clear head in all the chaos! *255 W 17th St (Seventh Ave) | www.barneys. com | subway: 18th St, 1*

CENTURY 21 (134 B4) (🗺 B17)

Designer brands and clothing at very low prices so go early and wear comfortable shoes! *22 Cortlandt St | between Broadway and Church St | www.c21stores.com | subway: Cortlandt St, N, R, 1*

DARLING (134 C4) (🗺 C11)

Unconventional, charming, sexy and very affordable best describes Ann French Emonts' fashion designs. Aside from her own creations she also carries fashions by other New York design talents. *1 Horatio St (Eighth Ave) | www.darlingnyc.com | subway: 14th St, A, C, E, L*

LIQUOR STORE (130 C2) (🗺 B15)

What was once a bar now houses the J.Crew's menswear boutique. The Steve McQueen-look is cultivated here. *Closed Sun | 235 W | Broadway | www.liquorstore tribeca.com | subway: Canal St, A, C, E, 1*

Who can resist these teddy bears from F.A.O. Schwarz?

FASHION & ACCESSORIES

MANOLO BLAHNIK (140 A4) (📖 G7)
Definitely the world's most famous shoe store thanks to *Sex and the City*. *31 W 54th St | between Fifth Ave and Sixth Ave | www.manoloblahnik.com | subway: Fifth Ave/53rd St, E, M*

MARC JACOBS (131 D1) (📖 D14)
His and her fashion and accessories by the crown prince of American designers. *163 Mercer St | between Houston and Prince St | www.marcjacobs.com | subway: Prince St, N, R*

NIKETOWN USA (140 A4) (📖 G7)
The interior design of Nike's New York outlet has made this their flagship store. Every kind of sporting equipment imaginable means that it is always very busy. *6 E 57th St (Fifth Ave) | www.nike.com | subway: 57th St, F, N, Q, R*

PRADA (131 D1) (📖 D14)
The Prada store offers a very 21st century shopping experience – its changing rooms have some very high-tech features – designed by the talented contemporary architect Rem Koolhaas. *575 Broadway (Prince St) | www.prada.com | subway: Prince St, N, R*

PUMA (131 D1–2) (📖 C14)
Showcasing everything that Puma has to offer since its *rebirth of cool* a number of years ago. *521 Broadway | between Spring and Broome St | www.puma.com | subway: Prince St, N, R*

SHANGHAI TANG (140 A–B4) (📖 G7)
Boutique offering contemporary Chinese fashion for women, men and children. *600 Madison Ave (57th St) | subway: Lexington Ave/59th St, N, R, 4–6*

Flagship store Niketown New York – the brand continues to be popular

UNIQLO (131 D1) (*map D 14*)
This Japanese chain sells simple high-end fashion, no logos and plenty of colours in their elegant and spacious store. *546 Broadway | between Prince St and Spring St | www.uiqlo.com | subway: Prince St, N, R*

URBAN ATHLETICS (144 B5) (*map J 3*)
When buying new trainers nothing beats a personal consultation by top NYC runner, the owner of Urban Athletics himself, Jerry Macari. *1291 Madison Ave (near 92nd St) | www.urbanathleticsnyc.com | subway: 96th St, 6*

SALONS & COSMETICS

AVEDA INSTITUTE (130 C1) (*map C 14*)
A beauty salon ideal for a quick treatment in between shopping. The institute is also a school so if you let trainees do your *facial* or colour, it could cost you half of what you would normally pay and the trainees tend to be twice as careful! *Closed Sun | 233 Spring St | between Sixth Ave and Varick St | tel. 1212 807 14 92 | www.avedainstituteny.com | subway: Houston St, 1*

FRÉDÉRIC FEKKAI (140 A4) (*map G 7*)
Stylist to the stars, his clients include celebrities like Liv Tyler and Naomi Watts. Very exclusive and this kind of luxury does not come cheap – a cut can cost you between $105 and an eye-watering $750 if it is by the master himself. *| 712 Fifth Ave (56th St) | tel. 1212 7 53 95 00 | subway: Fifth Ave, E, F*

KIEHL'S PHARMACY (135 E5) (*map E 12*)
Beautiful old-fashioned pharmacy famous for its own skin and hair care cosmetics line. *109 Third Ave | between 13th St and 14th St | www.kiehls.com | subway: 14th St–Union Square, L, N, Q, R, 4–6*

SEPHORA (131 D1) (*map D 14*)
This is where New York's glamour crowd go for their beauty tips. *555 Broadway | between Houston St and Prince St | subway: Prince St, N, R*

MALLS

WOODBURY COMMON PREMIUM OUTLETS (0) (*map 0*)
Located outside the city it is a popular attraction with its 220 outlet stores from world famous high-end brands like Prada, Miu Miu, Marc Jacobs, Armani and Gucci. *Take the Short Line bus from Port Authority (second floor) | Fare of $42 includes discount vouchers) | www.premiumoutlets.com*

MUSIC

JAZZ RECORD CENTER (135 D2) (*map D 10*)
The name says it all – all that jazz is what this store is all about. *Closed Sun | 236 W 26th St | between Seventh Ave and Eighth Ave, 8th floor | www.jazzrecordcenter.com | subway: 28th St, 1*

OTHER MUSIC (135 D6) (*map D 13*)
A true homage to independent music – the best selection in the city. Indie music, ambient, Francophile and psychedelic music and more. Nothing mainstream here! *15 E 4th St | between Broadway and Lafayette St | www.othermusic.com | subway: Broadway–Lafayette, B, D, F*

JEWELLERY

TIFFANY & CO. (140 A4) (*map G 7*)
The legendary New York jewellery store that has prices that are equally legendary! Head to the third floor for very affordable silver knick-knacks. *727 Fifth Ave (57th St) | www.tiffany.com | subway: 57th St, B, C*

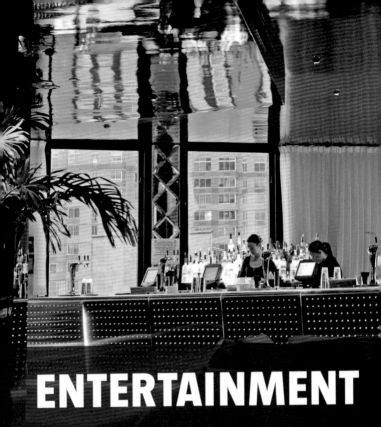

ENTERTAINMENT

CITY **WHERE TO START?**
New York's nightlife is as varied as the city itself. A musical in the renowned Theater District? Greenwich Village for some live jazz? Or one of the many smaller bars and live music clubs in the Lower East Side? The world is your oyster here and what better way to kick off your evening than at **Salon de Ning (140 A4)** (*ᴁ G7*) on the rooftop of The Peninsula hotel. From here you get the perfect overview – and insight into – of the glittering nightlife of the Big Apple.

In the entertainment capital of the world New Yorkers seldom head home right after work but prefer to meet for drinks in their favourite bar and then move on to an early dinner at the city's newest hot spot.

Straight afterwards they will head to the theatre, the opera, a musical or the movies ending the evening on a high note at one of the city's hip and trendy clubs. While visitors can feel quite overwhelmed, New Yorkers themselves are almost blasé about being spoilt for choice – they know what they like and often also check out what the newspaper critics have to say.

The Big Apple knows exactly how to lay it on with a limitless choice of musicals, theatre, jazz, opera, bars, discos and nightclubs

The clubs especially rely on what is in and their popularity is constantly in the throes of change. Some owners use this to their advantage by catering for a different clientele every evening. Who knows what tomorrow will bring! One thing is certain though, live music will always stand its ground in the Big Apple – and if its blues and jazz the loyalty of their audiences remains a constant.

BARS

Hotel bars are a popular meeting place for New Yorkers who gather there till late at night enjoying traditional New York cocktails such as Martinis, Manhattans, Gimlets or Whisky Sours. Hot spots are the *King Cole Bar* in *The St Regis*, the ❧ *Rise* in the *Ritz Carlton Battery Park* and the *Grand Bar* in the *Hotel Soho Grand*.

Balthazar – for a taste of France in the middle of New York

In the more sophisticated restaurants there are often bar sections with bartenders who prepare drinks behind a counter and in expensive establishments these bars will also serve a full spectrum of culinary fare as starters. It is important to carry some form of ID even if you clearly are 21 years or older – the minimum age at which you may order alcohol in the United States – as bars often request them before serving clients.

INSIDER TIP 230 FIFTH
(135 E2) (*∅ E10*)

This award winning roof terrace bar on Fifth Avenue – the city's largest – lies at the heart of Midtown's sea of lights. *230 Fifth Ave (27th St) | tel. 1212 725 43 00 | www.230-fifth.com | subway: 28th St, N, R, 6*

ALGONQUIN/BLUE BAR
(139 E6) (*∅ F8*)

Enjoy a leisurely drink and chat in the comfortable lounge of this historic hotel where New York's literati used to meet. *59 W 44th St | between Fifth and Sixth Ave | tel. 1212 8 40 68 00 | www.algonquinhotel. com | subway: 42nd St, B, D, F, Q, M, H*

INSIDER TIP APOTHÉKE
(131 D3) (*∅ D16*)

Here you will be served blazing shots of absinthe by barmen wearing white pharmacists' coats. The green liquid was prohibited for many years – now it is all the rage and this bar in Chinatown is packed every evening. *9 Doyers St | between The Bowery and Pell St | tel. 1212 4 06 04 00 | www.apothekenyc.com | subway: Canal St, N, Q, 6*

BALTHAZAR (131 D1) *(🗺 D14)*
Trendy without being ostentatious this French brasserie is perfect for celebrity spotting from its bar counter. *80 Spring St (Crosby St) | tel. 1212 9 65 14 14 | www. balthazarny.com | subway: Spring St, 6*

BARCADE (133 E4) *(🗺 K16)*
In this arcade game-style bar in Williamsburg you can play video games for only 25 cents and there are also a number of games that were popular in the 1980s available; Tetris, Centipede, Outrun, Galaga, Donkey Kong and Street Fighter. A whole range of draft beer is even more reason to stick around. *388 Union Ave | tel. 1718 302 64 64 | www.barcadebrooklyn. com | subway: Lorimer St, L*

BEMELMAN'S BAR
(140 C2) *(🗺 H5)*
The stylish interior of this piano bar in the Carlyle Hotel attracts a chic and elegant clientele. *35 E 76th St (Madison Ave) | tel. 1212 7 44 16 00 | subway: 77th St, 6*

THE BLIND BARBER (135 F6) *(🗺 F13)*
Have your hair cut in this nostalgic, old-school barber shop in East Village for only $40 or your beard trimmed for $30 and enjoy a cocktail included in the price. *339 E 10th St | tel. 1212 228 21 23 | blindbarber. com | subway: First Ave, L*

BRASSERIE 8½ (140 A4) *(🗺 G7)*
Its lively bar scene and retro décor makes this a Midtown hot spot for New York's *in-crowd. 9 W 57th St | between Fifth Ave and Sixth Ave | tel. 1212 8 29 08 12 | subway: Sixth Ave, B, Q*

CARNIVAL AT BOWLMOR LANES
(135 D5) *(🗺 D12)*
This venue is an extraordinary combination of a bar and a circus. Not only do you get snacks with your drinks but you will also be served up a repertoire of circus acts such as knife eaters and tightrope walkers. *110 University Place (13th St) | tel. 1212 2 55 81 88 | www.carnivalnyc.com | subway: 14th St–Union Square, L, N, Q, R, 4–6*

MARCO POLO HIGHLIGHTS

CIBAR LOUNGE (135 E4) (*⌖ E12*)
Amazing Martini selection which you can enjoy in front of the fireplace in the bamboo garden! *56 Irving Place | between 17th and 18th St | tel. 1212 4 60 56 56 | www.cibarlounge.com | subway: 14th St–Union Square, N, Q, R, 4–6*

HOLLAND BAR (138 C5) (*⌖ D8*)
Reasonably priced beers and a great vibe are to be had at this small bar in Hell's Kitchen. *53 29th Ave | tel. 1212 5 02 46 09 | subway: 42nd St–Port Authority, A, C, E*

KAÑA (130 B1) (*⌖ B14*)
This tapas lounge is the perfect spot to chill out and it is also a dance venue. *324 Spring St | between Greenwich and Washington St | tel. 1212 3 43 81 80 | www.kanatapasbar.com | subway: Spring St, C, E*

LOW BUDGET

▶ Crime writers, celebrities and politicians read from their works at *Barnes & Noble (→ p. 74).* Flyers at the stores carry scheduled events.

▶ The *Central Park Summer Stage* **(140 B2)** (*⌖ H5*) offers open air opera concerts free of charge in July and August. *Rumsey Playfield | at 72nd St | www.summerstage.org | subway: 68th St–Hunter College, 6*

▶ See the *Late Show by David Letterman* **(139 E4)** (*⌖ F7*) live. Free tickets can be booked by phone on the day from 11am. *Mon–Thu 5.30pm | Ed Sullivan Theater | 1697 Broadway, tel. 1212 2 47 64 97 | www.cbs.com/latenight/lateshow | subway: Seventh Ave, B, D, E*

KUSH (131 E2) (*⌖ D14*)
Hookahs pipes, exotic décor and dimmed lights has led one of the city's magazine's to dub Kush New York's best *make out-bar.* *191 Chrystie St | between Stanton and Rivington St | tel. 1212 6 77 73 28 | www.the kushnyc.com | subway: Second Ave, F, M*

MCSORLEY'S OLD ALE HOUSE (135 E6) (*⌖ E13*)
This is one of New York's oldest bars and was a men only bar right up to 1970. The floor is covered in sawdust and drinks are limited to a choice of *light* and *dark beer* and you have to order two drinks at a time. *15 E 7th St (Third Ave) | tel. 1212 473 91 48 | www.mcsorleysnewyork.com | subway: Astor Place, 6*

OLD TOWN BAR (135 E4) (*⌖ E11*)
Just like the New York's pubs of yesteryear: movie star clippings on the walls, long mahogany counters, dark wood and fast service. *45 E 18th St | tel. 1212 5 29 67 32 | www.oldtownbar.com | subway: 14th St–Union Square, L, N, Q, R, 4–6*

PAINKILLER (131 E3) (*⌖ E15*)
Polynesian style tiki bars are all the rage and this one has it all; strong rum cocktails, bamboo bar counters and Caribbean décor. Painkiller is a true island escape! *49 Essex St (Grand St) | tel. 1212 777 84 54 | www.painkillernyc.com | subway: Delancey St, F*

PRAVDA (131 D1) (*⌖ D14*)
The rosemary Martini served here is an absolute must! *281 Lafayette St (Prince St) | tel. 1212 2 26 49 44 | www.pravdany.com | subway: Prince St, N, R*

PRESS ● (138 C4) (*⌖ D6*)
Ink48's spacious hotel rooftop bar with pool and brilliant views. *653 W 48th St | tel. 1212 757 00 88 | www.ink48.com | subway: 50th St, C, E, 1*

A balmy summer evening on the Salon de Ning rooftop terrace

RODEO BAR (135 F3) (*ⅅ F11*)
Don your cowboy boots and enjoy a Tex-Mex meal in a typical southern-style bar with cow horns on the walls. Live bluegrass, country and rockabilly music every night. *375 Third Ave (27th St) | tel. 1212 683 65 00 | www.rodeobar.com | subway: 28th St, 6*

RUDY'S BAR (138 C5) (*ⅅ E7*)
There is always something on the go in this small pub. The waitresses rush around with huge *pitchers* (and the free *hot dogs* that go with them) and look like they are all in training for the Munich Oktoberfest. *627 Ninth Ave (45th St) | tel. 1212 974 91 69 | subway: 42nd St–Port Authority Bus Terminal, A, C, E*

SALON DE NING ★ ⋇
(140 A4) (*ⅅ G7*)
The glass enclosed terrace on the roof of the 23rd floor of *The Peninsula* hotel with an excellent view across the city's skyscrapers. *700 Fifth Ave (55th St) | tel. 1212 2 47 22 00 | subway: Fifth Ave, E, M*

SMITH & MILLS (130 B2) (*ⅅ B15*)
This charming and offbeat pub in a restored coach house is a great place to enjoy some cocktails. *71 N Moore St | tel. 1212 226 25 15 | www.smithandmills.com | subway: Franklin St, 1*

INSIDER TIP ▶ TOP OF THE TOWER ⋇
(136 C1) (*ⅅ H9*)
Take in the panoramic views of the East River from the Top of the Tower on the 26th floor of the Beekman Tower Hotel. *3 Mitchell Place | between 49th St and First Ave | tel. 1212 9 80 47 96 | subway: 51st St, 6*

XAI XAI (139 D4) (*ⅅ E7*)
A busy wine bar in Hell's Kitchen serving South African snacks with a great selection of South African wines. *365 W 51 St | tel. 1212 5 41 92 41 | www.xaixaiwinebar.com | subway: 50th St, C, E*

theatres are closed on a Monday. There are often matinees on a Wednesday, Saturday and Sunday.

Cielo Club – only New York's top DJs play here

BROADWAY & MUSICALS

New York has a remarkable 250 theatres to its name and its ⭐ *Broadway musicals* are the real money-spinners with more than ten million tickets a year being sold. The Theater District is where you will find almost all of the Broadway theatres. A number of shows have been box office hits for many years – *The Phantom of the Opera* has been going for 20 years. Every musical taste is catered for from the ABBA-based *Mamma Mia* through to the ballet-based *Billy Elliot*. Programme schedules and reviews can be found in the *New York Times* (Friday and Sunday), the *New York Magazine* and *The New Yorker*. Most

CLUBS & POP/ROCK

For event listings use the *New York, Time Out* or the *Village Voice.* The *New Yorker* or the Friday entertainment section of the *New York Times* is your best bet for live music. For club information go to *www. ny.com*. Most venues will charge a *cover charge (CC:* price for one place setting). It is unlikely that you will be admitted if you are dressed as a tourist, so be sure to dress up. Try a number of clubs as the doormen all have different tastes and with some you may stand a better chance of getting in.

ARLENE'S GROCERY (131 F2) *(⌀ E14)*
Loud music, a young audience and young bands. The musicians on stage change hourly and there is lots of loud noise and high energy. *Entrance fee $10 | 95 Stanton St (Orchard St) | tel. 1212 995 16 52 | www. arlenegrocery.net | subway: Second Ave, F*

BARBES ● (146 C4) *(⌀ 0)*
Here you can hear anything from jazz to eastern European wind instruments and world music and in the back area there is a small bar. Excellent live music, good acoustics and an eclectic mix of patrons of all ages have elevated this small gem in an excellent location in Brooklyn to cult status. *376 9th St (Sixth Ave) | tel. 1347 422 02 48 | www.barbesbrooklyn.com | subway: Seventh Ave, F, G*

INSIDER TIP THE BELL HOUSE
(146 C4) *(⌀ 0)*
One of the best new clubs to have opened their doors in New York with all kinds of interesting events from live bands and DJs to ping-pong and bingo contests and launch parties. Many events are free of

charge, the entrance fee for some from $5 to $10 – the occasional concert will be pricier. Visit their website for some inspiration and then take a trip to Brooklyn to dance and celebrate in this converted warehouse. *149 7th St / tel. 1718 643 65 10 / www.thebellhouseny.com / subway: 9th St–4th Ave, F, G*

BOWERY BALLROOM (131 E2) (*ⓜ D15*)
Hip up-and-coming indie bands and old independent names like Patti Smith take it in turns on the stage here. *CC $10–50 / 6 Delancey St / between Bowery and Chrystie St / tel. 1212 5 33 21 11 / www.boweryball room.com / subway: Delancey St, F*

BOWERY ELECTRIC (135 E6) (*ⓜ D14*)
A club on the Bowery with dance DJs and live rock concerts. It covers two floors with three bars complementing the live music and dance club. *327 Bowery (2nd St) / tel. 1 646 461 76 79 / www.theboweryelectric. com / subway: Bleeker St, 6*

CAKE SHOP (131 F2) (*ⓜ E15*)
Indie and underground music at its best can be heard in this vaulted cellar on the Lower East Side. Aside from beers being served upstairs, you can also order coffee and cake – the cupcakes are a huge hit! *152 Ludlow St (Stanton St) / tel. 1212 253 00 36 / www.cake-shop.com / subway: Delancey St, F*

CIELO CLUB (134 B3) (*ⓜ B11*)
Here world-class DJs turn the night into a party in the trendy Meatpacking District. *CC $5–25 / 18 Little W 12th St / tel. 1212 6 45 57 00 / www.cieloclub.com / subway: 14th St/Eighth Ave, A, C, E, L*

INSIDER TIP ▶ KARAOKE KILLED THE CAT
This is a unique dance party and karaoke combo. The weekly KKTC jam session is not your regular cheesy karaoke sing-along

but rather an exclusive and enthusiastic variation of karaoke with background singers and dancers Chris Goldteeth and Lord Easy. Entrance is free and whether you choose to join in or not you will be guaranteed an excellent time. *Wed 10pm: Fontana's Bar / 105 Eldridge St (Grand St) (131 E2) (ⓜ D15) / tel. 1212 334 67 40 / www.fontanasnyc.com / subway: Grand St, B, D; Fri 24 hours: Union Hall / 702 Union St (Sixth Ave), Brooklyn (146 C4) (ⓜ O) / tel. 1718 6 38 44 00 / subway: Union St, N, R, Park Slope/Brooklyn*

THE LIVING ROOM (131 E–F2) (*ⓜ E15*)
A very popular club with a casual lounge-style atmosphere. The Frames, Anna Ternheim and Kate Walsh have all appeared here. *154 Ludlow St / tel. 1212 5 33 72 37 / www.livingroomny.com / subway: Second Ave, F*

MARQUEE (134 C1) (*ⓜ C9*)
Funky house music, hip-hop or techno remix to get you into the groove. *CC $20 / 289 Tenth Ave corner 26th St / tel. 1 646 4 73 02 02 / www.marqueeny.com / subway: 23rd St, C, E*

INSIDER TIP ▶ MERCURY LOUNGE (131 F2) (*ⓜ E14*)
Very hip! Showcase for up-and-coming bands hoping to make their breakthrough. *CC $8–15 / 217 E Houston St (Essex St) / tel. 1212 2 60 47 00 / www.mercuryloungenyc. com / subway: Second Ave, F*

PIANOS (131 E–F2) (*ⓜ E15*)
Instead of buying some expensive concert tickets go to this bar in the Lower East Side and use the money to enjoy some drinks and excellent live music at a fraction of the price of concert tickets. *158 Ludlow St / tel. 1212 5 05 37 33 / www.pianosnyc. com / subway: Second Ave, F*

LE POISSON ROUGE ⭐

(134 C6) (*ΩΩ C13*)

The club with the best music in Manhattan – that is according to the *Village Voice*. *156 Bleeker St | tel. 1212 5 05 34 74 | www.lepoissonrouge.com | subway: West 4th St, A–F, M*

INSIDER TIP ROCKWOOD MUSIC HALL

(131 E2) (*ΩΩ E14*)

There are live concerts every evening and the band has to be small otherwise there isn't enough place for the guests. Red velvet curtains enclose this music bar where the admission is free, the music fantastic the patrons friendly. *196 Allen St (Houston St) | tel. 1212 477 41 55 | www.rockwoodmusichall.com | subway: 2nd Ave, F*

SAPPHIRE LOUNGE (131 E1) (*ΩΩ E14*)

Good dance music, great people! Soul, funk, pop and rock – the happening place to dance the night away in New York's famous and trendy Lower East Side. *249 Eldridge St (Houston St) | tel. 1212 777 51 53 | www.saphirenyc.com | subway: 2nd Ave, F*

INSIDER TIP S.O.B.'S

(134 B6) (*ΩΩ C13*)

The name is an abbreviation for the Sounds of Brazil so if Caribbean and Brazilian music or salsa and reggae are your thing then this is the place for you. *CC $10–40 | 204 Varick St (Houston St) | tel. 1212 2 43 49 40 | www.sobs.com | subway: Houston St, 1*

INSIDER TIP WARSAW CLUB

(133 F1–2) (*ΩΩ L14*)

One of the city's *hot spots* for rock, indie and punk! Except on a Saturday when couples 40 and over come here to dance the polka at their Polish club. *CC from $10 | 261 Driggs Ave (Eckford St) Greenpoint/Brooklyn | tel. 1718 3 87 05 05 | www.warsawconcerts.com | subway: Lorimer St, L*

JAZZ & BLUES

For the best overview of the jazz and blues music events refer to the weekend section in the Friday's *New York Times. Pop and Jazz Guide | www.nytimes.com*

THE BLUE NOTE (134 C5) (*ΩΩ C13*)

This famous club is very crowded because the music here is of the finest. Reservation essential! *CC $25–75 | 131 W 3rd St (Sixth Ave) | tel. 1212 4 75 85 92 | www.thebluenote.net | subway: W 4th St, A–F, M*

DIZZY'S CLUB COCA COLA ⭐

(139 E3) (*ΩΩ F6*)

This club in the Lincoln Center offers the crème de la crème of jazz. *Entrance fee $10–35 plus $10 minimum meal charge | Broadway and 60th St | tel. 1212 2 58 95 95 | www.jalc.org | subway: 59th St–Columbus Circle, A-D, 1*

KNICKERBOCKER BAR & GRILL

(135 D5) (*ΩΩ D12*)

A bar with wooden tables and leather chairs and absolutely outstanding pianists and bass players who play *only Fri, Sat from 9.45pm*, so phone ahead of time. *CC $3 | 33 | University Place (9th St) | tel. 1212 2 28 84 90 | www.knickerbockerbarandgrill.com | subway: Astor Place, 6*

KNITTING FACTORY (130 C3) (*ΩΩ K16*)

Avant-garde or traditional jazz, alternative rock and pop – this legendary club is also an entertainment business with its own record labels and branches around the USA. *CC $8–30 | 361 Metropolitan Ave | tel. 3 475 29 66 96 | www.knittingfactory.com | subway: Bedford Ave, L*

PARLOR ENTERTAINMENT ●

(147 D1) (*ΩΩ O*)

Every Sunday at 4pm Marjorie Eliot invites you in to her lounge in Harlem for a jazz

Village Vanguard hits the high notes with jazz lovers

concert. Entrance free of charge, voluntary contribution. *555 Edgecombe Ave (160th St), Apt 3F | tel. 1212 7 81 65 95 | subway: 163 St, C*

SMALL'S (134 C5) *(Ø C12)*
Outstanding jazz until the early hours – the jazz club only shuts its doors at 4am. *CC $20 | 183 W 10th St (Seventh Ave) | tel. 1212 2 52 50 91 | www.smallsjazzclub.com | subway: Christopher St, 1*

THE VILLAGE VANGUARD
(134 C4) *(Ø C12)*
A slick jazz club in Greenwich Village with top-notch renditions. *CC $35 and includes a drink, no credit cards | 178 Seventh Ave (11th St) | tel. 1212 2 55 40 37 | www.village vanguard.com | subway: 14th St, 1–3*

CINEMA & FILM

The latest film release can premiere in several cinemas at once. For movie listings check out the *New York Times* and the *New York Post*, as well as the weekly magazines *New York Magazine* and *The New Yorker*.

CONCERTS

The New York Philharmonic Orchestra plays in the *Avery Fisher Hall* in the Lincoln Center. The Chamber Music Society alternates with talented students of the Julliard School of Music and famous guest players at the *Alice Tully Hall*. New York's second largest concert hall seating 2760 is *Carnegie Hall.* Recordings are often held here thanks to its ideal acoustics.

New York would not be New York without its many open air shows held here in the summer. *Mostly Mozart* and *Classical Jazz* held in the Lincoln Center courtyard are all-time favourites. The Metropolitan Opera and philharmonic orchestras offer INSIDER TIP Concerts in the Park, four of them in Central Park. Traditionally spectators picnic on the park lawns before the concerts get underway. *Events schedule: Lincoln Center | tel. 1212 5 46 26 56 | www. lincolncenter.org*

AVERY FISHER HALL ⭐
(139 D–E2) *(𝄞 F5)*
The world's leading performing arts cen-
tre. *Lincoln Center Broadway/62nd St |
tel. 1 212 875 56 56 | www.nyphil.org, new.
lincolncenter.org | subway: 66th St, 1*

BARGEMUSIC ● 𝄢
(131 E5) *(𝄞 D18)*
Chamber music on a ship docked in
Brooklyn with a great view of Manhattan.
*Thu–Sat 8pm, Sun 3pm | Fulton Ferry
Landing, Brooklyn | tel. 1 718 624 20 83 |
www.bargemusic.org | subway: Clark St,
2, 3*

OPERA & BALLET

New York is home to two large opera
houses – the Metropolitan Opera and the
New York City Opera. The Met is legendary
and performing on its stage in the Lincoln
Center is something that every world-class
star aspires towards. The brilliant New York
City Opera always has an innovative repertoire and is known for fostering talent
and for giving the next generation of
American stars a platform.
Rivalry is also rampant in the ballet – the
prominent *American Ballet Theatre* (ABT,
www.abt.org) vies against the *New York*

A cathedral of culture – the world famous Met in the Lincoln Center

CARNEGIE HALL (139 E4) *(𝄞 F6)*
One of the world's most prestigious venues for both popular and classical music.
*Back stage tours mid Sept–June Mon–Fri
11.30am, 12.30am, 2pm, 3pm, Sat
11.30am and 12.30am, Sun 12.30am |
57th St (Seventh Ave) | entrance fee $10 |
tel. 1 212 2 47 78 00 | www.carnegiehall.
org | subway: 57th St, N, R*

City Ballet (www.nycballet.com) which pre-
fers to gives up-and-coming artists their
break.

CITY CENTER ⭐ (139 E4) *(𝄞F7)*
Completely renovation and reopened at
the end of 2011 it aims to attract as vast
an audience as possible to the perform-
ing arts. *131 W 55th St | between Sixth*

Ave and Seventh Ave | tel. 1212 5 81 79 07 | www.nycitycenter.org | subway: 57th St, N, R

DAVID H. KOCH THEATER
(139 E2) (⌖ F5)
Previously known as the New York State Theater today it is home to productions by the New York City Opera and the New York City Ballet. *Lincoln Center Broadway/ 62nd St–66th St | tel. 1212 8 70 55 70 | www.nycopera.com | www.nycballet.com | subway: 66th St, 1*

JOYCE THEATER
(134 C3) (⌖ C10)
A dance theatre staging performances from around the globe. *175 Eighth Ave (19th St) | tel. 1212 691 97 40 | www.joyce. org | subway: 18th St, 1*

METROPOLITAN OPERA ★
(139 E2) (⌖ E5)
Opera and ballet performances in one of the world's most famous and sought after opera houses. *Lincoln Center Broadway/ 62nd St–66th St | tel. 1212 3 62 60 00 | www.metopera.org | subway: 66th St, 1*

TISCH SCHOOL OF THE ARTS
(131 E1) (⌖ E13)
Excellent up-and-coming dancers – come and see tomorrow's stars in the making! *$5 (donation) | events' schedule: www. dance.tisch.nyu.edu | 111 Second Ave, fifth floor | subway: Second Ave, F*

THEATRES & OFF-BROADWAY

APOLLO THEATER
(147 D2) (⌖ 0)
A Harlem theatre dating back to 1914 where amateur entertainers perform every Thursday. *253 W 125th St | tel. 1212 5 3153 05 | www.apollotheater.com | subway: 125th St, 2, 3*

BLUE MAN GROUP (135 D5–6) (⌖ D13)
Long running and world famous. The group started in 1991 and do performances pieces that take the mickey out of the arts scene. *Astor Place Theatre: 434 Lafayette St (Astor Place) | www.blueman. com | subway: Astor Place, 6*

BROOKLYN ACADEMY OF MUSIC (BAM) ★ (146 C4) (⌖ 0)
This theatre and performance art venue have staged productions that include those by the acclaimed composer Philip Glass, works by avant-garde stage director Robert Wilson and musician and performing artist Laurie Anderson. *30 Lafayette Ave | between Saint Felix St and Ashland Place, Brooklyn | tel. 1 718 6 36 41 00 | www. bam.org | subway: Atlantic Ave, 2–5, B, D, Q*

INSIDER TIP ▶ FUERZABRUTA
(135 E4) (⌖ E12)
A high-energy and very impressive stage extravaganza from Buenos Aires. One scene is even performed in water. *Daryl Roth Theatre: 103 E 15th St | tel. 1212 2 39 62 00 | www.fuerzabruta.net | subway: 14th St–Union Square, L, N, Q, R, 4–6*

JOSEPH PAPP PUBLIC THEATER
(135 D5–6) (⌖ D13)
There are a number of stages one of which always has Shakespearean performances. The pub section is *Joe's Pub (tel. 1212 5 39 87 78) | www.joespub.com)* where musicians such as Mos Def, Alicia Keys and Joss Stone have performed. *425 Lafayette St (Astor Place) | tel. 1212 9 67 75 55 | www. publictheater.org | subway: Astor Place, 6*

THE KITCHEN (134 B2) (⌖ B10)
An important centre for performance, dance and video art. *512 W 19th St | between Tenth and Eleventh Ave | tel. 1212 2 55 57 93 | www.thekitchen.org | subway: 23rd St, C, E*

WHERE TO STAY

Either way be warned, a good hotel in New York will not come cheap. With skyrocketing real estate prices a hotel room for under $100 a night is an absolute rarity. The average is between $300 and $400.

In addition to the many tourists, it is business travellers with expense accounts that make up the high occupancy of New York's hotels. The rule of thumb is to book early – preferably online where you tend to get the best offers. Room prices fluctuate seasonally and an overnight stay is cheaper in January, February, July and August. It is wise to take your hotel's location into account. From Midtown Manhattan for example you will be in easy walking distance from the theatre, museums and shops. Whereas downtown Manhattan is home to plenty of restaurants and trendy bars.

It is customary in the United States to quote accommodation prices per room and not per person. If two people share a room i.e. a double, it is generally not more expensive than a single. When you budget remember that on top of the quote you will be levied an additional surcharge of 13.375 per cent in Hotel Sales Tax and additional $3.50 per night room tax. A double bed comes standard with most rooms. Rooms with two single beds are more

Photo: Gershwin Hotel

In New York your choice of hotel is important: must it be within walking distance to a theatre or right in the heart of the nightlife?

difficult to come by. Best to book the bed configuration you require in advance.

As a minimum requirement the hotels selected here come with air conditioning, en suite bathroom, television set and telephone. There are numerous phone shops where you can easily purchase a SIM or smart card for your mobile phone. Most hotels now also offer wireless internet access. Specials are often applicable to summer and weekend bookings, as well as to long stays. All-inclusive packages with accommodation and flights booked in Europe are often cheaper.

You need to check into your room by 6pm on the day of arrival, otherwise your reservation will be cancelled. It is imperative to advise the hotel of your late arrival as soon as possible on the same day. A hotel reservation by credit card is binding. The

its prix fixe menu of *$67 (79 from 6.30pm)* is a culinary experience that is both affordable and well worth it for the unrivalled panoramic views. *1886 rooms | 1535 Broadway | between 45th St and 46th St | tel. 1212 3 98 19 00 | www.ny marriottmarquis.com | subway: 42nd St/ Times Square, N, R, 1–3*

SOHO GRAND
(130–131 C–D2) (*C14*)

Average-sized rooms most of which look across the city from the hotel's location in the heart of SoHo. Also on the premises: *The Gallery* restaurant and *The Yard* a bar frequented by the in-crowd and as its name suggests is located in the courtyard. *369 rooms | 310 W Broadway (Grand St) | tel. 1212 9 65 30 00 | www.sohogrand. com | subway: Canal St, N, R*

THE STANDARD ★
(134 B3) (*B11*)

Looming large and unmistakable, The Standard stretches across the High Line as if on stilts. Hotelier André Balazs' prestigious hotel with its hip interiors in the trendy Meatpacking District offers spectacular views across the Hudson. Le Bain on the rooftop is ideal for a cocktail stop. *337 rooms | 848 Washington St | tel. 1212 6 45 46 46 | www.standardhotels. com/new-york-city | subway: 14th St, A, C, E*

W (140 A–B 5–6) (*G8*)

Designer hotel with a feel-good factor – the interior is based on the four elements. *688 rooms | 541 Lexington Ave (50th St) | tel. 1212 7 55 12 00 | www.whotels.com | subway: 51st St, 6*

LUXURY HOTELS

The Carlyle (140 C2) (*H5*)
Hailed by culinary critic Tim Zagat as 'probably the best run hotel in New York', it is a timeless art deco classic. *198 rooms | double rooms from around $755 | 35 E 76th St (Madison Ave) | tel. 1212 7 44 16 00 | www.thecarlyle. com | subway: 77th St, 6*

The Peninsula (140 A4) (*G10*)
Elegantly decorated with Asian antiquities this luxury hotel also has a topnotch fitness club on the upper floors; a ☆ pool with a view of the city's skyscrapers and the prestigious *Salon de Ning* rooftop bar (p. 87). *240 rooms | double room from around $650 | 700 Fifth Ave (55th St) | tel. 1212 9 56 28 88 | www.peninsula.com | subway: Fifth Ave, E, N, R*

Ritz-Carlton Battery Park ☆
(130 A5) (*A17*)
Five-star luxury with stunning views of New York harbour and at night enjoy the full splendour of the illuminated Statue of Liberty through your own private telescope. *298 rooms | double room from $450 | 2 West St | tel. 1212 3 44 08 00 | www.ritzcarlton.com | subway: South Ferry, 1, Bowling Green, 4, 5*

The St Regis (140 A4) (*G7*)
This gracious 1904 art nouveau hotel owned by John Jacob Astor remains an iconic landmark and ranks as one of New York's finest more than a century on. *256 rooms | double room from around $900 | 2 E 55th St (Fifth Ave) | tel. 1212 7 53 45 00 | www.stregis.com/ newyork | subway: Fifth Ave, E, M*

The Carlyle a refined Upper East Side landmark hotel

HOTELS: MODERATE

ACE HOTEL
(135 E2) (*m E10*)

This hip and reasonably priced hotel was designed by Roman & Williams, interior designers to Gwyneth Paltrow and Kate Hudson. The firm's signature is combining unusual objects salvaged from old houses with vintage furniture. The definition of trendy it also has a bar with some hip DJs. *260 rooms | 20 W 29th St | tel. 1212 6 79 22 22 | www.acehotel.com | subway: 34th St–Herald Square, B, D, F, N, Q, R*

BEACON ♨ (142 B6) (*m F3*)

Old apartment hotel on the Upper West Side with lavishly sized rooms and from the 20th floor upwards you even have views of Central Park. *244 rooms | 2130 Broadway | between 74th and 75th St | tel. 1212 7 87 11 00 | www.beaconhotel.com | subway: 72nd St, 1–3*

BELVEDERE HOTEL (139 D4) (*m E7*)

Since 1928 this art deco hotel has had no shortage of guests because of its ideal location in Midtown. You can have breakfast at the in-house café or it can be served from the small kitchenette in your room. *320 rooms | 319 W 48th St | between Eighth Ave and Ninth Ave | tel. 1212 2 45 70 00 | www.belvederehotelnyc.com | subway: 50th St, C, E*

HOTEL EAST HOUSTON
(131 E1) (*m E14*)

This modern affordable hotel with a rooftop garden is ideally located to explore the Lower East Side scene. The rooms are not big but stylishly decorated. The hotel is in an area full of restaurants, bars, cafés, small shops and galleries. It also has a roof terrace. *42 rooms | 151 E Houston St | tel. 1212 7 77 00 12 | www.hoteleasthouston.com | subway: Second Ave, F, Broadway-Lafayette, B, D, F*

INK48 ☪ (138 B4) (🗺 D6)

This new boutique hotel in Hell's Kitchen offers spectacular views across the Hudson and a number of services including music systems with iPod docking stations, stylish rooms, a spa and a gym. *222 rooms | 652 Eleventh Ave | tel. 1212 7 57 00 88 | www. ink48.com | subway: 50th St, C, E, 1*

INSIDER TIP THE JANE HOTEL ☪
(134 B4) (🗺 B11)

Within close walking distance from the Hudson, this was originally a hotel for seafarers. In 1912 the survivors of the Titanic spent a considerable period of time here. Extensive refurbishments have now given this historical establishment with great views of the river a new lease on life. The tiny rooms are called *cabins* and you can be forgiven for thinking you are on a ship or in a train compartment. Fresh bedding only once a week. Single room $99, double room $250 (own bathroom), ask about weekly rates. *211 rooms | 113 Jane St | between Washington and West St | tel. 1212 9 24 67 00 | www.thejanenyc.com | subway: 14th St, A, C, E, L*

The Jane Hotel – historical building with a maritime past

HOTEL GRACE ★
(139 D5) (🗺 F8)

Perfectly situated close to the hustle and bustle of Times Square, MoMA and the Rockefeller Center this hotel is synonymous with *style*. Simple but first-rate rooms, breakfast included and a sauna to relax after a busy day out and a pool with bar where you can swim any time of night. So pack your swimming costume and come prepared to relax. *140 rooms | 125 W 45th St | between Sixth and Seventh Ave | tel. 1212 3 54 23 23 | www.room-matehotels. com | subway: Rockefeller Center, B, D, F, M*

HOTEL 31 (135 F2) (🗺 F10)

Recently refurbished this is the big sister to Hotel 17 and is more comfortable and slightly more expensive. It is also fairly central. *60 rooms | 120 E 31st St | between Lexington Ave and Park Ave | tel. 1212 6 85 30 60 | www.hotel31.com | subway: 33rd St, 6*

HOTEL THIRTY-THIRTY ★
(135 F2) (🗺 F10)

Although it is relatively inexpensive, this hotel has definitely got class. The rooms are small but there are also a few that are slightly larger and come with a *kitchenette* so self-catering is an option (from $225). The Empire State Building is just around the corner. *350 rooms | 30 E 30th St |*

between Park Ave and Madison Ave | tel. 1212 6 89 19 00 | www.thirtythirty-nyc.com | subway: 28th St, 6

MARRAKECH HOTEL (143 D2) (*m* 0)

This Upper West Side hotel does justice to its name with a Moroccan and oriental laid back feel to it. The rooms are small but have internet access. *127 rooms | 2688 Broadway (103rd St) | tel. 1212 2 22 29 54 | www.marrakechhotelnyc.com | subway: 103rd St, 1*

MILBURN ⭐ (142 B6) (*m* F3)

Situated in the best Upper West Side residential area its two-room suites are modern and family friendly and come with a kitchenette. *112 units | 242 W 76th St (West End Ave) | tel. 1212 3 62 10 06 | www.milburn hotel.com | subway: 72nd St, 1–3*

RAMADA INN EASTSIDE (135 F3) (*m* F10)

This hotel belongs to the *Apple Core (tel. 1212 7 90 27 10)* chain of five basic and clean hotels. Breakfast is included – a big advantage in New York. *100 rooms | 161 Lexington Ave (30th St) | tel. 1212 545 18 00 | www.applecorehotels.com | subway: 28th St, 6*

RED ROOF INN (135 E2) (*m* E10)

This hotel has a lot going for it. It is family friendly and breakfast is included as is the use of their fitness centre. It is well located in an area dense with hotels and Korean restaurants and is close to the Empire State Building. Wifi throughout! *171 rooms | 6 W 32nd St | between Fifth Ave and Broadway | tel. 1212 6 43 71 00 | www.redroof.com | subway: 34th St–Herald Square, B, D, F, N, Q, R*

STAY THE NIGHT (143 F5) (*m* J2)

Stay the night in this B&B housed in the top three floors of a lovely *brownstone*

building that has been converted into suites, apartments and single rooms. There is a lovely garden in the back and you are only two minutes from Central Park's popular jogging path around the Reservoir. The Guggenheim and The Met are also close by. *7 rooms | 18 E 93rd St | tel. 1212 7 22 83 00 | www.staythenight. com | subway: 96th St, 6*

WASHINGTON SQUARE HOTEL (134 C5) (*m* C12)

A good value for money hotel located in Greenwich Village where you can also enjoy jazz brunch on a Sunday. *160 rooms | 103 Waverly Place (MacDougal St) | tel. 1212 7 77 95 15 | www.washingtonsquare hotel.com | subway: W 4th St, A–F, M*

WJ HOTEL (139 D4) (*m* E7)

Recently refurbished so has a light modern feel to it. For $15 you can get yourself a day pass to *Gold's Gym NYC. 127 rooms | 318 W 51st St | between Eighth and Ninth Ave | tel. 1212 2 46 75 50 | www.wjhotel. com | subway: 50th St, C, E*

HOTELS: BUDGET

CARLTON ARMS (135 F3) (*m* F11)

A little antiquated but its rooms are charming and are all designed by a different artist – in fact there is art all over the hotel. If you stay more than a night you will have to make your own bed but for $130 (or as little as $110 if you are willing to share a bathroom) it is a bargain. No TV. *52 rooms | 160 E 25th St | between Third Ave and Lexington Ave | tel. 2 212 6 79 06 80 | www.carltonarms.com | subway: 23rd St, 6*

CHELSEA LODGE (134 C3) (*m* C10)

A small hotel in a charming old building. The small but lovely rooms start at $150 are a giveaway in this quiet street in bus-

tling and trendy Chelsea. This is the perfect area to go out and do your shopping. *22 rooms | 318 W 20th St | tel. 1212 243 44 99 | www.chelsealodge.com | subway: 23rd St, C, E*

THE CHELSEA STAR HOTEL
(135 D1) (*D9*)

The best address for young tourists on a budget. The *superior rooms* are slightly more expensive and have DVD players. *30 rooms | dormitory from $35 per person, double room with communal bathroom from $110, double room with en suite bathroom from $190 | 300 W 30th St (Eighth Ave) | tel. 2 212 2 44 78 27 | www.starhotelny.com | subway: 34th St, A, C, E*

LOW BUDGET

▶ Some agencies also have apartments on their books. These apartments can be quite small but are a good alternative to a hotel room, often less expensive and less impersonal. Contact *New York Habitat (tel. 1212 2 55 80 18 | www.nyhabitat.com), City Lights (tel. 1212 7 37 70 49 | www.citylightsbandb.com), Affordable New York (tel. 1212 5 33 40 01 | www.affordablenewyorkcity.com), Petra Loewen (tel. 1718 3 73 22 26 | www.aptpl.com)* or go to *www.roomorama.com*

▶ You can often get accommodation cheaper from individual hotel websites or booking agencies such as *www.hoteldiscount.com* or *www.quikbook.com*

▶ For private offers go to *http://newyork.craigslist.org*

INSIDER TIP ▶ COLONIAL HOUSE INN
(134 C2) (*C10*)

This historic *brownstone* building dates back to 1850 and has 20 rooms and there is a rooftop area that is a great place to relax. It is particularly popular with the gay community. The most inexpensive rooms range from $130 to $150 while those with an en suite bathroom go for $180. *318 W 22nd St (Eighth Ave) | tel. 1212 243 96 69 | www.colonialhouseinn.com | subway: 23rd St, C, E*

GERSHWIN ★
(135 E3) (*E10*)

150 unassuming but clean rooms in an area of New York that has seen a big upturn thanks to its good restaurants and shops. Rooms with multiple beds cost from $39 per person (ten people) or $49 per person (four to six people). An all-time favourite among artists and the décor reflects this. Family suits with two rooms are also available. *7 E 27th St | between Madison Ave and Fifth Ave | tel. 1212 5 45 80 00 | www.gershwinhotel.com | subway: 28th St, 6*

THE HARLEM FLOPHOUSE ★
(146 C2) (*0*)

This beautifully refurbished townhouse almost comes across as an art gallery thanks to the passion of its owner Rene Calvo who collects art from Harlem. On offer at this B&B are four comfortable rooms with two bathrooms and the price is $100 for a single, $150 for a double room. Wifi is included in the price and in summer you may even be invited to an impromptu barbecue. Its location in northern Manhattan makes for an ideal opportunity to explore Harlem in all its diversity. *242 W 123rd St | between Frederick Douglass Blvd and Seventh Ave | tel. 1212 6 62 06 78 | www.harlemflophouse.com | subway: 125th St, A–D*

HERALD SQUARE HOTEL ⭐
(135 E2) (*⌘ E 10*)

This used to be Life magazine's editorial office. Today it is a very popular and affordable hotel. *120 rooms | 19 W 31st St | between Fifth Ave and Broadway | tel. 1 212 2 79 40 17 | www.heraldsquarehotel. com | subway: 34th St–Herald Square, B, D, F, N, Q, R*

INSIDER TIP HOTEL LE BLEU
(146 C4) (*⌘ 0*)

Its cool design and the fact that it offers a lot for relatively little (by New York standards) makes this trendy new hotel a popular choice: internet access, breakfast, a minbar and even a small balcony. It may be located in a semi-industrial area but this does not seem to deter its guests.

Hotel Le Bleu – boutique hotel where even the bedding has cool blue accents

LARCHMONT HOTEL
(135 D4–5) (*⌘ D12*)

The excellent price to performance ratio and its quiet location north of Washington Square Park puts the Larchmont very much in demand. A small kitchen and shared bathrooms on every floor. Breakfast is included in the price. *62 rooms | 27 W 11th St (Fifth Ave) | single rooms from $90, double rooms from $120 | tel. 1 212 989 93 33 | www.larchmonthotel.com | subway: W 4th St, A, B, C, D, E, F, M*

Only a block away is Brooklyn's Fifth Avenue with its many restaurants, bars and shops and with Prospect Park is only one subway station away. *48 rooms | 370 Fourth Ave (4th St) | tel. 1 718 625 15 00 | www.hotellebleu.com | subway: 4th Ave–9th St, F, G, R*

HOTEL NEWTON (142 C3) (*⌘ G1*)

In the northern part of the Upper West Side Close and close to Central Park this unassuming hotel has exceptionally large

Hotel 17 – an affordable option in a pricey metropolis

clean rooms at affordable prices and very friendly service. Suites come equipped with a microwave oven, mini fridge and iron. Children up to the age of 14 can stay in the same room as their parents free of charge. *110 rooms | 2528 E Broadway (95th St) | tel. 1212 6 78 65 00 | www.the hotelnewton.com | subway: 96th St, 1–3*

HOTEL 17 (141 F5) *(Ø E12)*
A no fills hotel ideal for young tourists (communal bathroom). *120 rooms | 225 E 17th St | between Second Ave and Third Ave | tel. 1212 4 75 28 45 | www.hotel17ny. com | subway: Union Square, 4–6, L, N, Q, R*

MORNINGSIDE INN (143 D1) *(Ø 0)*
Plain clean rooms in a renovated house exuding an old-world New York charm. *85 rooms | weekly and monthly rates also available | 235 W 107th St | between*

Broadway and Amsterdam Ave | tel. 1212 3 16 00 55 | www.morningsideinn-ny.com | subway: 110th St, 1

MURRAY HILL INN (135 F3) *(Ø F10)*
The rooms may be tiny and very basic in this hotel but it has the advantage that it is not very big and that it is located on a quiet street. Some rooms have a sleeper couch for an additional guest at an extra $15. *45 rooms | 143 E 30th St | between Lexington Ave and Third Ave | tel. 1212 545 08 79 | www.murrayhillinn.com | subway: 28th St, 6*

OFF SOHO SUITES (131 E2) *(Ø E15)*
The ideal district to experience Downtown on a budget and having your own kitchenette can help you reduce your spending even further. *38 rooms | 11 Rivington St | between The Bowery and Chrystie St | tel. 1212 9 79 98 15 | www.offsoho.com | subway: Second Ave, F*

INSIDER TIP ▶ POD HOTEL
(140 B6) *(Ø H8)*
Cheap and cheerful this hotel attracts a young hip crowd and has become such a success story that the owners now want to open a second one in Manhattan. A bunk bed here can be yours for the night from as little as $89. Small, value for money, minimalist rooms, some with bunk beds, but it is their modern amenities like flat screen TVs and Wifi that are the draw card. Also has a roof terrace. *156 rooms | 230 E 51st St | between Second Ave and Third Ave | tel. 1212 3 55 03 00 | www.thepod hotel.com | subway: 51st St, 6*

HOSTELS

CENTRAL PARK HOSTEL (143 E3) *(Ø 0)*
Practically unbeatable! New York's 200 cheapest beds: $32 to $95 each for two to eight people per room. *19 W 103rd St |*

between Central Park W and Manhattan Ave | tel. 1212 6 78 04 91 | www.centralpark hostel.com | subway: 103rd St, B, C

CHELSEA CENTER (135 D1) *(∅ D 9)*

Share with five to seven others for only $35 a night and you also get a small breakfast. Also available are double rooms from $100 a night. You will either be allocated a room in Lower East Side or in Chelsea. *Main office: Chelsea Center West, 313 W 29th St, between 8th and 9th Ave | tel. 1212 2 60 09 61 | www.chelseacenterhostel. com | subway: 23rd St, C, E; 28th St, 1*

COLUMBUS CIRCLE HOSTEL (139 D3) *(∅ E 5)*

A traditional youth hostel with bunk beds. Choose from a segregated dorm for guys or girls, or a combined dorm. Four to 14 guests per room but at only $30 to $40 a night it is very easy on your budget which makes it worthwhile. Free Wifi in the lobby. *18 rooms | 120 W 60th St (Columbus Ave) | www.cchostel.com | tel. 1212 247 76 76 | subway: 59th St–Columbus Circle, A, B, C, D, 1*

HOSTELLING INTERNATIONAL (143 D2) *(∅ 0)*

Affordable, basic and clean. From $30 you can have a bed for the night in a room that sleeps six people. *624 beds (dorms all sleep 154 and there are 5 single rooms) | 891 Amsterdam Ave | between 103rd St and 104th St | tel. 1212 9 32 23 00 | www. hinewyork.org | subway: 103rd St, 1*

INSIDER TIP PINK HOSTELS (144 B2) *(∅ 0)*

Only for female guests. Rooms for four to eight persons and you have access to the kitchen, the internet and laundry. From $25. *10 rooms | 137 W 111st St | tel. 1646 3 71 93 69 | www.pinkhostels.com | subway: 110th St–Central Park North, 2, 3*

VANDERBILT YMCA (140 B6) *(∅ G 8)*

You will find a YMCA in just about every borough of New York. There are three in Manhattan, two in Brooklyn and two in Queens. Depending on availability you can opt to sleep in a mini single room or in rooms for two, three or four persons. Communal bathroom. The nicest and also the most centrally located is the Vanderbilt. *370 beds | single room from $100, double room from $120, special weekly prices | 224 E 47th St | between Second Ave and Third Ave | tel. 1212 9 12 25 00 | www.ymca nyc.org | subway: Grand Central, 4–7*

POD Hotel – simple and stylish

WALKING TOURS

The tours are marked in green in the street atlas, pull-out map and on the back cover

1 STRANGE WORLDS

Contemporary art and exotic ethnic enclaves are what this walking tour through SoHo, Little Italy, Chinatown and East Village has in store. Duration: around six hours.

This Downtown ramble begins in Washington Square Park → p. 40 with its triumphant arch. The recently refurbished park was a cemetery until the 18th century. Today students from neighbouring New York University (NYU) hang out here and it has an atmosphere all of its own with street artists, strains of guitar music, dogs

romping around – in a playground set aside specially for them – and chess players vying against one another in the park's most southerly corner. Now cross Bleecker Street, once the centre of the folk music scene in the 1960s, today a magnet for young people. The route takes you via West Houston Street to one of the city's most interesting architectural districts: SoHo → p. 34 with its *cast-iron* buildings that once housed multi-floor factories, shops and warehouses. Artists and students discovered them in the 1960s and converted them to huge lofts. Today they fetch exorbitant prices and are only for the very well off. A typical example of a

Photo: East River promenade

MON TO FRI
10 AM TO 16 PM
USE THRU STREET

No other American city is as pedestrian friendly as this metropolis on the Hudson and East Rivers making it perfect to explore on foot!

refurbished loft is 101 Spring St, corner of Mercer Street, which was once home to the *sculptor Donald Judd*. The property is earmarked to become a museum and the collection with works by Judd, Dan Flavin and Claes Oldenburg can be viewed by appointment only *(tel. 1212 2 19 27 47)*. Take Spring Street and cut across this neighbourhood with its narrow streets, boutiques and inviting restaurants and cross over Greene Street with its distinctive cobblestones, a feature from the past that is now seldom seen in the city.

Next up is Broadway → p. 36 with its really good selection of shopping attractions. There is the Prada → p. 80 store designed by architect Rem Koolhaas, the Puma → p. 80 sports and lifestyle store and definitely worth popping into for an espresso, the Dean & DeLuca → p. 75 gourmet

store. Carry on up Spring Street where and you will be walking in the area often frequented by New York's celebrities. If you are intent on celeb spotting drop in at the French-style bistro Balthazar → p. 85. By the time you reach Mulberry Street you may feel that you that you are no longer in New York. Here the brick buildings are only five floors high and there is not a skyscraper in sight. This is Little Italy's → p. 35 high street with its alluring array of specialty food shops and Italian restaurants – sadly though Little Italy is fighting for its life.

Chinatown → p. 34 is fast encroaching. Originally Canal Street → p. 36 formed its border but it is now bursting at the seams spreading north. Running east-west Canal Street is the undisputed heart of Chinatown's main fish, meat and vegetable traders. Here there are endless restaurants to choose from or if you prefer you can also buy a bite to eat on the street corner. Knock-off Chanel handbags and Gucci sunglasses are also sold in Chinatown but a word of caution: if customs finds them on you, it could land you in hot water.

Once you turn left into the Bowery the Asian atmosphere disappears entirely. Walking to Orchard Street via Grand Street you will have noticed the Pearl River Mart → p. 77 an emporium selling everything Chinese. Enter a district in the throes of change: the Lower East Side → p. 37 is becoming quite fashionable. Jewish immigrants from Eastern Europe shaped this part of the city in the 19th century. Synagogues, grocery stores and restaurants still bear testimony to this heritage and still pervades the neighbourhood today, although trendy bars and boutiques are fast taking over.

North of Houston Street and there are more cultural contrasts in store. Many German immigrants moved into the small, basic apartments in the heart of East Village → p. 37 from 1850 onwards and gave the area its nickname Little Germany. In the 1960s Avenue A and Tompkins Square Park were a hippie strongholds in turn evolved into punk rock strongholds in the 1970s. Today many up-and-coming artists live in this area and there are increasing numbers of young bankers and attorneys moving in because they can afford its skyrocketing prices. Here you will also find the occasional hints of Russian and Ukrainian life and to experience it first hand Veselka → p. 40 is where to go and where *blintzes* – pancake specialities with a cream cheese filling – are the order of the day. Now take in the easy-going lifestyle that typifies East Village as you make your way to St. Marks Place → p. 39.

2 DISCOVERING DOWNTOWN

This walking route to the most southerly tip of Manhattan takes you to the Statue of Liberty and to Brooklyn Bridge, also to Ground Zero, the World Trade Center Site where the city's history changed the forever. Duration: around six hours.

Starting at the Municipal Building → p. 29 this route takes you past the Federal Plaza administrative buildings to Duane Park. The antique shops you find here today will give you an idea of the kind of life the merchants 1700s led here in Manhattan's most southerly tip.

Take Duane Street to Broadway. The African Burial Ground is located on the corner of Duane Street and Broadway and it is estimated that some 15,000 slaves from Africa were buried here *(www.nps.gov/afbg)*. You can get more information at the Visitors' Center at *290 Broadway*. From there head south to City Hall → p. 29. Built between 1803 and 1812 New York's City Hall

has since become too small to accommodate the city's administrative functions and only the mayor has offices here today. These overlook the Woolworth Building (Broadway, between Barclay St and Park Place) with its distinctive copper dome.

Vesey Street is where you will find St. Paul's Chapel → p. 32, Manhattan's only church that dates back to colonial times. The small chapel was an important contact point for volunteers and those seeking comfort during 9/11. Vesey Street takes you to Ground Zero, the former World Trade Center Site → p. 31, whose twin towers once attracted thousands of visitors daily prior to their destruction. On the corner of Church Street is the Path Train Station, the best vantage point to observe the reconstruction.

Now head along Church Street in a southerly direction, past Trinity Church which is nestled between the skyscrapers of the financial district. It was Manhattan's tallest building (80 m, 281 ft) up to 1890 and it served as a beacon for arriving ships.

Just before the southerly end of Broadway you will come across the massive bronze sculpture of a bull that has become synonymous with Wall Street as a symbol of aggressive financial optimism and prosperity. From Battery Place and First Place looking in a southerly direction you will get a stunning ☀ view of the tree-lined promenade. It is from here that you will be able to take the iconic photo of the Statue of Liberty → p. 33, Ellis Island → p. 30 and the Verrazano Bridge all in one. A view of Lady Liberty is also guaranteed if you take the Staten Island Ferry → p. 33, which departs from the terminal at the end of Battery Park.

Battery Place is where the Skyscraper Museum → p. 32 is located. From there continue walking to the Robert Wagner Jr. Memorial Park where the Museum of Jewish Heritage → p. 32 is situated. Not far from here lies Castle Clinton where immigrants to the new world were processed up until 1860 and where you can buy your ferry ticket to Ellis Island, the island that served as a transit station for immigrants from 1860. Another ferry leaves from here for Liberty Island → p. 33 where New York's iconic Statue of Liberty

Make the free Staten Island Ferry crossing for a perfect view of Lady Liberty

holds aloft the torch that is the country's symbol of freedom. Passing through Battery Park you reach the Alexander Hamilton Customs House on the Bowling Green. It is no longer in use by customs today but instead it houses the **National Museum of the American Indian → p. 32**. Look out for **Fraunces Tavern** where Broad Street intersects Pearl Street, a pub that has been around since 1763. From Pearl Street turn into **Wall Street → p. 34** enter the world of the stockbrokers and dealers and the street that has become synonymous with crises in the international financial world. The entrance to the **Stock Exchange → p. 33** is on Broad Street but it is closed to visitors.

Take Pine Street to reach the **Chase Manhattan Plaza**, the first skyscraper built in the *international style* of the 1960s to make its appearance in New York. In front of it you will be able to admire the sculptures by Jean Dubuffet. Pass the Federal Reserve Bank of New York and take Maiden Lane cross Water Street (once flanked by bars and brothels in the 19th century). At the end of it, the historic **South Street Seaport** – part shopping mall part scenic area – awaits you and this is a good spot for your lunch. If you prefer to move on, then access **Brooklyn Bridge → p. 29** from Park Row. There is a pedestrian and cycle own lane (above the street traffic) to cross this iconic suspension bridge built in 1883 and lauded at the time as the eighth wonder of the world. Take the stroll across is at dusk when the massive glass façades of the skyscrapers reflect the of colours of the setting sun.

3 THE BEST OF BOTH WORLDS

Culture, wealth and style and a trip through Central Park – this walking tour shows you New York's elegant and finer side. Duration: around six hours.

The impressive Egyptian temple at The Metropolitan Museum of Art

Right in the heart of Manhattan at the centre of a huge office and shopping complex there is a gilded statue of Prometheus in the shadow of the **GE Building** → **p. 45**. The complex does not carry the name of the Greek god – the legendary watcher and custodian of fire and hence knowledge – but rather that of the famous American oil magnate John D. Rockefeller. In 1929 he commissioned the 14 buildings between 48th and 51st Street and Fifth and Sixth Avenue that came to be known as the **Rockefeller Center** → **p. 45**. A quarter of a million people pass through here every day. It is worth heading north from to visit the time-honoured department store **Saks Fifth Avenue** (*No. 611*) with its impressively large cosmetics department. Drop in and have one of their beauticians do your make up for you in the season's latest look.

Now take a stroll along New York's iconic Fifth Avenue with its big international designer names like **Versace** (*No. 647*) and **Cartier** (*No. 653*), and brand names such as **Gap** (*No. 680*). Two blocks on in the boulevard you can admire the jewellery collection at **Tiffany's** → **p. 81**. Now walk back to 55th Street and turn left, past **The St Regis Hotel** → **p. 98** and amble along Madison Avenue in a northerly direction – through the **Sony Building** → **p. 46** lobby where the electronics giant also has a museum, the (free entry) **Sony Wonder Technology Lab** a must for anyone interested in technology and the media.

The upscale department store **Bergdorf Goodman** → **p. 75** and the toy haven **F.A.O. Schwarz** → **p. 78** are also good for a brows through – at the very least their ground floor. Had enough of the shopping hustle and bustle? Then head for **Central Park** → **p. 50** and its expansive green areas and parklands that will come as a welcome change. If you need to rest your wary feet take a horse and carriage ride through the park (*20 minutes $35*) or rest on one of the wooden benches and watch New York's parade of life go by. You can even hire a bicycle and take a cycle through the park (*p. 50*).

Opposite 72nd Street West in front of the **Dakota Building** → **p. 51** is **Strawberry Fields** a commemorative garden established by Yoko Ono, the widow of John Lennon (the famous Beatle), in memory of her husband and his music. On 8 December 1980 the pop star was shot dead in front of the building by a mentally deranged fan. If you head diagonally across the park you will reach Upper Fifth Avenue, where the city's most luxurious apartments are found and some of the world's most interesting museums. Among them the **Frick Collection** → **p. 52** on the corner of 70th Street, housed in a stylish *townhouse* from the turn of the 19th century. In the glass-covered atrium of this mansion it is hard to imagine that you are in the centre of New York, it is an oasis of peace and calm.

Now carry on to **Madison Avenue** → **p. 43** which is lined with American and European designer boutiques. Everything is upscale, stylish and decorative. Return to Fifth Avenue from 80th Street where the **Metropolitan Museum of Art** → **p. 53** with its impressive outside staircase awaits you. This mega museum's collection remains unrivalled and showcases more than two million items – from the Egyptian temple of Dendur to paintings by Edward Hopper. From its ☀ roof you can admire the tree-tops of Central Park. On 86th Street the **Neue Galerie** → **p. 54** displays German and Austrian art from the early 20th century and you can treat yourself to an authentic Austrian coffee shop experience when you order their delicious apple strudel. Three blocks on you will find yourself standing in front of the **Guggenheim Museum** → **p. 52** – architect Frank Lloyd Wright's masterpiece.

TRAVEL WITH KIDS

NEW YORK AQUARIUM (146 C5) *(🕮 O)*
Its sharks, seals and penguins make this outing to Coney Island a must. *602 Surf Ave | corner West 8th St | Brooklyn | adults $17, children $13 | www.nyaquarium.com | subway: West 8th St, F, Q*

BRONX ZOO (147 E1) *(🕮 O)*
Some 4200 animals and next door is the *New York Botanical Garden. Mon–Fri 10am–5pm, Sat, Sun 5.30pm, end Oct–end March until 4.30 pm | Bronx Park 2300 Southern Blvd/Corona Parkway | adults $16, children $12, Wed voluntary donation | www.bronx zoo.org | bus: BxM 11, Liberty Lines, bus stops on Madison Ave, subway: Pelham Parkway, 2 Express Brooklyn*

BUILD-A-BEAR (140 A6) *(🕮 F8)*
Here teddy bears are tailor-made to your child's every whim. *565 Fifth Ave | corner 46th St | www.buildabear.com | subway: 47th St–50th St, B, D, F, M*

CHILDREN'S MUSEUM OF ART
(131 D2) *(🕮 D15)*
Children under twelve can create their own works. *Wed, Fri–Sun noon–5pm, Thu noon–6pm | 182 Lafayette St | entrance $10 | tel. 1212 9 41 91 98 | www.cmany.org | subway: Spring St, 6, Canal St, N*

CHILDREN'S MUSEUM OF MANHATTAN (142 C5) *(🕮 F2)*
A highlight here is the television studio where children can make their own shows. *Tue–Sun 10am to 5pm | 212 W 83rd St | entrance fee $10 | tel. 1212 7 21 12 34 | www.cmom.org | subway: 86th St, 1*

DISCOVERY ROOM (142 C6) *(🕮 G3)*
The American Museum of Natural History has an excellent interactive room for five to twelve year olds. *Daily 10am to 5.45pm | 79th St | Central Park West | entrance fee adults $16, children $9 | www.amnh.org/education/youth/discovery.html | subway: 81st St, B, C*

INSIDER TIP ▶ DYLAN'S CANDY BAR
(140 B4) *(🕮 H7)*
Two floors of sweet delights – one of the world's largest sweet stores. *1011 Third Ave | corner 60th St | tel. 1 646 7 35 00 78 | www.dylanscandybar.com | subway: Lexington Ave/59th St, N, R, 4–6*

Have a meal in a 'space station', build your own teddy bear or fly on a trapeze – New York is a dream come true for children

MARS 2112 (139 D4) (🗺 F7)
Space-themed restaurant that transports children into another world – Star Trek with a hamburger. *Noon–9pm | 1633 Broadway/ 50th St | tel. 1212 5 82 21 12 | www.mars 2112.com | subway: 50th St, 1 | Moderate*

MUSEUM OF THE MOVING IMAGE (147 D3) (🗺 0)
Here in Queens, children can make their own animated films, try out sound effects and watch movies. *Tue–Thu 10.30am–5pm, Fri 10.30am–8pm Sat/Sun 10.30am–7pm | 37-01 35th Ave (37th St) | adults $12, children $6 | www.movingimage.us | subway: Steinway St, E, M, R*

ROOSEVELT ISLAND TRAMWAY (140 C4) (🗺 H7)
An aerial cableway rides every 15 minutes across the East River to Roosevelt Island. *6am–2.30pm | entrance: 59th St and Second Ave | price $2.25 | www.tioc.com | subway: Lexington Ave/59th St, N, R, 4–6*

TOP OF THE ROCK (139 E5) (🗺 F7)
The observation terrace on the 70th floor of the Rockefeller Center is a great experience for the whole family. An expo and film help to make waiting time manageable. *Daily 8am–midnight | Rockefeller Plaza, entrance 50th St | entrance $22 | tel. 1212 6 98 20 00 | www.topoftherocknyc. com | subway: 47th St–50th St, B, D, F, M*

INSIDER TIP ▶ TRAPEZE SCHOOL (134 A6) (🗺 B13)
Here aspirant trapeze high flyers can live their dream. *Mon–Thu 10.45am–10.30pm, Fri–Sun 8.30am–10.30pm | Hudson River Park, in line with Houston St | price (2-hour course, 10 pupils): $47, $65 on weekends | tel. 1 917 7 97 18 72 | www.newyork.trapeze school.com | subway: Canal St, A, C, E, 1*

FESTIVALS & EVENTS

You have at least three comprehensive weekly magazines to choose from to come to grips with the sheer volume of what's on offer – *New York, Time Out* and the free *Village Voice.* Another good option is the Weekend section of the *New York Times* on a Friday.

The following are bank/public holidays when government offices, post offices, businesses and most shops are closed: **1 Jan** – *New Year's Day;* **last Monday in May** – *Memorial Day;* **4 July** – *Independence Day* (United States' national day); **first Monday in Sept** – *Labor Day;* **fourth Thursday in Nov** – *Thanksgiving;* **25 Dec** – *Christmas Day* (Boxing Day is not a holiday in the United States). Government offices are closed on the following days, most other businesses however remain open (many stores have special *sales*): **third Monday in Jan** – *Martin Luther King's Birthday;* **third Monday in Feb** – *Presidents' Day;* **second Monday in Oct** – *Columbus Day;* **first Tuesday in Nov** – *Election Day;* **11 Nov** – *Veteran's Day*

EVENTS

JANUARY/FEBRUARY
▶ *Chinese New Year*: ten-day festival with fireworks in Chinatown

MARCH
On the 17th ▶ *St Patrick's Day*: procession on Fifth Ave between 44th St and 86th St

APRIL
▶ *Easter Sunday*: Easter Parade with costumes and outlandish hats on Fifth Ave in the vicinity of 48th St to 57th St

MAY
Beginning of the month ▶ *TriBeCa Film Festival*: hosted by Robert De Niro. *www. tribecafilmfestival.com*

JUNE
▶ *Museum Mile Festival*: Fifth Ave between 82nd St and 104th St with jugglers, clowns and musicians; The Met offers exciting evening INSIDER TIP ▶ *open air concerts* in various parks free of charge; ▶ *Gay and Lesbian Pride Day (Christopher Street Day)* parade at the end of the month

There is aways something on — from cultural events like the TriBeCa Film Festival to street events like the Halloween Parade

JULY

▶ *Independence Day*: fireworks display on the East River or Hudson River at 9pm on 4 July. The best views are from FDR Drive or from West Side Highway but enquire about the actual launch site beforehand

SEPTEMBER

▶ *11 September*: Commemoration of the victims of the 9/11 World Trade Center terror attacks in 2001

▶ *Steuben Day Parade*: A Fifth Ave celebration by nationals of German origin held on a Saturday in the second half of Sept *(www.germanparadenyc.org)*. In Mulberry Street south of Houston Street the ▶ *Feast of San Gennaro* an annual market in honour of the patron saint of Naples runs for ten days mid Sept *(www. sangennaro.org)*

End of September to the beginning of October ▶ *New York Film Festival*: held in the Museum of Modern Art in the Lincoln Center *www.filmlinc.com*

OCTOBER

▶ *Halloween*: celebrated on Sixth Avenue on the last day of the month by tens of thousands flaunting outlandish costumes to keep evil spirits at bay

NOVEMBER

▶ *New York Marathon*: first Sunday of the month. Starts at Verrazano Bridge and ends in Central Park *(www.ingnycmarathon.org)*

▶ *Thanksgiving Day Parade*: on the fourth Thursday of the month this parade with massive balloons sets off from Central Park West and 77th Street all the way to Macy's At the end of Nov ▶ *Rockefeller Christmas Tree Lighting*: no holiday highlight is quite like this elaborate ceremony — the light chains span some 5 miles *(www.rockefeller center.com)*

LINKS, BLOGS, APPS & MORE

LINKS

▶ www.notfortourists.com is a guide that aims to help the visitor explore the city like a local. Full of tips about secret city spots, bars and restaurants even local hardware stores. The website is well worth a visit

▶ www.theskint.com has daily updates advertising free and cheap entertainment in the city. Also has links to sites with free music downloads and listings for the free admission days for the museums

▶ timeoutnewyork.com/blog online version of the city magazine with tips about shopping, exhibitions, concerts and shows

▶ www.villagevoice.com is the website for the alternative newsweekly for hip, political New Yorkers

▶ www.dailycandy.com is a website that showcases a selection of things that are fun, fashionable, food related and culturally stimulating

▶ rightherenyc.com find out where Bob Dylan, Hemingway and Janis Joplin lived and take a walk around their neighbourhood. Lots of listing for famous actors, poets, painters, writers and musicians past and present

▶ www.nycinsiderguide.com is a local site targeted at visitors wanting to live like a 'real New Yorker' aimed at the sophisticated traveller looking for more than the typical tourist attractions

BLOGS

▶ trustneely.com is a New York blog that is focused on entertainment, food, drink, art and fashion. Lots of up to date restaurant tips.

▶ newyorkdailyphoto.blogspot.com a witty and original photo blog that shows a slice of New York life

▶ www.scoutingny.com a blog by a film location scout who spends his time looking for unique locations

Regardless of whether you are still preparing your trip or already in New York: these addresses will provide you with more information, videos and networks to make your holiday even more enjoyable

BLOGS

▶ www.newyorker.com/online/blogs/goingson the online version of the weekly *The New Yorker* that has articles on the life, culture and politics of the city

▶ tugster.wordpress.com Will van Dorp blogs about the ships, coastal life and waterways of the port of New York

VIDEOS & PODCASTS

▶ www.nyc.gov/html/film/html/news/podcast_main.shtml the city's website has a series of podcast Walking Tours highlighting the history of film. They are downloadable for free and are read by well known figures in entertainment

▶ www.newyorkminuteshow.com podcast and blog that is a multimedia guide to New York City. Try the video podcasts of a tour through Chelsea, a snowstorm in Manhattan or a stroll on Fifth Avenue

▶ theboweryboys.blogspot.com website run by two New York historians. It lists entertainment and information as well as weekly podcasts

APPS

▶ The Scoop is a free app from *The New York Times* which gives an insiders' guide to the city and has tips on where to shop, where to find the best cafés, bars, coffee shops (under 'Filter'), restaurants and boutiques as well as events and outings (under 'Outings')

▶ NYC mtrip a free app for iPhone, iPod and iPad with offline maps and navigation and lots of information about places to visit, recommended itineries and a feature that allows you to personalise your travel interests

NETWORK

▶ twitter.com/CouchSurfNY tips and listings for Couchsurfing per tweet

▶ twitter.com/#NewYorkology tweets with news and events and updates from the independent travel site NewYorkology

▶ www.airbnb.com/New-York-city for private accommodation at bargain prices

TRAVEL TIPS

ARRIVAL

✈ Most flights from abroad arrive at *John F. Kennedy Airport (JFK)* in Queens. There are several ways to reach the city from the airport. To book a New York Airport Service shuttle bus to Manhattan go to the *Ground Transportation Center* at baggage claim *(every 20–30 min. travel time 60–75 min. $15, return trip $27 | tel. 1718 8 75 82 00 | www.nyairportservice.com)*.

A taxi takes 60 to 75 min. to Manhattan and will charge you a $45 flat rate plus toll and a 15–20 per cent tip. The return journey to JFK by taxi is approx. $50. Warning: only take the official taxis i.e. the yellow cabs. Other taxi drivers may offer you a cheaper ride but these are best avoided. Your cheapest option from the airport will be the subway. Take the Airtrain *(travel time 12 min. $5 | www.panynj.gov)* in front of the terminal to the Howard Beach Station. Change trains and take the

A train to Manhattan *(Metrocard $2.25 | travel time approx 1.5 hours)*. On the return journey only take the A trains in the direction of Far Rockaway/Mott Avenue or Rockaway Park Beach (as far as the Howard Beach–JFK Airport Station). Or take the Airtrain to Jamaica Station, change trains to the Long Island Rail Road *(travel time 35 min. $12)* – congestion free until Penn Station and the perfect answer if your return flight falls into *rush hour*.

If your flight arrives at *Newark (EWR)* in New Jersey take the Olympia Trails Bus to Midtown Manhattan *(every 15–20 min. travel time 60 min. $15, return trip $25 | tel. 1212 9 64 62 33)*. Or take the Airtrain or Amtrak to NJ Transit, then head on to Penn Station *(travel time 45–60 min. $11–15 | www.airtrainnewark.com)*. A taxi will take you about 60 min. and cost approx. $60 plus tip. A surcharge of $15 is applicable from New York.

National flights normally arrive at *La Guardia Airport (LGA)* in Queens. Bus: NY Airport Express *(travel time approx.50 min. $10)*. Express Shuttle *(travel time approx. 60 min. to Manhattan $13)*. Taxi: 45 min. approx. $30 plus tip.

RESPONSIBLE TRAVEL

It doesn't take a lot to be environmentally friendly whilst travelling. Don't just think about your carbon footprint whilst flying to and from your holiday destination but also about how you can protect nature and culture abroad. As a tourist it is especially important to respect nature, look out for local products, cycle instead of driving, save water and much more. If you would like to find out more about eco-tourism please visit: *www.ecotourism.org*

CITY SIGHTSEEING TOURS

BY BOAT

A popular choice for tourists is the ● *Circle Line Sightseeing Tour:* a three-hour boat ride around Manhattan *(mid April–Oct 10am–4.30pm, in winter once daily | Circle Line Plaza, W 42nd St/Hudson River | price $34 | tel. 1212 5 63 32 00 | www.circleline42.com*

BY BUS

Gray Line of New York: offers around 20 different tours – also to Harlem *(2–8*

From arrival to weather

Holiday from start to finish: the most important addresses and information for your New York trip

hours from $25). Other excursions go to Atlantic City for its casinos or take you into the Hudson Valley (*New York Port Authority Bus Terminal's northern wing | 42nd St, between Eighth Ave and Ninth Ave | tel. 1800 6 69 00 51 | www.newyork sightseeing.com*).

Harlem Spirituals: a tour through Harlem, Wed and Sun mornings with a visit to a Baptist church ($55), Mon, Thu and Sat evenings ($135 per person per group of eight) with a visit to a jazz club; two cocktails and dinner are included in the price (*690 Eighth Ave, between 43rd and 44th St | tel. 1 212 3 91 09 00 | www.harlemspirituals. com*).

BY AIR

Liberty Helicopters: 12–15 minute flips $180/person, 18–20 minutes $245/person, while a private helicopter for four persons for 18–20 minutes will cost $995 (plus $30/person fee). *Pier 6, to the left of the Staten Island Ferry | tel. 1 212 9 67 64 64 | www.libertyhelicopters.com*

BY BICYCLE

Bike the Big Apple: a range of tours through New York's different districts ($90, includes bicycle and helmet | tel. 1 347 878 98 09 | www.bikethebigapple.com*).

BY YACHT

Dinner cruises by World Yacht Cruises are not only a culinary delight but also a feast for the eyes as you watch the moon poised above the Statue of Liberty from your choice window seat. *April–Dec Thu–Mon, boarding at 6pm | Pier 81, W 41st St (Hudson River) | dinner approx. $110 | tel. 1 212 6 30 81 00 | www.worldyacht.com | subway: 23rd St, C, E*

BUDGETING

Espresso	2.50 dollars	*for a shot at a stand-up bar*
Hot dog	2 dollars	*if you do not have a telltale tourist accent*
Cinema	12 dollars	*starting price for a ticket*
Soft Drink	2.50 dollars	*for bottled water/ Coca Cola*
Taxi	10 dollars	*approx. for a short trip (2 miles)*
Subway	2.20 dollars	*per ticket*

CONSULATES & EMBASSIES

BRITISH CONSULATE GENERAL

Mon–Fri 9–12 closed Wed | 845 Third Avenue | tel. 1 212 7 45 02 00 | www.ukin usa.fco.gov.uk | Subway line 6 at 51st Street

CANADIAN CONSULATE

Mon–Fri 9–12, 1pm–3pm | 1251 Avenue of the Americas | tel. 1 212 596 16 28 | www.canadainternational.gc.ca/new_ york | Subway line F at 47–50th Streets

IRISH CONSULATE GENERAL

Mon–Fri 9–15 | 345 Park Avenue, 17th Floor | tel. 1 212 319 25 55 | www.consulate ofirelandnewyork.org | Subway line 6 at 51st Street and Lexington Ave

CUSTOMS

The following goods can be imported duty-free into the USA: 1 litre of alcohol over 22 percent, 200 cigarettes and gifts up to a value of $100. Many foodstuffs, especially fresh food, may not be imported. The following goods can be imported duty-free into the EU: 1 litre of alcohol over 22 percent or 2 litres of wine, 200 cigarettes, 50g of perfume or 250g of eau de toilette and other goods up to a value of 390 pounds/430 euros.

ELECTRICITY

110 Volt/60 Hertz. Small devices brought from Europe like hair dryers or shavers work with an adapter. Larger devices might require a transformer (available from electronics stores like Radio Shack). Otherwise charging can take a long time.

EMERGENCY

Tel. 911 is the free emergency number for police and medical assistance.

EVENTS

For what's on, consult the *New York Times (Fri, Sat)*. The *New York Post* and the *Daily News* publish a cinema programme daily. *New York Magazine (Mon)* lists cultural, sporting and other events. Also on a Monday *The New Yorker* gives an overview of what is on in the music and cinema scene, and much more. On a Wednesday *Time Out* publishes the most comprehensive and current information on clubs and concerts i.e. *music venues*. The free publication *Village Voice* gives weekly reviews and lists of cultural and political events. The best pre-selection of what is on makes its appearance at INSIDER TIP ▶ *www.flavorpill. com* on a Tuesday.

HEALTH

It is recommended that you take out travel health insurance when travelling to the United States. Accident and emergency departments (called emergency rooms, ER) are obliged to treat all patients, but they demand a credit card from non-US citizens.

The *Travelers Medical Center (952 Fifth Ave Suite 1D | tel. 1 212 7 37 12 12 | www.travel md.com)* also comes highly recommended as a recognised 24-hour service and will also call on patients in their hotels.

IMMIGRATION

To travel to the United States you need a machine-readable passport and must register online at least 72 hours before starting your journey *(https://esta.cbp.dhs. gov)* for an application.

Passports issued after October 2005 must have a digital photo. Passports issued after October 2006 must be electronic passports with a digital chip containing biometric information. The ESTA approval is valid for two years. Children must have their own passport, and for a stay longer than three months a visa is required.

You are also obligated to fill out a form with your personal particulars before your trip. Your travel agency will be able to assist you with this. Among others the first address (hotel, vehicle hire point) where you will be staying has to be stated otherwise you will be charged a $14 fee.

INFORMATION

OFFICIAL NYC INFORMATION CENTER
Information about everything from hotels to sightseeing tours. Also available here is the City Pass *(from $79 | www.newyork pass.com)* which offers great discounts,

savings and other privileges and also means you can avoid long queues. They also sell tickets for basketball and football games and Broadway musicals. *Mon–Fri 8.30am–6pm, Sat, Sun 9am–5pm | 810 Seventh Ave/53rd St* (139 E4) *(𝄞 F 7)*, *tel. 1212 4 84 12 22 | www.nycgo.com | subway: 50th St*

BROOKLYN TOURISM COUNCIL
Located in downtown Brooklyn, information and brochures on events, sightseeing and walking tours in Brooklyn, as well as on its history. *Mon–Fri 10am–6pm | 209 Joralemon St* (146 C4) *(𝄞 0) | tel. 1718 802 38 46 | www.visitbrooklyn.org | subway: Borough Hall, 2, 3, 4, 5*

TIMES SQUARE INFORMATION CENTER
(139 D5) *(𝄞 E 7)*
Metrocards, Broadway tickets and stamps also obtainable here. *Mon–Fri 9am–8pm, Sat/Sun 8am–8pm | 1560 Broadway, between 46th and 47th St | tel. 1212 869 18 90 | www.timessquarenyc.org | subway: 42nd St, N, R, 1–3, 7*

INTERNET
There is no other city that uses the internet to convey information to the extent that New York does – from the hotel reservation service of the Visitor Center *(www.nycgo.com)* to jazz clubs and museums. Go to *www.allny.com* for a good overview. The websites of the city magazines *www.nymag.com* and *www.timeoutny.com* are also an excellent source.

You can surf the internet free of charge up to 30 minutes in all *public libraries.* It is a good idea to have the addresses of the websites you will be consulting on you before you arrive: *www.nypl.org.* Some cafés have computers but are increasingly moving towards wireless access for PCs. Wifi access is often free of charge.

CURRENCY CONVERTER

$	£	£	$
1	0.70	1	1.40
3	2.10	3	4.20
5	3.50	5	7
13	9.10	13	18.20
40	28	40	56
75	52.50	75	105
120	84	120	168
250	175	250	350
500	350	500	700

For current exchange rates see www.xe.com

MONEY, BANKS & CREDIT CARDS

1 dollar = 100 cents. *Bills* come in the following denominations: one, five, ten, 20, 50, 100 dollars. *Coins* in denominations of one, five, ten, 25, 50 cents and one dollar. Coins may also be referred to as follows: *penny* (1 cent), *nickel* (5 cents), *dime* (10 cents) and *quarter* (25 cents). The proverbial *buck* equals one dollar.

Most of the centrally located banks in New York have foreign exchange facilities *(Mon–Fri 9am–3pm),* however they do not necessarily change cash or other currencies, but do take traveller's cheques and pay out cash on presentation of credit cards. Processing through these can often be expensive. You can buy dollars in cash at booths in airports and hotels. Credit cards are the most popular method of payment. Problems with a European card can occur, e.g. at a petrol station, if the security procedures require you to give a postcode. Traveller's cheques issued by *American Express (in case of loss tel. 1 800 5 28 48 00)* and *Visa (tel. 1 800 8 47 29 11)* are also accepted everywhere as a payment

method. You can get money at a cash point (ATM) using an EC and ATMs can be found at all banks and in many *delis*. Make enquiries with your bank back home to find out whether it has an associated institution where you can draw money at no charge and whether your debit/credit card is valid in the United States. On arrival be sure to have some cash and especially small denominations on you so you can pay your taxi, bus fare or porter. Taxi drivers are not obligated to give you change for notes higher than $20.

PHONE & MOBILE PHONE

Dial 0 to get the operator, who can help to set up a return call (*collect calls* only within the United States), or with phoning using US phone credit cards. A call from

BOOKS & FILMS

▶ **25th Hour** – A drama by Spike Lee (2002) in which a convicted drug dealer roams the hot spots of New York with two friends contemplating his life ahead of serving a jail term.

▶ **Gangs of New York** – This epic film by Martin Scorsese (2002) takes you back to the New York of 1863. The streets are violent, its citizens volatile and there is the pervading threat of knife-bearing Bill the Butcher around every corner. Starring Leonardo DiCaprio und Cameron Diaz.

▶ **Night at the Museum** – At night when its visitors have deserted the building, the New York Museum of Natural History comes to life – even the prankish giant dinosaur gets up to its tricks. Entertaining comedy (2006) starring Ben Stiller followed by an equally funny sequel.

▶ **New York Trilogy** – Set against the backdrop of New York – a three-part sequel in which Paul Auster's protagonists go in search of themselves (1985–87) in the Big Apple.

▶ **The Bonfire of the Vanities** – In this satire on New York of the 1980s an arrogant investment broker inadvertently knocks down an African American male with his Mercedes Benz in the Bronx – and his world turns upside down. The film is based on the novel by Tom Wolfe (1987) starring Tom Hanks, Melanie Griffith and Bruce Willis.

▶ **Extremely Loud and Incredibly Close** – A film adaptation of Jonathan Safran Foer's novel narrated from the perspective of nine-year-old Oscar Schell, an intellectually curious and sensitive child. He gives a movingly funny and endearing account of how he tries to follow in the footsteps of his father killed in the terror attack on the World Trade Center on 9/11 (2005).

▶ **The Sopranos** – This popular television series is about the mafia boss Tony Sporano and his clan in New York and revolves around his life and his struggle to balance his home life and his responsibilities as a crime boss (1999–2007).

▶ **Mad Men** – An award-winning television series that is set in the New York of the 1960s – dramas of success and social upheaval unfold in a world of advertising and glamour.

a phone booth costs approx. 50 cents. Details on how to make a call are shown on the phone device.

Hotels charge more – sometimes much more (at least $1 per unit), so it pays to check before you dial. For a cheaper alternative, buy a phone card at a kiosk, petrol station or supermarket (compare prices per minute!). By using a free number and a card code you can use a phone card to make calls from private landlines without paying cash. These cards are not suitable for making local calls from public phones, as the connection charge is fairly high.

European mobile phones work in the United States only if they are GSM tri-band phones (remember to reset the phone to GSM). If you have one of these find out about roaming charges before you go. The snag is that you can incur very high roaming costs so it is worth getting a prepaid SIM card for a local GSM network operator in the United States (Cellular One, T-Mobile USA, Verizon). You can also incur high charges from your mobile phone's messaging service. Best to switch it off even before you leave your home country!

In New York the *area code* always forms part of the phone number. For long-distance calls in the US: dial 1 before the area code (the numbers in this guide include the area and the long distance code); toll-free calls operate on the codes 800 and 888. Code for calling overseas from the US: 011 followed by country code, e.g. UK 01144, Ireland 011353. Code for calling the US: 001. Dial (411) for information (¢50 per enquiry) or go to *www.411.com*.

You will come across the alternative kiosks in New York that sell prepaid cards ($5, $10 and $25). These will dial you up to the local exchange and with a pin number some will make it possible to phone worldwide for as little as 3 cents/minute.

You will be able to use these with your GSM tri-band mobile phone, provided that your network operator is part of the international roaming agreement.

POST

The *General Post Office (Eighth Ave/33rd St)* is the only one that is open around the clock. Other post offices are generally open: *Mon–Fri 9am–5pm*. Stamps are also available from the vending machines outside post offices or in some pharmacies and delis. The price of a stamp for a postcard to Europe is 70 cents. Letterboxes are blue with a flap slot.

PUBLIC TOILETS

Public toilets or rest rooms are a scarce commodity in New York. With that said, atriums and lobbies accessible to the general public in a number of skyscrapers and shopping centres like Trump Tower and Citicorp will have public toilets for visitors. Another alternative are the toilets located in the lobbies of big hotels, in department stores, in bookstores and in outlets of Starbucks and McDonald's.

PUBLIC TRANSPORT

BUS AND SUBWAY

The New York subway and bus network is seamless and will get you anywhere in the city. It is worth knowing that the NY subway express trains only stop at around every fifth station. Normal trains are called local trains. Some train stations have separate entrances for Uptown and Downtown trains. The price for a single trip is $2.25. The city's magnetic card, the *Metrocard* has a number of advantages: free transfers between the NY subway and buses, bulk discounts and a weekly ticket for $29 and is especially recommended for tour-

ists. The *Metrocard* is obtainable from NY subway stations, many kiosks, some delis and from the *Times Square Visitors Center.* You can also pay cash, $2.25 in coins, when catching a bus. Since the NY subway network is constantly being repaired expect detours and temporary suspensions – particularly on weekends. Information: *www.mta.info* or at the stations

CAR HIRE

If you are planning to travel New York by car it is best to get your hire car at the airport. You get cheaper deals (from $50/day) than in Manhattan. Even more cost effective is to reserve your hire car before your trip. If you book from outside the United States, damage insurance (CDW) and additional third party cover are normally also included which can be expensive if booked after arrival. Some hire firms have a minimum age requirement of 25 years. Parking is a huge problem in Manhattan. There are too few parking spaces and the risk of break-ins and theft means that it is a better option to use parking garages (daily rates approx. $40). For chauffeur-driven *limos* or *town cars* (from $90 per hour with a minimum of two hours plus 20 per cent tip and tax), call *Farrell Limousine Service (tel. 1212 988 44 41).*

TAXI

Authorised *yellow cabs* are not that expensive. The basic rate for the first third of a mile is $2.50, for every further fifth of a mile 40 cents. 25 blocks will cost you around $8.50 plus tip (15 per cent). A night surcharge of 50 cents applies from 8pm to 6am and on a weekday there is a surcharge between 4pm and 8pm. Added to this is a $1 surcharge for bridge and tunnel *toll.* Leave the non-yellow cabs to the pros prepared to haggle!

TICKETS

Telephonic reservations can be made via *box offices* but it is rare for most shows not to be booked out. Ticket services add a percentage surcharge to the ticket price and are available 24 hours. *Telecharge (tel. 1 212 2 39 62 00 | www.telecharge.com)* and *Ticketmaster (tel. 1 800 745 30 00 | www.ticketmaster.com).*

Often hotel concierges will be able to assist you. Remember to tip them commensurate with services rendered. Half-price tickets for same day shows can be obtained from: *TKTS at Times Square (W 47th St/ Broadway) among others. Daily 3pm–8pm, tickets for matinees Wed and Sat 10am–2pm, Sun 11am–3pm plus $2 service charge.* Get them equally cheap without a waiting time at: *www.entertainment-link.com*

TIME

New York is five hours ahead of London in the Eastern Standard Time (GMT – 5 hrs) zone. Daylight savings time is valid from the second Sunday in March until the first Sunday in November. NB: these dates do not coincide with when the UK changes its clocks.

TIPS

In New York, *tipping* is not only welcomed, it is expected. European visitors should remember that in the United States tips are regarded as a part of the salary, not an added extra. Service staff need gratuities to earn a decent living. Your bill, or check, will include *tax.* New Yorkers simply multiply the *tax* by two and this is the figure they will give as a *tip.* Some restaurants fear that foreigners will not give a *tip* and add their own *gratuity* especially in tourist hot spots – this speaks for itself and the tip becomes obsolete. Headwaiters

and *maître d's* in top class restaurants expect at least $10 for special favours like a window table, even as much as $20. Hotel bellboys expect at least $1 per piece of baggage and at least $5 in the upscale ones. Chambermaids should get $5 at least and for longer stays a $1 per day. Concierges providing special services (e.g. booking of show tickets or restaurant tables) should get at least a $10 tip. Taxi drivers expect a 15 per cent tip.

WEATHER, WHEN TO GO

New York's weather can be extreme. In winter it is often bitterly cold, in summer very humid sometimes reaching temperatures of up to 104° F (40° C). It is a good idea to carry a light jacket around with you to avoid catching a cold when moving between air-conditioned interiors and the hot outdoors. Best time to go is from May to mid June and mid September to end October.

Temperatures will always be indicated in Fahrenheit (not Celsius) in the United States. To convert Celsius to Fahrenheit multiply the Celsius figure by 1.8 and add 32. 32° Fahrenheit equals 0° Celsius. Simple but not a rule of thumb: Fahrenheit minus 30, divided by two gives you Celsius.

50° F = 10° Celsius, 68° F = 20° Celsius
86° F = 30° Celsius, 95° F = 35° Celsius

WEATHER IN NEW YORK

	Jan	Feb	March	April	May	June	July	Aug	Sept	Oct	Nov	Dec
Daytime temperatures in °C/°F	4/39	5/41	9/48	14/57	21/70	25/77	28/82	27/81	24/75	18/64	12/54	6/43
Nighttime temperatures in °C/°F	−4/25	−4/25	0/32	5/41	11/52	17/63	19/66	19/66	16/61	10/50	4/39	−2/28
Sunshine hours/day	4	6	7	8	8	10	9	8	8	6	5	4
Precipitation days/month	8	7	9	9	8	7	7	7	6	5	8	8
Water temperatures in °C/°F	3/37	2/36	4/39	8/46	13/55	18/64	22/72	23/73	21/70	17/63	11/52	6/43

NOTES

MARCO POLO TRAVEL GUIDES

ALGARVE
AMSTERDAM
BARCELONA
BERLIN
BUDAPEST
CORFU
DUBROVNIK &
  DALMATIAN COAST
DUBAI
EDINBURGH
FINLAND
FLORENCE
FLORIDA
FRENCH RIVIERA
  NICE, CANNES &
    MONACO

IRELAND
KOS
LAKE GARDA
LANZAROTE
LONDON
MADEIRA
  PORTO SANTO
MALLORCA
MALTA
  GOZO
NEW YORK

NORWAY
PARIS
RHODES
ROME
SAN FRANCISCO
STOCKHOLM
THAILAND
VENICE

- PACKED WITH INSIDER TIPS
- BEST WALKS AND TOURS
- FULL-COLOUR PULL-OUT MAP
  AND STREET ATLAS

STREET ATLAS

The green line ▬ indicates the Walking tours (p. 106–111)

All tours are also marked on the pull-out map

Photo: Statue of Liberty

Hudson River

Holland Tunnel (Toll)

TRIBECA

Hudson River Park

BATTERY

PARK

CIVIC CENTER

CITY (U.C.)

LOWER MANHATTAN

FINANCIAL DISTRICT

World Financial Center

Holocaust Mem.
Mus. of Jew. Herit.
R.F. Wagner Jr. Park

Battery Park
South Ferry
Castle Clinton Nat. Monument

Battery Park

U.S. Coast Guard

Liberty Island

Ellis Island

Brooklyn Battery Tunnel (Toll)

Staten Island Ferry Terminal

Downtown Manhattan Heliport

Battery Maritime Bldg.
Governors Island Ferry

South Street Seaport Mus.

Wall Street Ferry

1 Edgar Street
2 Marketfield Street
3 Hanover Street
4 Counties Alley Slip
5 Moore Street
6 Gouverneur Lane

130

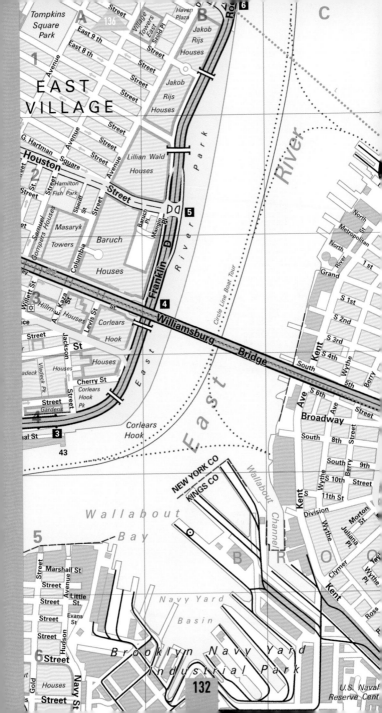

Tompkins
Square
Park

A

136

East 9 th

East 8 th

Street

Street

Village
Towers
East

Szold Pl

B

Ro

6

Haven
Plaza

Jakob
Rijs
Houses

C

Street

1

Avenue

**EAST
VILLAGE**

Street

Avenue

Street

Street

Street

Jakob
Rijs
Houses

G. Hartman Square

Houston

Avenue

Street

Avenue

Street

Avenue

Street

Lillian Wald
Houses

2

S. Hamilton
Fish Park

Street

Park

River

River

North

Metropolitan

North

1 st

River

Grand

Samuel
Gompers Houses

Masaryk

Towers

Baruch

Columbia

Houses

Baruch

Mangin

Franklin

D

D

5

River

S 1st

S 2nd

S 3rd

Willett St

Hillm

A.E. Kaza St

Lewis St

Corlears

Hook

4

Williamsburg Bridge

Kent

Wythe

S 4th

South

5th

Berry

3

Jackson

St

Houses

adeck Pk

Houses

Cherry St

Corlears
Hook
Pk

East

South

8th

Broadway

Wythe

9th

Street

Street

Berry

Kent

Ave

Street

Street

Gardens

4

al St

3

43

Corlears
Hook

South 10th

Division

S

Kent

11th St

Wythe

Circle Line Boat Tour

Street

Morton
St.

Juliana
Pl.

NEW YORK CO

KINGS CO

Wallabout Channel

B

R

O

Wythe
Pl.

5

Wallabout

Marshall St

Street

Avenue

Little
St.

Street

Evans
St

Street

Bay

Clymer

Kent

Ross

6

Street

Hudson

Houses

Navy St

Navy Yard

Basin

Brooklyn Navy Yard

Industrial Park

132

U.S. Naval
Reserve Cent

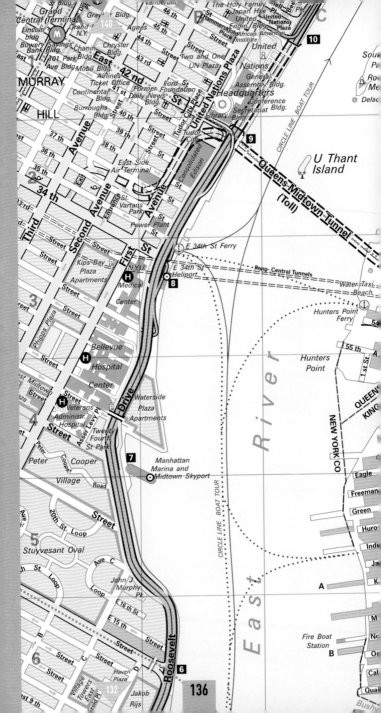

H

Point

evelt
orial
te Geyser

25

141

Queens Plaza

23 rd Street
23 rd

Street

Street

Street

Blvd

43 rd
43 rd

Street
Street

44th

9th

11th
Road

Street

12th

13th

Street

Silvercup
Studios

42nd

Dutch Kills

21 st

22 nd
Avenue

Crescent

Avenue

Hunter

St

44 th

44 th Street

5 th Street

10th

45 th

Road

24 th

QUEENS

Drive

M

45th

Street

Road

Street

P.S. 1
Contemp.
Art Center
& Museum

23 rd

Ave

M

Court
House

Thomson Ave

Purves St

2

46th

46 th

Street

47 th

48th

49th

50 th

Center Blvd

Street

Road

11th

Street

Avenue

Road

Road

Avenue

Ave

Davis St

Queens
City Prison

Crane St

Five
Points

Jackson Ave

Pearson St

Court St

Court Sq

4 th St

Pearson Pl

47 th

Chocolate Factory
Theater

5 th Avenue

Vernon

Ave

Jackson

Hunters
Pt. Station

Skillman

Pearson

Court

St

Long Island

50th

495

51 st

Street

Borden

Toll

11th St

Pulaski Bridge

Long Island
City-station

Avenue

Ave

Avenue

M

21th

Avenue

Hunters

Ave

Dutch

Point Ave

3

Long Island

M

51st

23rd St

Street

25th St

Ave

27th

Ave

Avenue

29th

4

Newton

Creek

Ash St

Street

Box

Street

Manhattan

McGuinness

Paidge

St

Ave

Provost

Street

Street

Street

Street

Kingsland

Av

Commercial

Clay

Dupont

point

Franklin

Newtown Creek
Water Pollution
Control Plant

Greenpoint Avenue

Kingsland

5

Street

Street

Street

Blvd

Avenue

McGuinness

Humboldt

Russel

North

Monitor

Street

Greenpoint

M

Street

Street

Leonard

Eckford

Newel

Diamond

Jewel

Calver

Moultrie

Avenue

Henry

Street

Street

Lorimer

Street

Guernsey

Street

Clifford
Pl

Banker

Ge

Meserole

Dobbin

Street

St

Norman

200 yd

250 m

6

Sutton

137

133

Nassau

Street

WEEHAWKEN

200 yd
250 m

Hudson

River

NEW JERSEY
HUDSON CO
NEW JERSEY
NEW YORK CO
NEW YORK

CIRCLE LINE BOAT TOUR

99
98
97
96
95
94

92

90

88

86

84

81

79

78

76

N.Y. City Passenger
Ship Terminal

Intrepid
Sea-Air-Space
Museum

Pier 83
Circle Line Cruises

World
Yacht

West-Midtown
Ferry

CIRCLE LINE BOAT TOUR

Lincoln Tunnel (Toll)

Lincoln Harbour

Penn-Central
Tunnel

West 30 St
Heliport

Clinton
Cove Park

De Witt
Clinton
Park

Women's
Int.
Arts Center

Irish Arts
Ctr. Theater

Joe

Dimaggio

West

West

West
Power
Plant

West

West
Avenue

West

West

West

Clinton

Bell Teleph
Systems

Sac

N.Y. S
of Pri

St. Clem

Twelfth
Avenue

Avenue

West

West

West

West

West

West Highway

West

West

West

West

West

West
Side
Theaters

Manhattan Plaza

St. Raphael

Theater
Complex

Ho
Cro

Port Authority
Bus Terminal

West

Dimaggio

West

30 th St
Terminal

West 32nd St

Eleventh
Avenue

Tenth
Avenue

J.K. Javits
Exhibition and
Convention
Center of
New York

YMCA-
Sloane House **34 th**

General

33 rd

Ninth
Avenue

Eighth

38 th

37 th

36 th

35 th

GAR

Nelson

West

West

134

138

8

9a